WHO ATE ALL
THE SQUID?

WHO ATE ALL THE SQUID?

FOOTBALL ADVENTURES IN SOUTH KOREA

DEVON ROWCLIFFE

First published by Pitch Publishing, 2020

Pitch Publishing
A2 Yeoman Gate
Yeoman Way
Worthing
Sussex
BN13 3QZ
www.pitchpublishing.co.uk
info@pitchpublishing.co.uk

ISBN 978 1 78531 681 4

Typesetting and origination by Pitch Publishing
Printed and bound in India by Replika Press Pvt. Ltd.

CONTENTS

Acknowledgements 7

Busan I'cons Squad List 8

Introduction – Chief Executive Chokeholds 9

1. Stadium Moats and Cracked Skulls 14

2. The Silly Bowing Dance (or, Don't Forget to Shake Your Muffler) 19

3. Rocket Launchers and 12-Lane Motorways (or, You Can't See Me!) 28

4. Sober Supporters and Player Punch-Ups 39

5. Supporters Have Kit, But Players Don't 49

6. Alcohol – No; Stolen Military Flares – Yes 57

7. Sleep-Deprived and Without a Toilet 67

8. Could You Switch Off the Floodlights? The Air Force is Cross 79

9. Plagues of Locusts and Flashy Foreigners 87

10. Democracy Protesters Support the Military Team 95

11. Death By Electric Fan (or, Don't Forget to Smear Red Bean Paste on Your Door) 105

12. Football? On a Saturday?!? Ridiculous! 115

13. Friday Naiveté (or, Build, Build, Build) 123

14. *Colgó los Guayos* (Hang Up the Football Boots) 132

15. We'll Show Those Neo-Colonialist Bastards 143

16. The Confrontation (or, Even Manchester United Took Time to Build) 148

17. Cureton's Debut (or, Busan's Treble of Embarrassment) 162

18. The British Revolution 171

19. Squad Squabbles and Empty World Cup
   Stadiums   181
20. Airing Dirty Laundry in the Newspapers   191
21. Best Mates with Local Derby Rivals   204
22. Dog Injures Player (or, Pregnancies Aplenty)   215
23. Big Bugs and Bodyguards (or, Uninterested
   Club Owners)   225
24. Divorces and Drubbings   237
25. Greener Pastures and Manitoba Dreamin'   243
26. Food Poisoning and a 335kph Breeze   249
27. Baseball Riots, Vanishing Nepalese and Furious
   Chickens   259
28. Smashing Chairs and Perilous Buses   266
29. Football Hooligans and Picnicking Families   274
30. Match Fixing and Farewell Letters   281
31. Season of Sorrow   289
   Epilogue   300
   Sources   317

ACKNOWLEDGEMENTS

TO THE Pride of Pusan members, particularly then-president Jang Seok-ho, for kindly inviting me to accompany them and for enduring my presence during bleak matches and tortuous bus journeys (sans toilets) across the Korean peninsula.

To Mark Trevena and the eclectic users of the (sadly defunct) ROKfootball.com forum, without whom this book would not have been possible.

To my late father, who bestowed in me a passion for writing and a predisposition for interests in niche topics, as well as providing me the freedom to be exploratory and independent from a young age.

To my mother, who exposed me to numerous cultures and languages as a child, which likely served as the genesis of my eventual interest in North East Asia.

And most of all to my irreplaceable spouse, who was supportive of my mid-life career change, encouraged me to follow my passions (even if our bank balance suffered), and persisted through 17 years of my incessant blathering about an embryonic manuscript that never quite seemed to approach completion. The mythical book is finally real; may your ears now find tranquillity.

BUSAN I'CONS SQUAD LIST

(squad number, name, position, age at start of season, year of birth)

1 Jung Yoo-suk (정유석), goalkeeper, 25 (1977)
2 Jon Olav Hjelde, defender, 31* (1972)
3 Dušan Šimić (Душан Шимич), midfielder, 22 (1980)
4 Zoran Urumov (Зоран Урумов), midfielder, 25 (1977)
5 Shim Jae-won (심재원), defender, 26 (1977)
7 Jang Dae-il (장대일), defender, 30 (1973)
8 Noh Jung-yoon (노정윤), midfielder, 31 (1971)
9 Gwak Kyung-keun (곽경근), striker, 30 (1972)
10 Harry Castillo, striker, 28 (1974)
11 Jeon Woo-keun (전우근), midfielder, 26 (1977)
12 Jamie Cureton, striker, 27 (1975)
15 Yoon Hee-joon (윤희준), defender, 30 (1972)
17 Ryu Byung-hoon (류병훈), defender, 26 (1976)
18 Lee Jang-kwan (이장관), defender, 28 (1974)
19 Lee Jung-hyo (이정효), defender, 27 (1975)
20 Lee Lim-saeng (이임생), defender, 31 (1971)
21 Kim Soo-hyung (김수형), midfielder, 19 (1983)
22 Han Jae-ung (한재웅), defender, 18 (1984)
26 Lee Yong-ha (이용하), midfielder, 29 (1973)
27 Kim Chang-oh (김창오), striker, 25 (1978)
29 Choi Kwang-soo (최광수), midfielder, 23 (1979)
30 Boo Young-tae (부영태), midfielder, 17 (1985)
33 Doh Hwa-sung (도화성), midfielder, 22 (1980)
35 Hwang Cheol-min (황철민), striker, 24 (1978)
38 Kim Tae-min (김태민), midfielder, 20 (1982)
40 Kim Yong-dae (김용대), goalkeeper, 23 (1979)
44 Tommy Mosquera Lozano, striker, 26 (1976)
45 Ahn Hyo-yeon (안효연), striker, 25* (1978)
46 Shin Young-rok (신영록), midfielder, 21 (1981)
50 Andy Cooke, striker, 29 (1974)

* *age when joined the squad mid-season*
(note: list excludes 13 squad members who did not receive any playing time)

INTRODUCTION

CHIEF EXECUTIVE CHOKEHOLDS

돌다리도 두드려 보고 건너라
– Look before you leap
(literally, 'even a stone bridge should be tested by
banging on it before crossing')

'WHO IS your boss? *Who is your boss?!?'*
Scottish football manager Ian Porterfield, in the dressing room for half-time, is pinned up against the wall. The club's CEO shouts as he punches Porterfield's arms and squeezes the Scot's throat. The team is losing 1-0 at home. The CEO is enraged.

'What are you going on about? I just want to do my job,' responds Porterfield as he gasps for air. He attempts to wriggle free from the CEO's grasp.

After five additional minutes of this physical and verbal barrage, the CEO releases Porterfield from the wall and swings open the dressing room door. The playing squad enters for their half-time team talk, likely unaware of the assault that has just transpired.

After a brief motivation session from a flustered Porterfield, the players saunter back out to the stadium tunnel for the second half. As the last player exits, the CEO slams the dressing room door shut again. He turns back toward Porterfield, then lunges at him.

'Who do you think you are?' barks the CEO, as he resumes his grip around Porterfield's neck, pushing the Scot down on to the team's massage table.

'I am Ian Porterfield.'

'Oh, do you think you are tough?' asks the CEO. 'Is it because you are white that you think you can talk to us that way?'

After several further minutes of the altercation, the CEO finally releases Porterfield.

'You had better get out of Ghana because you and I cannot work together,' says the CEO. 'I won't pay your salary so why don't you just fuck off!'

'I want to go out and win the game for the boys and the supporters,' says Porterfield.

'Why do you want to go out there?' asks the exasperated CEO, as if to suggest Porterfield shouldn't bother returning to the pitch for the second half.

'I just want to do my job,' says Porterfield.

The Scot's team perform a second-half comeback, scoring twice and winning the Ghana Premier League match. After brief celebrations, Porterfield strides toward the club's VIP area, where the CEO usually watches the games. But before Porterfield arrives, the CEO has already launched into a tirade against the Scot's wife, Glenda, yelling, 'You should both just leave Ghana! And you should watch your backs until you go, because I am a powerful man and you don't know who you are messing with.'

The above are highlights from Ian Porterfield's account of his alleged treatment at Ghanaian football club Kumasi Asante Kotoko. Porterfield would attempt to sue the club and its management for wrongful dismissal, breach of contract, assault and battery, as well as uttering threats, before ultimately settling out of court.

Mere weeks after leaving Ghana, the former Chelsea manager would accept his next international assignment: taking charge of struggling South Korean club football giants Busan I'cons. South Korea had a reputation among international football journeymen as a reliable country that paid on time, respected contracts and rarely screwed people around. After several 'eventful' football management stints around the globe, Porterfield looked forward to the stability and predictability of leading a club in North East Asia, his first job in the region.

* * *

Had I chosen the worst time in decades to travel to South Korea?

Events looked tumultuous as I boarded a Korean Air flight, destined for a season of football in the Hermit Kingdom. The United States of America had begun its foolhardy invasion of Iraq the day prior to my departure, causing unease for those still brave enough to venture on to an international aircraft. The mood in the airport was noticeably sombre.

North Korea's usual cacophony of threats to bomb their enemy *du jour* into oblivion, which I had always dismissed nonchalantly in the past, suddenly took on an entirely new relevance – my new home in Busan would be within missile range of the Dear Leader's pariah country.

South Korea had just been ravaged by a vicious subway fire that melted carriages – as well as the unfortunate passengers encaged within.

Anti-American sentiment had swollen into months of street protests across South Korea – and although I wasn't from the USA, it wouldn't be difficult to be misidentified as an American by agitated locals.

And the World Health Organization had just declared the Severe Acute Respiratory Syndrome (SARS) virus – centred in East Asia – a 'worldwide health threat' and issued an emergency travel advisory.

But like any self-respecting youngster, I ignored adversity. I boarded the aircraft and welcomed the adventures ahead – no matter how eventful they threatened to become.

My first impressions of Korea took place aboard the flight, prior to actually stepping foot in the country. Having previously only been subjected to airlines from Western nations, I wasn't expecting to be enamoured by the journey. But to my surprise, I was impressed by the exceptional standard of service and mesmerised by what was then the pinnacle of technology for an in-flight experience. Being familiar with squinting at small, overhead airplane televisions that either displayed flickering movies (when they weren't on the blink) or hung switched off as if passively participating in industrial action, I was captivated by massive plasma screens mounted throughout the aircraft that beckoned my attention like prominent pieces of artwork.

And then came the movies. I am perhaps resorting to exaggeration, drawing upon memories tainted by over-excitement as they solidified in my mind, but witnessing high-definition plasma screens in action for the first time – in an aeroplane, of all places – was surreal. Aware that South Korea was at the forefront of technological innovation, I thought that if this was the experience on a Korean plane, enthralling adventures must abound inside the actual country. I wasn't usually one to get excited by material things, yet there I was, enchanted like a small child, pondering what other surprises awaited.

A prospect even more exciting than futuristic television sets was the local football scene I was about to immerse myself in. As a football-mad youngster, I planned to spend an entire season following my local South Korean club to all of their K League matches, home and away.

But why South Korea? A surprising destination for someone enamoured with football, you might remark?

Surely not. The country had been one of Asia's dominant football powers for decades, and its K League was the continent's first professional domestic competition. South Korea also co-hosted the 2002 World Cup less than a year prior to my arrival, the country now bejewelled with state-of-the-art World Cup stadiums. Football fans from around the world remarked about the passion that Koreans displayed during the country's matches. Even FIFA president Sepp Blatter was delighted, remarking in 2003: 'The future of football is Asia.' The country I was travelling to was no footballing backwater.

With visions of an Asian football Mecca and a high-tech utopia dancing through my imagination, my flight neared South Korea. After a brief connecting flight to Busan, my year-long adventure was about to begin.

Also arriving in South Korea around the same time was one Ian Porterfield, still revered by Sunderland fans for scoring the goal that won the club the 1973 FA Cup. He had toiled as a football manager for almost a quarter of a century by this point, but his most dramatic highs and lows were all experienced during his recent decade working abroad. These varied from an honorary national freedom award and a visit by a country's president, through to employment under the Mugabes as well as alleged assault and threats from a club chairman.

Would Porterfield prove a success in North East Asian football? Did he possess the skills – and the favourable circumstances beyond his control – to dramatically improve a slumbering Korean football club? Would this job end in Porterfield once again being declared a national hero, or would he repeat the humiliation of being tossed out on his ear in just a matter of months?

CHAPTER 1

STADIUM MOATS AND CRACKED SKULLS

SOUTH KOREA VS. COLOMBIA
INTERNATIONAL FRIENDLY
SATURDAY, 29 MARCH 2003
BUSAN ASIAD WORLD CUP STADIUM

*'The [Korean World Cup] stadiums are like none
I've ever seen. I think there must have been some
strong competition nationally between Korea and
Japan to make the best facilities because they are
very well designed.'*

– Lamar Hunt, American soccer philanthropist

WHY DID I choose to live in Busan?

The majority of Western expats in South Korea opt to reside in or around Seoul, the country's capital. As the most developed region of Korea, Greater Seoul is the most cosmopolitan and offers the best employment, public transport and entertainment.

What tourist brochures cleverly fail to mention is that the Seoul Capital Area is jammed full of people, and lots of them – 26 million, or half of South Korea's total population, making it the fifth most populated urban area in the world. Other impressive features of Seoul include its sea of concrete, plentiful air pollution and meagre green space.

Weighing the options, I decided to give South Korea's capital a miss in favour of Busan, a city later known by Westerners thanks mostly to the 2016 zombie thriller movie *Train to Busan*. As the country's second most populous city, Busan contains a mere third the people of Seoul, is situated adjacent to the Pacific Ocean, boasts several mountains that make for great hiking or a quick escape when urban life becomes overwhelming, and enjoys a relatively temperate climate – more akin to the UK's moderate weather than Seoul's frozen winters.

Busan's location on the Korean peninsula offers additional advantages over Seoul. The south-eastern city is farther away from the Gobi Desert, where the infamous 'Asian dust storms' originate each spring before sweeping across the continent and causing people to develop sandpaper-like mucus. Busan is also more distant from the factories that dot China's east coast, the primary source of fine particulate matter that plagues North East Asian air quality. And whereas Seoul is a mere 50km from the North Korean border, Busan is a much more comforting 350 clicks away from the nuclear-armed pariah regime.

For Scottish football manager Ian Porterfield, Busan represented an opportunity to resurrect his career. Other than initial success in charge of Trinidad and Tobago's national team that ultimately proved short-lived, Porterfield's four jobs prior to Busan each ended in disappointment, either on or off the field – and in some cases, both. Yet he clung to fond memories of achievements from earlier in his managerial career, including one instance he was declared a national hero. Busan I'cons represented an opportunity to repeat such heroics: to depart a completed managerial gig loved rather than loathed.

After recent assignments fraught with interfering and impatient bosses, or beset by petty politics beyond his control, Porterfield was excited to sign a three-year contract as manager of Busan. Although there is always an element of uncertainty in joining a new club, he was impressed by Busan's chairman and felt assured rather than apprehensive. The K League had an air of security and safety compared to other settings Porterfield recently toiled in. The Scot was keen to begin work.

* * *

Barely a week after settling in Busan, an opportunity arose to attend some football: South Korea versus Colombia in an international friendly. Admittedly it wasn't the most glamorous of fixtures, but it was a chance to watch recent World Cup semi-finalists South Korea – and their ardent supporters who had become the envy of the footballing world – take on a decent South American side in a newly built stadium. This would also mark the first national team match in Busan since the well-attended World Cup, ensuring a large and enthusiastic crowd.

Like many new football grounds in the UK, Busan Asiad World Cup Stadium seemed to be located in the middle of nowhere. After negotiating a circuitous public transport route that involved two subways and a bus – because building a sporting venue near the subway or vice versa would be far too logical – I eventually arrived at the massive pantheon, nestled into the eastern base of Baek-yang Mountain. With one of the largest capacities among Korea's new stadiums, Asiad had hosted three group-stage matches during the 2002 World Cup. Most prominent was South Korea's initial game of the tournament, which doubled as their first-ever win at a World Cup: a historic 2-0 victory over Poland. Asiad also served as the centrepiece of the 2002 Asian Games, which unfortunately necessitated a colossal running track between the pitch and the stands. Oh well, who needs atmosphere at a football venue?

Approaching Asiad, its gargantuan size was hypnotising. The venue was more than 300m long, with three expansive walkways to feed people into the stadium. The structure's base was a mass of drab concrete, capped with a luminously white membrane surface similar to the Mound Stand roof at Lord's Cricket Ground in London.

Walking inside Asiad, the expansive concourse teemed with vendors. Some sold food, while others hawked gaudy merchandise emblazoned with the ubiquitous 'Be The Reds!' slogan made famous during the recent World Cup. Disappointing the salespeople who hoped to make a quick buck unloading World Cup leftovers on to an unsuspecting foreigner, I made my way through to the heart of the stadium. Emerging from the dark tunnel, I was struck by a cacophony of bright colours. The stadium seats, rather than being painted the colours of the home football club, were instead coated with a garish assortment of brilliant hues. I eventually recognised a pattern: waves of neon yellow and royal blue, with sprinkles of other colours – turquoise, red, pink, orange and green, in seemingly random order – filling the gaps. All right then.

Fixing my gaze downward, I couldn't help but marvel at the flawless grass pitch that anchored the stadium. The dark emerald surface looked more like an immaculate billiards table than a living organism. Encasing the pitch was a maroon running track, covered with white lines to demarcate lanes for athletics competitions. Surrounding the track was yet another buffer: an un-utilised space covered with lime-green artificial turf. And if that wasn't enough, there was a third layer that separated the pitch from the stands: the infamous moat.

When I hear the term 'moat', my mind summons images of flooded ditches protecting castles from hordes of unruly invaders. I wasn't aware these devices served a functional role in football as well.

The Koreans and Japanese, soon after winning hosting rights for the 2002 World Cup, quickly shifted their focus to how to keep barbarian visitors from finding their way on to stadium pitches and causing a nuisance during matches. The Korean organisers had undoubtedly watched footage from the 1970s and 1980s of English hooligans marauding their way through stadium terraces – as well as each other's skulls – and were terrified about such scenes being replicated on North East Asian soil. Never mind that such footage was 20 to 30 years old, and that all-seater English stadiums by now catered primarily to families and the wealthy; surely violence must be embedded within the genetic make-up of the English football fan. The Korean planners were determined to prevent any fan disturbance lest they risk embarrassment in view of the entire world.

And so football stadium moats, alarmingly reminiscent of alligator pits, were imported into North East Asia and incorporated into most of the new World Cup venues. Moats had been in place for decades in grounds across South America and select parts of Europe, but would never pass modern health and safety muster in the UK. Just ask Scotsman Jack Elliot, who fell head-first into the moat at the Jeonju World Cup Stadium during a 2002 World Cup group-stage match between Portugal and Poland. His minor tumble resulted in a broken skull, severe bleeding of the brain and a nice little cat-nap in the form of a coma.

There I was, amid a crowd of 45,000 announced as 60,000 in the 55,000-capacity Busan Asiad World Cup Stadium. I looked forlornly down towards the moats, wondering how many other skulls would be figuratively – and perhaps literally – cracked during the 2003 K League season to come.

The match begins. South Korea field a strong side similar to the one that competed in the World Cup, flaunting numerous big names. They're spurred on by deafeningly loud home fans, almost entirely clad in red, who repetitively serenade the players with the familiar chants of '*Dae-Han-Min-Guk*' ('Republic of Korea'), and '*Oh, Pilseung Korea*' ('Korea must win'). Unfortunately the crowd atmosphere is the only aspect of interest, as the match turns out to be a languid 0-0 draw. Neither the Korean nor Colombian players, dragged away from their glamorous European clubs to contest this unimportant friendly, can be bothered to muster their full effort lest they risk injury. But despite the uninspiring game, I leave satisfied, having been to a new World Cup stadium and witnessed a large football crowd in full voice. I return home buzzing and with ears ringing as if I had attended a rock concert.

With this enjoyable but meaningless international friendly out of the way, I was eager to watch some competitive club football. The wait would be short, as I would attend my first Busan I'cons Football Club match the very next afternoon.

The 2003 K League season awaited. Would the experience measure up to the passion and atmosphere produced at South Korea's national team games?

Tomorrow would also mark Ian Porterfield's first home match in charge of Busan I'cons. With this latent giant of a club moving to a state-of-the-art World Cup stadium, constructing a new clubhouse and hiring a foreign manager with an impressive CV, Busan supporters expected a rapid resurrection in the months ahead.

CHAPTER 2

THE SILLY BOWING DANCE (OR, DON'T FORGET TO SHAKE YOUR MUFFLER)

BUSAN I'CONS VS. POHANG STEELERS
SUNDAY, 30 MARCH 2003
K LEAGUE ROUND 3
BUSAN ASIAD WORLD CUP STADIUM

식은 죽 먹기
— Piece of cake (literally, 'like eating cold rice porridge')

THE 2003 K League season did not begin promisingly for Busan I'cons and their new Scottish manager, Ian Porterfield.

After starting the year with a narrow win away to league whipping-boys Bucheon SK, Busan I'cons were thrashed 5-1 at Jeonbuk Hyundai Motors. The squad returned to Busan demoralised, yet still optimistic about playing their first home match of the season. Today began a new era for the club, as it marked Busan's first game as tenants of the sparklingly new Busan Asiad World Cup Stadium.

Sadly, it wasn't just match results that weren't unfolding in Busan's favour. To the horror of club staff, attendance at this loudly trumpeted home opener was dreadfully low: just over 6,000 punters in a 55,000-capacity venue.

It would be the only attendance across the K League this weekend that didn't surpass four figures.

The new stadium sired an alarming dissonance. During the World Cup, and even at yesterday's unimportant international friendly, this venue throbbed with excitement as it hosted boisterous crowds. But less than 24 hours later, Busan Asiad Stadium was completely transformed. Without warning, it had become a vacant white elephant, devoid of atmosphere. Today's K League match would not be the same spectacle of frenzied enthusiasm witnessed just one day earlier – and that was being polite.

Just yesterday, when I entered the stadium concourse and attempted to negotiate my way into the stands during a national team match, I was forced to navigate a gauntlet of salespeople hawking T-shirts. I had expected a similar swarm of insistent vendors endeavouring to shift Busan I'cons wares today. Instead, the K League match offered a striking absence of concourse commotion. There was no Busan I'cons merchandise, no club shop, no matchday programmes. It was as if the city's astute salespeople had already known this K League match attendance would be pitiful compared to yesterday's Korea–Colombia friendly.

If the new Asiad World Cup Stadium was intended to be one of the crown jewels of Busan I'cons' new K League season, the capture of Ian Porterfield as manager was another source of early optimism. Busan finished second-last the previous year, the club's worst-ever K League result. Busan needed to prevent the rot of recent years from becoming terminal, and turned to Porterfield to help reverse the club's ailing fortunes.

John 'Ian' Porterfield had been a footballer with considerable potential, but due to injury his playing career was cut short and was mostly uneventful. Uneventful, that is, except for scoring one of the most important goals in the history of the FA Cup. Porterfield tallied in the 1973 FA Cup Final for second-tier Sunderland, leading them to a remarkable 1-0 upset over a Leeds United side that dominated English football and competed in Europe. It had been more than 40 years since a club from the Second Division lifted the FA Cup, and many had already consigned such fairy-tale upsets to a bygone era. But with a single boot of a ball, Porterfield orchestrated one of the most unexpected results in the history of English club football, garnering him cult status in Wearside that continues to this day.

Now in management, Porterfield was an impressive signing for beleaguered Busan I'cons. While some of his more recent international adventures as a two-decade journeyman manager may not have floored club officials, Porterfield was previously in charge of Chelsea and succeeded Alex Ferguson at Aberdeen. Local context is also important: Koreans had just bestowed god-like status upon another European football manager, Dutchman Guus Hiddink, for leading South Korea's national team to an unprecedented fourth-place finish at the 2002 World Cup. With the concept of the 'genius foreign manager' still in vogue months later, Busan were determined to get a piece of the overseas action and snap up their own *waygookin*, or foreigner. Porterfield was their man – the first British manager in the K League.

Rather wisely, Porterfield was quick to temper expectations, suggesting he would deliver 'slow and steady progress' to embattled Busan I'cons.

* * *

It takes just seven minutes for someone to score – the first-ever K League goal at Busan Asiad World Cup Stadium. It's credited to a striker wearing the name 'Konan' in Hangeul, the Korean language script, on his back. His real name is Goran Petreski, a striker who briefly played for Macedonia's national team during the mid-1990s, primarily as a substitute.

Unfortunately the front of Petreski's shirt is emblazoned with the club crest of Pohang Steelers, rather than the home side. Busan trail 1-0.

The Busan supporters, comprised predominantly of middle-school girls but complemented with a spattering of slightly older males masquerading as leaders, lower their heads in collective frustration.

* * *

For many Koreans, supporting a football club is a serious, structured and scripted occasion – requiring substantial preparation, social hierarchy, discipline, obedience and strict cohesion.

Think back to the 2002 World Cup, in which South Korea impressed billions of television viewers by filling their new stadiums with an animate mass of red shirts chanting at full volume without respite. While such scenes were indeed stirring, upon closer scrutiny they had a sense of artificiality to them. It was as if the Koreans had been put up to the task, and were acting with coordinated behaviour not naturally characteristic of large crowds.

Now imagine a similar degree of enthusiasm, but from 50 fervent supporters instead of 50,000. That is exactly the scene at this Busan I'cons match.

A male in his 20s stands at the front of the red-clad Pride of Pusan (or 'POP' for short), the official supporters' club of Busan I'cons. With his back turned to the match action, he faces his fellow POP members and fixes his attention entirely upon them. Lifting a plastic megaphone to his mouth and raising his other arm in dramatic anticipation, he barks out the first word of a chant. Almost immediately, the entire group is singing along with alacrity. They all know the lyrics. When the leader sings, each POP member dutifully joins in with tremendous eagerness.

Why a megaphone is necessary for a small group of 50 supporters huddled closely together, buffered from the normal fans by section upon section of empty seats surrounding them, is beyond me. Is the megaphone meant as a symbolic crown, tangibly asserting the authority of the leader? Or is it meant to amplify the minor racket made by the Pride of Pusan in the hope of attracting more people to join the 'hardcore' supporters by reverberating their minute cacophony throughout the stadium?

The head supporter seamlessly shifts into another song, as do the rest of the devoted Pride of Pusan members. They stand under a home-made banner fluttering from the upper tier of the stadium that reads, 'Always be on the top!' – which presumably refers to where they want Busan I'cons to ascend in the K League table, rather than an unabashed admission of boudoir preference.

Drummers stand on both ends of the front row, one on each side of the head supporter, as if lieutenants-in-arms flanking their general. The remainder of the group is a motley ensemble. Roughly 70 per cent of the supporters are teenage girls, eager to catch a glimpse of Busan's mediocre players as if they're local celebrities. The young ladies let out startling shrieks whenever Busan players have possession, particularly if one of their preferred 'stars' is on the ball. A few females with seniority stand nearby and display more composed behaviour, undoubtedly muted by numerous seasons of accumulated cynicism. The rest of the pack is filled by males ranging in age mostly between middle-school through university, with only one or two adults. Compared to terraces dominated by 18- to 45-year-old males found around most of the world, this adolescent and oestrogen-laden group is an unexpected assemblage.

Perhaps most interesting is the lack of spontaneity. Of course the odd person will let out a word of encouragement on their own initiative when it looks as if Busan might score, and the occasional expletive is quietly muttered under someone's breath when a chance is squandered. But there's only one person leading songs for the entire 90 minutes: the man with the mighty megaphone. And while the concept of a head supporter leading songs can also be found in European and South American football, the precision and compliance from this group's members is startling. The experience is the polar opposite of UK stadium culture.

At British football, fans will chant, talk with their friends or partners, chew on their fingernails in anticipation of the result, tap on their smartphones, take photographs, stuff their gobs with chip butties and even excuse themselves mid-match to use the toilet. But Korean supporters? They sing, loudly and proudly, with an adherence that causes individual-minded Britons slight alarm. Put it down to cultural differences.

The Pride of Pusan members make as much of a spectacle as possible with just 50 people amid a gargantuan stadium. They tie football scarves (or 'mufflers' as they call them) around their wrists, made of thin, breathable material suited to Korea's warmer climate and summer-based league, and madly wave their arms around in rhythmic circles. When each Busan-supporting individual represents what would be one thousand people at a South Korean national team match, you had better believe they put an earnest effort into their role as a club abettor.

Harry, Busan's diminutive Colombian attacker, races up the pitch in a burst of speed. He receives possession of the ball. The Pride of Pusan inhale with anticipation, expecting a goal. But as the nimble striker rounds a Pohang defender, the referee halts action. Offside. Harry throws his head back in exaggerated frustration as a guilty grin forms on his face.

Harry German Castillo Vallejo was a gifted footballer from a young age. Gregarious and with a baby face, he had a disarming personality.

After beginning his professional career as a midfielder with Millonarios, Harry bounced between several other Colombian clubs as well as a team in Peru. But with South American football leagues battered by economic turbulence in the late 1990s – wages were regularly late or withheld, and contracts not always honoured – Harry looked enviously across the Pacific to South Korea, a country selected to co-host the World Cup. His agent informed him that South American players were in demand, able to fetch a much higher salary in Korea than at home, and the K League was largely exempt from financial shenanigans and dubious club owners.

Convinced, Harry left for the Hermit Kingdom in 2000, signing with Suwon Samsung Bluewings – a new and affluent club that had just won the K League title in its third season. But he didn't fit in well, only scoring once in five appearances, leading to a mid-season move to Busan I'cons.

At Busan, Harry thrived as an attacking midfielder who scored and set up goals for team-mates. But with an exodus of strikers from Busan after the 2002 season, Porterfield asked Harry to move up front to become a forward. Today he was proving to be a handful for Pohang's back-line.

Just then, a pivotal moment of the match. Busan score. *Busan score!* Zoran Urumov, a Serbian utility player and arguably Busan's best attacker, equalises for the home side in the 22nd minute from a penalty, scoring the club's first goal at Asiad Stadium. The small crowd, and the Pride of Pusan in particular, explode in uproarious delight, galvanised by Busan's revival. The Eastern European goalscorer traipses around the pitch in a disorganised celebration, showing definite signs of spontaneity. Is this the fresh start to the 2003 season that everyone at Busan has so desperately wanted? Will the goal lead to a comeback victory and hopefully larger crowds at future Busan matches?

Forget the future – it's time to celebrate. The Pride of Pusan's two drummers hammer away furiously while the rest of the hardcore assemble closely together into two tightly packed rows, arms embraced around each other's shoulders. The supporters bow several times in unison. From there, with arms and shoulders interlinked, they begin to bounce together in celebratory unison – long before 'the Poznań' had become a familiar sight in British stadiums. One row joyfully hops to the left, the other to the right.

With gleeful smiles on their faces, the two lines bounce in opposite directions, spilling into the surrounding sections with amusing effect. Then, without missing a beat, the two sideways conga lines switch directions and merrily jump back toward each other.

The curious performance continues back and forth several times, and finishes as it began with another series of collective bows. The Busan supporters, some of whom are strangers except for the replica shirts they share on matchdays, break free from each other's grasp and offer a slight bow to their immediate neighbours. Giggles fill the air. Everyone has a silly smirk on their face; the group now shares a greater bond.

And then: the unthinkable. They all break out in a spontaneous, self-congratulatory yet self-deprecating round of applause.

Perhaps Korean football supporters aren't so different from their Western counterparts after all.

* * *

Pohang are not happy. The 1-1 scoreline belies their significant stature in Korean football, especially compared to a Busan side that were woeful last season. Before the smiles have subsided from the faces of Busan's players, Pohang are on the attack. Goran Petreski (or 'Konan' if you prefer), who scored Pohang's opener, is determined to earn their second goal. He blasts forward with the ball, pushing and shoving Busan's midfielders in an unsportsmanlike manner. His dirty tactics receive a hearty round of boos from the Pride of Pusan.

Horribly outnumbered, Pohang's Petreski is eventually stripped of the ball by Busan right-back Shim Jae-won. Keen to launch a quick counter-attack, Shim blasts the ball optimistically up the pitch, intending to feed Zoran Urumov, Busan's earlier goalscorer. To everyone's surprise, the temerarious pass travels almost the entire field and lands between Urumov and Pohang's bleach-blond goalkeeper, Kim Byung-ji.

Kim was famous for much more than his outlandish hairstyles: he had played for the South Korean national team for eight years before recently retiring from international duty. The Pride of Pusan brace themselves for a crucial encounter between Busan's best striker and one of Asia's former leading goalkeepers.

But there would be no test of skills between Urumov and Kim. The long-range pass lands with such velocity it sails over goalkeeper

Kim. Urumov, foreseeing the miscalculation, cheekily rounds Kim while the ball is mid-flight, calmly collects it and taps it into Pohang's goal. 2-1 for Busan in the 26th minute.

The Pride of Pusan howl with elation. They launch into another silly bowing-hopping-bowing dance, with perhaps even more enthusiasm this time around. Their equivalents, the Pohang Marines, slink forlornly into their seats in the mostly empty opposite end of the stadium.

Urumov flashes a grin as he's mobbed by celebrating teammates. This is the Serbian's fifth season at Busan, an unusually long spell for a foreign player at a single K League club.

Although Urumov began his early career at Red Star Belgrade as a left-back, Busan are exploiting his pace and eye for goal in an attack-oriented role. As with Harry, Busan manager Porterfield asked Urumov to take on much of the scoring responsibility. He's adjusted to the new task surprisingly well, scoring all four of Busan's goals this young season and being named in the league's unofficial 'best 11' for the week.

Urumov is well-liked among the squad: affable and eager to enjoy life. Despite his family living with him here in Korea, the Eastern European is known to sneak away to enjoy Busan's colourful nightlife and often drinks the rest of the squad under the table.

The 2-1 scoreline persists for the remainder of the match. Pride of Pusan's members, beaming in victory, exchange pleasantries as they exit the stadium and go their separate ways.

Did today's victory portend a season of improvement and success for Busan? Would the club be able to repeat such winning performances consistently throughout the remainder of this 44-match K League season, unprecedented in length?

And perhaps just as importantly, would today's victory lead to larger crowds at Busan matches? Attempting to fill the mammoth Asiad Stadium could prove a daunting task for the club in the months ahead.

ROUND 1

Bucheon	**0-1**	**Busan**
Daegu	0-1	Suwon
Seongnam	1-0	Daejeon
Gwangju	0-1	Ulsan
Pohang	3-4	Anyang
Jeonbuk	1-1	Jeonnam

ROUND 2

Jeonbuk	**5-1**	**Busan**
Seongnam	2-0	Daegu
Gwangju	0-0	Suwon
Bucheon	0-1	Daejeon
Pohang	2-1	Ulsan
Jeonnam	0-0	Anyang

ROUND 3

Busan	**2-1**	**Pohang**
Jeonnam	0-0	Daegu
Anyang	1-0	Jeonbuk
Ulsan	2-1	Bucheon
Daejeon	2-0	Gwangju
Suwon	1-2	Seongnam

K LEAGUE TABLE

Seongnam Ilhwa Chunma (Pegasus)	9
Anyang LG Cheetahs	7
Daejeon Citizen	6
Ulsan Hyundai Horang-i (Tigers)	6
Busan I'cons	**6**
Jeonbuk Hyundai Motors	4
Suwon Samsung Bluewings	4
Jeonnam Dragons	3
Pohang Steelers	3
Gwangju Sangmu Bulsajo (Military Phoenix)	1
Daegu FC	1
Bucheon SK	0

CHAPTER 3

ROCKET LAUNCHERS AND 12- LANE MOTORWAYS (OR, YOU CAN'T SEE ME!)

DAEGU FC VS. BUSAN I'CONS
SUNDAY, 27 APRIL 2003
K LEAGUE ROUND 6
DAEGU WORLD CUP STADIUM (A.K.A. BLUE ARC)

달도 차면 기운다
*– One cannot expect to be dominant forever
(literally, 'even the moon wanes once it is full')*

I RECEIVED an unexpected phone call a few days after the win over Pohang. It was the Pride of Pusan's president, inviting me to accompany the Busan I'cons supporters to Daegu for an away match. The trip would involve travelling more than 100km north-west to Daegu on the supporters' bus and taking in my first K League away game at the new Daegu World Cup Stadium. Busan would face recently formed Daegu FC, which had just joined the league this season, thus offering a reasonable chance of witnessing another Busan win.

During our brief chat, the POP president volunteered that he was not only the leader of the Busan supporters but also one of the senior members of the Red Devils, South Korea's fervent national team supporters. He seemed excited at the prospect of meeting someone genuinely interested in Busan I'cons, probably because there were only a few dozen such supporters in this city of 3.6 million people.

The day of the match arrived quickly. I followed the instructions to the meeting spot, emerged from the underground subway and ended up on the side of a busy street in Seomyeon, Busan's city centre. I had never seen such a massive thoroughfare in my entire life. Ten lanes of traffic surged in front of me, cars madly darting in and out with only a minimum of warning (if that), sometimes simply with the blare of a horn rather than an indicator light. It ranked somewhere between the pace of traffic that I was accustomed to and an F1 race, leaning toward the latter. And all this took place smack in the middle of the city centre, adjacent to a busy pedestrian footpath.

Several dozen people congregated near a bus stop were wearing Busan I'cons shirts, so I went over and introduced myself. A large bus appeared on the horizon, turned rapidly on to the busy street and barrelled towards the small crowd of football day-trippers. The Busan supporters boarded the vehicle, destined for Daegu, and eagerly settled into their seats for the first group away trip of the season.

We soon set off, and the supporters let slip their enthusiasm by tentatively humming football chants that only minutes later would resonate at full voice throughout the narrow coach. A few POP members pulled back the bus window drapes and tied their club-branded 'mufflers' (scarves) to the metal rod instead, keen to announce their footballing allegiance to the baseball-mad city of Busan. The younger girls were more interested in primping themselves, equipped with the ubiquitous make-up kit and mirror that so many Korean females below the age of 25 carry around and constantly fuss with in public, as if part of a national uniform. Heaven forbid if they were to meet one of the Busan I'cons pop stars – errr, players – and not have five layers of misty eye shadow perfectly applied.

Just as quickly as the singing, chattering, scarf-tying and fanatic cosmetic-administering had begun, a silence unexpectedly swept over the bus. I was puzzled. Had the POP president, the last person to board the supporters' coach, become so irritated with the incessant din that he surreptitiously covered each young supporter's mouth with a chloroform-soaked tissue in a desperate attempt at temporary respite? I turned in my seat and looked back at the Busan supporters. A loud snore tore through the quiescence. Everyone was fast asleep. Boarding the bus, selecting seats, yapping away, applying make-up and falling comatose – all within 15 minutes. Talk about efficient.

* * *

'I saw the [South Korea-USA World Cup] game and the street scenes were unbelievable. That was the greatest atmosphere I've ever felt at a sporting event. Part of it was the stunning stadium in Daegu, but it was mostly the fans.'

– Lamar Hunt, American soccer philanthropist

The Busan supporters' bus soon arrived in the City of Apples. Unlike the dilapidated Daegu Civic Stadium located in the city centre, the new Daegu World Cup Stadium (or 'Blue Arc') sat tucked away in a remote, mostly uninhabited, agricultural corner of the city, nestled up against the foot of a mountain.

Daegu's new venue was the largest of Korea's World Cup stadiums with a capacity of more than 65,000. Not content with merely hosting sport, the complex featured three underground levels, conference centres, open-air theatres, restaurants, a rock-climbing and bungee-jumping facility, a jungle gym and even an outdoor wedding hall. If the young, female Busan supporters applied their eye shadow flawlessly during the bus journey to Daegu, we might be in for some nuptials after the conclusion of the match.

The Busan supporters disembarked from the bus. There were 'ooohs' and 'aaaws' as many of them admired the impressive new stadium for the first time. I was equally surprised by the size of the neighbouring motorway, which spanned an extraordinary 12 lanes – more than Britain's M25 ring road that encircles London – despite being in the middle of nowhere. Koreans certainly loved their cars and concrete.

As the Busan supporters' fascination with the facility waned, they bellowed out several ditties at the top of their lungs and elevated their 'mufflers' with fierce bravado, triumphantly announcing their presence to the locals. Unfortunately there was no one else around for miles. We had arrived more than 90 minutes prior to kick-off.

We entered the stadium. I was surprised to see Daegu's supporters already inside the ground well before kick-off, busily tying massive banners into place with ropes. Some were hung boastfully from the upper tier while others concealed swathes of empty seats. The banners exuded buoyant messages meant to evoke courage and enthusiasm from the Daegu players, yet were primarily in English – a language most of them couldn't comprehend. The plethora of slogans included:

> *Eleven: Be Crazy with Daegu F.C*
> *I was born to love Daegu*
> *LASTMAN STANDING*
> *Voce e da hora* (Portuguese for 'You of the hour' – a nod to Daegu's several Brazilian players)
> *I'LL BE WITH U*
> *WE ARE BOUND TO WIN*
> *YOU CAN'T SEE ME!*

The inadvertently amusing banners were accompanied by an enormous, sky-blue tarp shaped like a Daegu FC shirt. Similar to the banners, the oversized shirt helped hide unoccupied seats from sight, covering several stadium sections.

After recently beating Pohang, Busan found themselves level for third place, a frothy league position for a club that finished second-bottom just last year. Unfortunately Busan's subsequent match was a 2-0 thumping at home, which temporarily deflated any heady thoughts of championship-chasing and returned the supporters to their familiar cynicism. However, the club followed that disappointment with an impressive draw away to Anyang Cheetahs, a powerful team that finished fourth last season. The hope and cautious optimism that sprung from the Pohang victory, although now tempered, still lingered in the imagination of the Busan supporters, or at least among the more optimistic.

That idealism exemplified what was fantastic about the early stages of each new football season: the Busan faithful still had hope. Mathematics had yet to conspire against their chances, however remote, of hoisting the K League title. The possibility persisted. A key win here, an upset victory there, and who knows? Busan could become the unexpected champions of South Korea, and even proceed to the Asian Champions League.

It had only been several years since Busan last achieved such a feat as a dominant K League side. But such history teased and mocked today's Busan supporters, who had come to expect far less achievement. Busan's era of dominance ended so recently that senior members of the Pride of Pusan could regale their younger peers with exciting tales of silverware being lifted and jubilant celebrations. And yet, to the youngsters who had only been supporting the club for the past few years, such stories seemed too alien, too unfamiliar, too laden with triumph to possibly be about the club they knew. Busan I'cons? Champions of South Korea? Surely not.

Busan were now in seventh place, a significant plummet from just two matches previous. But just as it was easy to tumble down the league table early in the season, so too was it feasible to quickly charge back up. That was exactly what Busan I'cons supporters had in mind today. Defeat this newly assembled team of players rejected by other K League clubs, of recent university graduates, of ageing veterans desperate to extend their career for just one more season. In theory, Daegu FC should be the weakest side Busan face all season. Depending on other results, victory could see Busan boomerang back into the upper half of the league table.

* * *

Goal. First half, 44th minute, just before the break. Daegu striker Yoon Joo-il ventures deep into Busan's half with little resistance. Sensing the threat, Busan goalkeeper Kim Yong-dae rushes forward, hoping to shut down the approaching attacker. But it's no use: Daegu's Yoon leaps into the air to meet the ball after its first bounce and pokes it well above the reach of Kim. The ball sails into the goal.

The Daegu supporters are ecstatic. Flags are fervently undulated. Confetti rains down upon empty seats.

1-0 Daegu.

On the opposite side of the stadium, the Busan supporters are distraught, perplexed, forlorn. Surely this hasn't happened. Surely Busan aren't losing to Daegu. Surely this recently assembled, motley collection of players – who likely wouldn't be playing professional football if not for the formation of the K League's newest team – haven't just scored against the former champions of Asia! The match is not meant to unfold this way. The Busan supporters had naively assumed victory against Daegu today and already considered how they would fare the following week. But instead, this! Losing to a club that should be the K League's whipping boys. The unthinkable is happening. And before the Busan players can put together a response, the referee blows his whistle to signal for half-time.

Could this new season prove to be just as disastrous as the last for Busan I'cons, or – heaven forbid – even worse?

* * *

John Ian Porterfield was born in Scotland in February 1946, conceived just weeks after the surrender of Nazi Germany. Raised in the Fife mining town of Lochgelly, he was the son of a humble coal miner, but his mother refused to let him work down in the pits. After dropping out of school at age 15, Porterfield began a football career with juniors Lochgelly Albert and quickly attracted interest from clubs across the British Isles. The youngster was invited to trials at prominent Scottish teams including Rangers and Hearts, and was even courted by Don Revie's eminent Leeds United, where Porterfield slogged for a month before succumbing to homesickness. Porterfield ultimately signed for Raith Rovers as a part-timer because it was closer to home, still painting and decorating on the side to earn sufficient income.

'I played against him when he was with Raith Rovers,' Alex Ferguson, then manager of Manchester United, wrote in a 2007 statement. 'He was an exceptional footballer, blessed with a lot of natural talent.'

Porterfield became known as 'the Bull' at Raith, powering through opponents as a physical midfielder. According to the Scot, he was soon courted by Liverpool, Manchester City and West Ham United. Eventually he signed for top-flight Sunderland, despite having never seen the Tyne and Wear region of England. He would initially return to Scotland every other weekend to avoid missing home.

Sunderland fell victim to relegation and began to flounder, but were galvanised by the mid-season arrival of new manager Bob Stokoe, who greatly inspired Porterfield.

Just months into Stokoe's tenure with the Second Division strugglers, Sunderland progressed to what was then the world's most important match: the FA Cup Final, English football's only game shown on live TV at the time. They would face the mighty Leeds United, still managed by the same Don Revie that Porterfield briefly trialled for years earlier. Leeds were one of the most powerful sides in England, and the general consensus was that they would make light work of Sunderland, a team toiling to avoid dropping down to the league's third tier. But Porterfield would score the only goal of the match, a messy scramble in which a corner kick eventually made its way to the Scot, who settled the ball with his preferred left foot and then surprisingly scored with his self-professed brick of a right.

'I was engulfed by red and white shirts,' Porterfield wrote (with John Gibson) in *The Impossible Dream* of the goal celebrations. 'I couldn't see and my eardrums were almost pierced by the noise.

'No one outside our tightly knit little community believed that we could do it to football's most professional team, but we did.'

One swing of his leg instantly transformed Porterfield into a Wearside legend, revered with cult status for the remainder of his life and beyond. The 1973 win persists as one of the greatest upsets in FA Cup history, with Sunderland the only team in the 20th century to win the cup without any full international players. Almost five decades later, it remains Sunderland's last major trophy victory, ensuring the Porterfield mythology lives on.

* * *

Busan I'cons manager Ian Porterfield stands by the touchline, his storied Korean club trailing 1-0. He had promised 'entertaining soccer' to Busan fans after agreeing to the laborious assignment of correcting an embattled K League team. Porterfield had wisely attempted to temper unrealistic expectations, remarking that the club's first ten matches of the season would likely be 'wobbly', and that results would gradually get better from there.

'I have no complaints; we are going in the right direction,' Porterfield told *Soccerphile*'s John Duerden. 'We are laying a foundation and I hope that we keep improving in my time as coach here.'

The Pride of Pusan members, however, expect swift improvement.

Controversially, Porterfield promoted Busan's young, second-choice goalkeeper to the starting position. Kim Yong-dae had signed for Busan a season earlier, a talented prospect who played at the

Under-20 World Cup and attended the 2000 Sydney Olympics. Kim trialled for the senior national team under Guus Hiddink ahead of the 2002 World Cup, but was ultimately cut during the final round of player evaluations. Less than a year later, Kim's new Scottish manager has taken a shine to him; this season is his big chance.

The second half of the match is a lacklustre affair. Busan's supporters can only muster the energy to chant intermittently. Daegu are determined to derail Busan's positive start to the season. Wave after wave of Busan attacks prove fruitless, casually brushed aside by Daegu's back-line. Mopishly trotting around the pitch, the Busan players sense their efforts are in vain. They become increasingly recumbent as the clock nears the 90-minute mark, already psychologically conceding a 1-0 defeat to the K League's newest members.

But matters worsen. Busan midfielder Kim Tae-min misjudges the speed of a pass he intends to intercept, putting in a sliding effort that inadvertently awards the ball to Daegu striker Hong Soon-hak and allows him to advance toward goal unmarked. Busan goalkeeper Kim Yong-dae has no choice but to come running out from goal for the second time this match, but Hong astutely swerves the ball beyond him.

Goal. 87th minute. 2-0 Daegu.

* * *

Daegu is perhaps best known outside of South Korea as the country's COVID-19 epicentre during the 2020 pandemic, due to the notorious Shincheonji cult inadvertently spreading the virus in large numbers after returning from proselytising trips to China.

Like many of Korea's cities, Daegu had suffered from an eventful history, particularly over the previous century. The metropolis spawned numerous secret societies intent on liberating Korea from Japanese colonial rule in the early 1900s. During the Korean War in the 1950s, communist Northern forces advanced south to the outskirts of Daegu and induced the region into major conflict. The nearby village of Waegwan was the site of war crimes committed by both North Korean and American soldiers, with both forces desperate to control bridge crossings along the Nakdong River.

After the war, Daegu's population ballooned, increasing tenfold in just several decades. The city took on a political tinge, becoming the heartland of Park Chung-hee's autocratic military dictatorship and subsequently the bedrock of South Korean conservatism, which it remains today.

One month prior to the 2003 K League season, Daegu was battered by a vicious subway fire that killed almost 200 people. Just eight days after the blaze, as Daegu FC were about to contest their inaugural K League season, the club announced the result of an online poll to determine which of several logos the fans preferred. Inexplicably, the new logo selected to represent Daegu FC was a swirling flame.

* * *

The Daegu supporters leap into the air, ecstatic about a second goal that surely means victory for their young club. Full time quickly arrives. Busan's dreadful loss to Daegu FC is confirmed.

Not only is this an embarrassing defeat for Busan – it's the first-ever win for Daegu. Busan I'cons, a once feared opponent, would forever be known as the first team to lose to the neophyte side from the City of Apples.

The Daegu players are near-delirious. They rush over to their sky blue-clad supporters and offer applause, followed by a deep and prolonged bow – the norm in South Korean football.

At the expense of Busan, Daegu double their season point tally in a single match, jumping to six points – just one below Busan. Busan's supporters looked stunned. Their club's promising start to the season was dissipating. Fortunately other results that afternoon were favourable for Busan, meaning that the south-east club remained in seventh place. But the damage had been done. Realistically, Busan's title aspirations for 2003 had been dashed barely one month into the new season. The Busan players might as well have announced it over the stadium loudspeakers, their heads hung in shame as they aimlessly meandered around the field in shock. Manager Porterfield looked annoyed, not speaking with any of the squad.

Likewise, not a single word was exchanged between the distraught Busan supporters as they sulked back to the car park. One girl was in tears, utterly inconsolable. Visibly crestfallen, the Pride of Pusan ruefully boarded their bus. Heads bowed, eye contact strictly avoided. It would be a tedious journey home.

Busan manager Porterfield had endeavoured to immunise himself from criticism by insisting his early reign would be shaky. However, none of the supporters foresaw a sapless loss against a newly formed opponent. Porterfield was under the assumption he remained safely ensconced within the cocoon of his recent appointment, but the Busan supporters already began to doubt whether he was the right person to lead the team.

There was cause for some optimism, though: that weekend, Busan signed an impressive Korean striker, still in his mid-20s, from Japanese club Kyoto Purple Sanga. Would his addition help transform Busan I'cons into a formidable team again?

ROUND 4

Busan	**0-2**	**Jeonnam**
Daegu	1-1	Anyang
Ulsan	1-2	Jeonbuk
Daejeon	2-1	Pohang
Suwon	1-0	Bucheon
Seongnam	2-1	Gwangju

ROUND 5

Anyang	**1-1**	**Busan**
Bucheon	2-4	Seongnam
Pohang	0-0	Suwon
Daegu	1-1	Gwangju
Jeonbuk	0-0	Daejeon
Jeonnam	1-2	Ulsan

ROUND 6

Daegu	**2-0**	**Busan**
Ulsan	0-3	Anyang
Suwon	1-1	Jeonbuk
Seongnam	2-0	Pohang
Daejeon	3-2	Jeonnam
Gwangju	2-1	Bucheon

K LEAGUE TABLE

Seongnam	18
Daejeon	13
Anyang	12
Jeonbuk	9
Suwon	9
Ulsan	9
Busan	**7**
Jeonnam	6
Daegu	6
Gwangju	5
Pohang	4
Bucheon	0

CHAPTER 4

SOBER SUPPORTERS AND PLAYER PUNCH-UPS

BUSAN I'CONS VS. ULSAN HYUNDAI
HORANG-I (TIGERS)
WEDNESDAY, 30 APRIL 2003
K LEAGUE ROUND 7
BUSAN ASIAD WORLD CUP STADIUM
호랑이도 제 말하면 온다
*– Speak of the devil (literally, 'if you talk about
the tiger, it will appear')*

JUST NINE minutes into the match, Lee Chun-soo – the South Korean national team's little caramel-haired darling – scores for Ulsan. Striding down the right side of the pitch without any support, Lee manages to advance all the way into Busan's 18-yard box, where he duly smacks the ball past the haemorrhaging backline and into goal.

Busan manager Ian Porterfield looks up at the heavens in frustration and saunters back to the dugout. Despite promising to deliver entertaining football to the people of Busan, his match tactics appear alarmingly old-fashioned: a typical British 4-4-2 formation that relied on 'kick and run' to move the ball up the pitch. Will his Korean squad be able to flourish by desperately launching long balls and outmuscling opponents?

* * *

Success.

It had been simple and achievable in the past. Something so expected, so routine for Busan during their first 17 years in the K League. The words 'success' and 'Busan' had been synonymous in Korean football for almost two decades; but now, the words verged on forming an oxymoron. Abruptly, seemingly overnight, success became elusive. Rot rapidly set in, threatening to topple this once-proud football club into obscurity.

Busan were founding members of the K League in 1983, the team initially known simply as 'Daewoo'. Like most North East Asian football clubs created during that era, they were owned and funded by a wealthy business conglomerate – in this case, the Daewoo Group. Despite only having amateur status that first season, Daewoo performed well, finishing as league runners-up. In the subsequent close season, the club embraced professionalism and expanded their name to Daewoo Royals. The gambit to convert the squad to full-time paid off immediately as the club concluded the 1984 season as Korean champions.

Triumph became the norm for Daewoo Royals. Over the next several seasons, the Busan club won two additional K League titles as well as its most prestigious accomplishments: the 1986 Asian Club Championship (since renamed the AFC Champions League) and the inaugural Afro-Asian Club Championship. That same year Busan also had a player invited to participate in a FIFA World Stars vs. Americas XI friendly.

In 1997, under the elongated moniker Busan Daewoo Royals, the club achieved a domestic treble, winning its fourth K League title and two league cups. Busan were drawing some of the largest crowds and revelled in what would later be perceived as the club's glory days.

But the 1990s weren't all fun and games for football in Busan. Enter 1999, when Busan's only professional football club came precariously close to being shut down. South Korea, and much of East Asia, was battered by an unprecedented financial crisis in the late 1990s. The country's large business conglomerates, which owned and bankrolled most K League clubs, teetered on the brink of fiscal collapse. And indeed, one corporate giant did crumble: Daewoo, South Korea's second largest conglomerate.

With the equivalent of US$80bn in debts, Daewoo's demise marked perhaps the largest corporate bankruptcy in world history at the time. Its chairman, Kim Woo-jung, left his wife behind and fled abroad to avoid arrest on an array of potential charges, including embezzlement and accounting fraud. Interpol put out a half-hearted appeal for Kim's arrest, although the lack of a suspect profile on Interpol's website suggested the South Korean government preferred Kim to remain in exile. Daewoo workers responded to their abandonment by burning Kim in effigy and plastering 'wanted' posters featuring their former chairman.

The calamity left Busan Daewoo Royals in an existential lurch. Without a major benefactor to bleed money to the football club, its existence was in jeopardy.

In response, South Korea's footballing powers twisted the arm of Hyundai – the nation's largest conglomerate – to save the club from extinction by assuming ownership. As Hyundai had just been forced by the government to split into numerous separate entities, financial responsibility for the football club would be shouldered only by one Hyundai subsidiary. The (un)lucky recipient was Hyundai Development Company (HDC), the conglomerate's real estate and construction group. Whether they liked it or not, as of the 2000 K League season, HDC would be required to hand over billions of Korean *won* every year to an endeavour that had nothing to do with land development and offered little if any return on investment.

Even worse, as Hyundai needed to improve its finances, HDC was instructed to increase its profit margin – despite just being saddled with the cost of bankrolling Busan's professional football club. Newly adopted Busan instantly became the red-headed stepchild of Hyundai's stable of football clubs.

No longer under Daewoo ownership, the club was rechristened 'Busan I'cons', the moniker purportedly a portmanteau of the words 'I'Park' (a brand of apartments built by HDC) and 'construction' blended together. Creative genius.

Busan I'cons got off to an inauspicious start under HDC guidance. The club's 2000 season resulted in a disappointing sixth-place finish – their worst performance since 1994. Attendances plummeted during the second half of the year, well below their usual five-figure mark.

Life began slowly in 2001 for results and attendance, but both improved as the season unfolded. The year ended in a mediocre, mid-table position.

But then, in 2002, disaster struck. Busan I'cons finished second-bottom, the club's worst-ever league performance. As always, attendance mimicked team results: the final three home matches saw crowds barely above 2,000.

Coffers had been significantly reduced compared to the Daewoo Royals glory days. Busan's finances were limited to whatever the relatively small HDC could afford to spare.

Overall, the club's achievements during the initial three years of HDC ownership had been poor. The success of the '80s and '90s era had vanished, leaving the club and its fans facing perdition. Busan I'cons had entered a new period in its history: as a skint team that now struggled to complete with opponents from much smaller cities. The club had reached an unprecedented low, with little hope evident for its beleaguered future.

This was the sombre scenario ahead of Busan's 2003 K League season. Club officials attempted to put a positive spin on matters before the year began, highlighting the team's move to the brand-new Asiad World Cup Stadium. It was portrayed as a symbol of rebirth, hope, ambition, glory – that better things were in store for Busan.

But if such a marketing campaign intended to balloon attendances early in the 2003 season, reality proved bereft. Busan's first match in the new stadium, as mentioned earlier, attracted a measly crowd of 6,236 – an embarrassing figure that should have been at least five times larger. One reason for the small gate, in addition to poor match results in recent years, was that punters didn't fancy the remote location of the new venue. The old Gudeok Stadium, used until 2002, may have become antiquated but it was convenient to get to and was inside an entertainment district. In contrast, the new World Cup venue, as bright and shiny as it may have been, was located much further north in an unfancied area nowhere near a subway station (until Busan opened its third subway line in late 2005). The land was part of an existing stadium complex situated with future population growth in mind. But that mattered little now for Busan I'cons Football Club, which couldn't even draw a half-respectable attendance figure for a club debut and season opener in a new stadium.

The ever-entwined binary of winning games and attracting fans continued to prove inseparable. Early season results were slightly better than 2002, but once again, Busan did not exhibit the appearance of would-be champions. Or anything even close to it. Other forms of entertainment also ate away at Busan I'cons' gates. Baseball was a big competitor, as the city's baseball club was by far the most popular in all of South Korea. Even worse, the new Asiad Stadium where Busan I'cons relocated was immediately adjacent to the baseball ground – meaning that if punters were going to travel to attend professional sport, they were much more likely to opt for the cult-like following of Lotte Giants rather than struggling Busan I'cons.

* * *

It was a tepid Wednesday evening, already cooling rapidly from the day's peak temperature of 20°C due to an afternoon deluge of rain. Busan were to host Ulsan, a neighbouring city that leans adversarially against Busan's north-east border. Having just been beaten – if not thoroughly humiliated – by a club founded less than one year ago, Busan's players and supporters were uneasy about this evening's fixture against one of the behemoths of the K League. Ulsan had finished 2002 as league runners-up – losing the title on the last day of the season – and as League Cup finalists. The difficult fixture offered Busan the opportunity to salvage an unexpected, morale-boosting win, but the more likely outcome was a thorough trouncing.

And yet, for Busan's dauntingly masochistic supporters, a sense of hope somehow prevailed. Many members of the Pride of Pusan had already consigned the 2003 K League championship to an opposing club, particularly in light of Sunday's 2-0 drubbing by Daegu. But their collective hubris urged them back into the stadium, match after subsequently painful match. After all, despite Ulsan's mighty stature, they were also stumbling at the moment and looked ripe for the picking. What better antidote for football supporters' wounded pride than a surprise victory against local rivals? Ulsan were immediately above Busan in the league table; a result for Busan today would see them leap-frog their neighbours.

While that may have been incentive enough for ardent Busan I'cons supporters to attend the match, most Busan residents couldn't be bothered, as today's paltry crowd of 3,633 suggested. Weeknight matches were particularly cumbersome; an earlier Wednesday night game only attracted a beggarly 1,569. Club officials could potentially spin tonight's attendance as relatively healthy, but the truth was painfully obvious: Busan simply weren't pulling in the punters.

However, Porterfield has a trick up his sleeve today. Busanites who bothered to turn up for the match are being treated to the debut of a new foreign player: Tommy Mosquera Rosano, known simply as Tommy. The Colombian striker has just been signed on a short-term loan by Porterfield, at the behest of fellow Busan attacker and countryman Harry.

Tommy looks ecstatic to be in South Korea, constantly flashing a beaming smile. After spending a precarious decade toiling in South America's turbulent leagues, he feels relieved to enjoy the stability of the K League.

Tommy had joined Colombian giants Millonarios – where Harry also began his career – in the mid-1990s on a verbal contract, playing for their youth and reserve teams. He was eventually called up to the senior squad that would compete in the 1997 Copa Libertadores, the South American equivalent of the UEFA Champions League. However, just months later, he was abruptly cut and stopped receiving his salary. After enquiring about his future, he was told he could play for the club's C-team and receive 60 per cent of his former senior-team pay, but the offer didn't materialise.

Not getting paid, but with Millonarios still possessing his playing rights, Tommy requested his release. The club ignored him. Despairing, he sought legal advice and took the club to Colombia's Constitutional Court for breach of contract – and won. Tommy's ordeal exemplified the perilous work situation faced by many professional footballers in Colombia.

But today, Tommy is determined to make an impressive K League debut. Just minutes after Ulsan's opening goal, a long ball is barrelled up the right side of the pitch that lands fortuitously in front of Busan striker Gwak Kyung-keun. Racing to control the ball's vehement pace before it bounces astray, Gwak sends it low across goal with Tommy approaching. Anticipating the play, Ulsan goalkeeper Seo Dongmyung trots out toward the trajectory of the ball. But Tommy intercepts it first, controls it as he springs over the diving goalkeeper and softly swats the ball into Ulsan's net. An equaliser for Busan. 1-1.

The phalanx of Pride of Pusan members are overjoyed, just as thrilled to learn that their new striker can actually score as they are with the equaliser. A sense of relief, and perhaps even confidence, overcomes the north end of the stadium – completely empty except for Busan's modest collection of supporters. The small group begins bellowing several chants; the cadence echoes throughout the mostly empty venue. The youngsters jump and sway, waving their cascading arms in temporary glory.

Then a surreal moment that reinforces this is not Western football fare. Two senior Pride of Pusan members quickly distribute short sticks to the Busan hardcore. Next, small white packets are passed around for everyone. I am confused, lacking the faintest idea what I'm observing.

I eventually comprehend what's unfolding. The small white packets are matches. And the sticks? Sparklers. Every supporter duly lights their sparkler and oscillates it frantically. All two-dozen Pride of Pusan members, huddled together in a small but sturdy cluster, are involved in this adorable act of polite pyromania. Who needs flares when you can have a veritable birthday celebration at the football ground?

* * *

Busan's Serbian attacker, Zoran Urumov, obtains possession of the ball. With an opposition midfielder nipping at his heels, Urumov veers toward goal. Approaching the rear corner of the six-yard box, and with a difficult angle to overcome, he slots a low ball narrowly past the extended reach of Ulsan's ponytailed goalkeeper. Urumov races away, raising his arms in celebration. The Serbian pauses to kiss his wedding ring and allow his team-mates to mob him. Busan are ahead, 2-1, in the 26th minute.

Busan's normally cynical supporters are now delirious, overjoyed to the point of bewilderment. Busan are unexpectedly ahead of Ulsan, the side that finished second last season. A few of the Busan hardcore look astonished – shocked so thoroughly they almost have to be reminded to rejoice.

But barely ten minutes later, a ruinous – if perhaps slightly predictable – setback. Busan concede an equalising goal. An Ulsan striker comfortably makes his way through Busan's penetrable back-line. He engineers an adroit and selfless pass across the penalty area to a midfielder who converts the ball with ease. Busan's lead instantly disappears. The momentum of the match abruptly shifts to last season's league runners-up. The small collection of travelling Ulsan supporters begin bouncing near their banner which proclaims *GET WINNING GOAL*.

Under sustained pressure, Busan's back-line buckles in disturbing submission, allowing Ulsan's attacking players to move the ball around Busan's 18-yard box with the sort of arrogance usually reserved for the training ground.

The Pride of Pusan grow apprehensive. Fingernails, some newly emerged from expensive manicure shops, are nervously gnawed.

As the match resumes, Porterfield shoots up off his seat and waves his arms, barking out orders in a Scottish tone most of his squad members still struggle with. Lowering his head, as if already consigned to defeat, he silently makes his way back to the dugout. Porterfield's body language discloses his disappointment.

The whistle for half-time reverberates throughout the stadium, echoing off thousands of empty plastic seats. The break provides a temporary reprieve for the two-dozen Busan supporters. They trek languidly up concrete steps to the stadium concourse, desperate for a 15-minute distraction from the maelstrom on the pitch.

During K League matches, Busan's stadium concourse is pragmatic and austere: it only offers nourishment. Food in the form of rolled *kimbap* (similar to sushi but not containing raw fish) or a hot cup of instant noodles (the Hermit Kingdom's answer to Bovril) during inclement weather. Beverages such as fizzy drinks or cans of lager, which fans may take into the stadium seating. And for more adventurous – or perhaps more demoralised – Busan punters, some bring small glass bottles of hard liquor into the stadium, primarily *soju*.

For some inexplicable reason, none of the Busan supporters are partaking in alcohol. I am perplexed. Certainly, many of them have not reached legal drinking age; but even the older supporters, who have suffered through more seasons and have grown bitter and cynical, refrain from drinking.

An enormous supply of Korean lager is being sold for roughly 50p a can, but not a single member of the Pride of Pusan is indulging, even though it would help dull the frustration of Busan's unravelling lead.

The Busan supporters noisily slurp their instant noodles, refraining from speaking, not wanting to dwell on the inevitable loss likely to unfold in the second half. As the last of the polystyrene bowls and wooden chopsticks are thrown into a large rubbish bin, the Busan faithful quietly saunter back to the stadium's northern end, psychologically readying themselves for the disappointment ahead.

Three minutes is all it takes for a goal that would prove deciding. Incredibly, it isn't Ulsan that score. Somehow, Busan I'cons re-establish their lead. Unfancied defensive midfielder Ryu Byung-hoon – bizarrely redeployed by Porterfield as a striker today – attempts to convert a free kick but instead nutmegs himself, an unusual move that appears more error than wizardry. The ball sails unimpeded into Ulsan's net.

Ryu trots away with the cheekiest of grins, perhaps acknowledging that the intricate goal was as much a surprise to him as it was to everyone else. The Pride of Pusan members are elated but temper their celebrations, as 42 minutes still remain.

Busan stubbornly hang on to their narrow lead. Discipline unravels and after a veritable taekwondo display, the referee dishes out two quick red cards and blows his whistle to signal full time. Porterfield pumps his fist in celebration of Busan's victory over a formidable opponent.

The Pride of Pusan members pull technologically advanced mobile phones, years ahead of Western equivalents, out from their pockets to check other scores. Jeonbuk lost to league leaders Seongnam as expected – meaning Busan have leapfrogged not only Ulsan, but Jeonbuk as well. Unexpectedly, Suwon Bluewings – the K League giants bankrolled by the enormous Samsung corporation – only managed to draw at home. Busan were now level for fifth place, with the same number of points (ten) as Suwon.

Was it possible this wouldn't be such an agony-filled season for Busan after all?

A match this coming weekend against the K League's other newly created member – Gwangju, the military's club – would prove whether Busan could claw their way back to being championship contenders. Victory would be a must for Ian Porterfield's team.

ROUND 7

Busan	**3-2**	**Ulsan**
Bucheon	1-1	Daegu
Pohang	2-1	Gwangju
Jeonbuk	0-3	Seongnam
Suwon	1-1	Jeonnam
Anyang	0-0	Daejeon

K LEAGUE TABLE

Seongnam	21
Daejeon	14
Anyang	13
Suwon	10
Busan	**10**
Jeonbuk	9
Ulsan	9
Jeonnam	7
Daegu	7
Pohang	7
Gwangju	5
Bucheon	1

CHAPTER 5

SUPPORTERS HAVE KIT, BUT PLAYERS DON'T

BUSAN I'CONS VS. GWANGJU SANGMU
BULSAJO (MILITARY PHOENIX)
SUNDAY, 4 MAY 2003
K LEAGUE ROUND 8
BUSAN ASIAD WORLD CUP STADIUM

벙어리삼년, 귀머거리삼년, 장님삼년
*– A bride must be able to forgive the annoyances
brought on by her new mother-in-law during the
initial three years of marriage (literally, 'a bride
must be three years deaf, three years dumb and
three years blind')*

FEMALE REFEREE Im Eun-ju pulls a red card out of her
pocket and raises it sternly above Busan attacker Urumov. With
the Serbian's early dismissal, Busan are ahead 1-0 thanks to his
earlier goal but are now down to ten men.

The opponent of the day is Gwangju Sangmu Bulsajo (or
'Military Phoenix'). This is South Korea's armed forces club, a
squad of footballers fulfilling their obligatory two-year military
service, as virtually all males in South Korea must eventually (and
reluctantly) do.

With the K League eager to expand and the Korean FA
keen to find tenant clubs for the country's new World Cup
stadiums, the military team was persuaded to join the K League
in 2003. They would play in the south-western city of Gwangju,

marking the first time the military team would represent a particular city.

Busan I'cons were apprehensive about playing Gwangju, having already earned the unflattering accolade of being the first team to lose to this season's other new K League club, Daegu FC. Luckily for Busan, Gwangju had already won a match this season, saving Busan from the potential embarrassment of being the first club to slip against the military side. But a hypothetical loss today would earn Busan the ignominy of being the first club to lose to the newcomer pair of Daegu and Gwangju, and would mark Gwangju's first away win. With Urumov's frivolous red card for dissent, such a worst-case scenario must be flashing through the minds of Busan's players and supporters. The confidence gained from beating Ulsan just four days earlier is quickly evaporating.

And then – a goal.

* * *

As South Korea's armed forces club, Gwangju Sangmu is perhaps more similar to a national C team than a typical K League club. Its squad is composed entirely of players on loan from other K League clubs – the very best of whichever players were currently fulfilling their military service. As such, Gwangju can't offer permanent contracts, nor can they sign any foreign players. The team suffers from 100 per cent squad turnover every two years, as on-loan players eventually complete their military service and return to their permanent K League clubs.

However, the one big advantage the military club does enjoy, unlike normal new clubs building a nascent squad, is access to some top talent. Almost all Korean men have to serve a stint in the nation's military – even the very best K League footballers. Because of this, most of the league's famous players eventually serve a stint with this military team. Given the choice between being woken up every morning at 4am for shooting practice and cleaning toilets, or playing in the K League for Gwangju Sangmu, the league's big names always choose the latter.

Lee Dong-gook was one such big-name player. His CV boasted of playing for Werder Bremen in the German Bundesliga, as well as being a key part of the South Korean national team at the 1998 World Cup in France. However, he was passed over by

Guus Hiddink for the 2002 World Cup due to a supposed lack of stamina and speed. Hurt by the exclusion, Lee didn't watch a single match of the tournament, and instead spent the summer consoling himself by drinking heavily, earning the hapless nickname 'Lazy Genius'.

Sure enough, Lazy Genius is playing for Gwangju today against Busan, having recently joined the military club. Busan supporters are fascinated by his presence, wondering whether they would see the striker that won the 2000 Asian Cup golden boot, or perhaps the more recent scallywag who just couldn't be arsed.

Busan start the match versus Gwangju with a distinct swagger, having just beaten last season's league runners-up Ulsan. The surprising result meant a decent crowd of more than 10,000 flocked to the Busan Asiad World Cup Stadium to see today's match, which Busan were favoured to win as they had accumulated twice as many points as Gwangju at this early point in the season.

The match begins well, with Urumov scoring in the sixth minute. Unfortunately, his subsequent red card sabotages Busan's confidence and momentum. Even more troubling for Busan is that unpredictable striker Lee Dong-gook looks to have conquered his off-field issues, exhibiting an alacrity he hasn't displayed for months.

As a footballer, Lee is hungry again. He wants to prove his doubters wrong. He desires to show European scouts that he is still as capable as, if not even sharper than, his previous exploits at Werder Bremen. Lee is intent on demonstrating to Humberto Coelho, the new manager of the South Korean national side, that he is worth capping. And perhaps most of all, he's desperate to affirm just how utterly wrong Guus Hiddink was to exclude him from the 2002 World Cup.

Lee is determined to eviscerate whichever club may be foolish enough to step between him and his comeback. And it just so happens that Busan I'cons stands in the way today.

Goal. Lee Dong-gook scores a cracker in the 18th minute, one of such majestic beauty that it belies his status as a mere K League player. After the goal, Lee does not smile nor does he celebrate, for such jubilation would suggest contentment. Lee was not yet satisfied. Not even close. His pursuit to annihilate his opponent of the day had only just begun.

Thud! The heads of the Busan players drop in an instant. *Poof!* Gone is the moderate arrogance they started the match with. Busan are a man down, and have the rotten luck of attempting to thwart quite possibly South Korea's best striker as he launches a steadfast career comeback. *Pop!* Lee's exquisite goal bursts what little sense of morale the Busan players developed during the last four days.

The Pride of Pusan members quietly slink down into their seats. A moribund atmosphere ensues. 'We're going to lose, aren't we?' their collective faces sob. Lose to some pathetic pseudo-club that had only just joined the K League. Lose to yet another crap opponent that any decent team should be able to effortlessly obliterate. Spend yet another weekend supporting a hopeless bunch of losers who couldn't win a string of matches if their lives depended on it.

Pride of Pusan leader Seok-ho closes his eyes. A look of scorn pushes his mouth uncomfortably over to the side of his face. It seems a seminal moment. Had he reached a breaking point? Seok-ho had spent years supporting Busan, once a mighty and proud club that could take on the finest in Asia. And just last year, South Korea had advanced to the semi-finals of the World Cup. Such a sweet taste of success must still simmer poignantly in his memory! But now this. Supporting a loathsome and degenerate group that didn't deserve to be called footballers. His disdain is obvious, found within every fold of anger and each wrinkle of disappointment that maps out his face. Sharing his pain, I look away, unable to stomach the sight of any more despondent Busan supporters. I close my own eyes, and find myself sharing in the collective remorse.

* * *

The effects of Busan I'cons' new financial restraints were painfully apparent. The football club had been under the ownership of Hyundai Development Company for a few seasons now, and witnessed reductions in the playing budget. Compared to the old Daewoo glory days, the club was now skint. A few of the better Daewoo era players briefly remained with the club after it was rechristened as Busan I'cons in 2000, but they were eventually transferred to other clubs – such as 2002 World Cup star Song Jong-gook's move to Feyenoord, as well as 2002 K League golden boot runner-up Woo Sung-yong and defensive lynchpin Lee Min-sung both heading to league rivals Pohang. The club's owners were happy to accept the transfer fees, despite the obvious pillaging of their best footballers.

By 2003, they had all left. Busan I'cons now suffered from a dearth of talent. As Leo Mendoza – the club's Spanish–English translator – would later remark, the 2003 squad was of a similar ability as the 2002 reserve side. Those who remained were either ageing veterans perilously close to retirement or pimple-faced kids fresh out of school – a motley, bipolar mixture. There were precious few mid-career players who could draw upon a mixture of both speed and experience. If anything was to be salvaged from the 2003 season, it would have to be earned through heroic efforts at every match, and would require exceptional management and coaching.

'Clubs like … Suwon … and Jeonbuk, the money these clubs are spending … I would love to have the budget that these people have, it would make my job a lot easier,' Porterfield told *Soccerphile's* John Duerden.

'Our club is not in that position.'

This wasn't going to be an easy year for Busan I'cons Football Club.

Busan midfielder Noh Jung-yoon places the ball down on the emerald Asiad pitch, rotating it several times until satisfied with its placement. He prepares to initiate an attacking play from a free kick. If a young/old dichotomy characterised Busan's squad, Noh was definitely part of the latter. Now at the age of 32 – but arguably with the body of a 40-year-old – Busan's decision to sign Noh illustrated their desperation.

Noh had enjoyed a decent career as a footballer. As a youngster he was one of Korea's fastest players, able to run 100m in 11 seconds, and became a star member of the Korea University side of 1992. Noh was whisked off to Japan to participate in the much-heralded debut season of the J.League, the first South Korean to do so. He remained there for almost a decade, sandwiched around a brief spell in the Dutch Eredivisie. Noh also appeared in the 1994 and 1998 World Cups.

Unfortunately, Noh picked up a major injury during his final season in Japan. He was informed he would likely never play football again. Most clubs no longer wanted anything to do with him.

Up stepped cash-strapped Busan I'cons. Unable to bring talented players to the club through expensive transfers, Busan hoped that signing Noh Jung-yoon on the cheap and rehabilitating him back to his old form would deliver to them a superstar, while barely scratching the player budget.

It was an audacious gamble. On one hand, Noh was starting most games for Busan, and he scored the quickest goal in K League history – 23 seconds after kick-off – just several weeks ago. Two games later he would score again, earning himself the club's 'most valuable player' award for the months of March and April.

On the other hand, he was being substituted out early each match – sometimes even during the first half.

Noh trots forward and arcs a powerful ball that swings toward goal. Busan defender Yoon Hee-joon, making a rare appearance in the opposition's 18-yard box, leaps up into the air and whacks the ball toward goal with impressive velocity. Gwangju's goalkeeper isn't paying attention to the unfancied Busan defender, and thus doesn't expect the dart of a header that sails into the right side of his goal.

2-1 Busan.

We are ahead again. The Busan supporters leap to their feet. The earlier wave of optimism and hope, brushed aside by the quick succession of a red card and a Gwangju equaliser, come roaring back.

Down a man, Busan are perhaps only hoping to ride out the match for a draw. But they've scored again! Busan, with a pitiable squad and down a player, have scored! Already beginning to take the result for granted, the Busan supporters begin to speculate how many more K League clubs they would leapfrog if the scoreline holds.

The whistle for half-time echoes throughout Asiad World Cup Stadium. The Pride of Pusan jump and dance as if they've already won.

Then, a Busan player jogs toward the supporters and begins an intense exchange. Someone from the club erred, as one of the Busan players was entered on to the team sheet with an incorrect number: 21. That was unfortunate – but the disaster is that the club doesn't have a clean uniform with number 21 on it. The affected substitute player comes over to the supporters to ask if they had a top with '21' on it that he could borrow for the second half, lest the referee not let him enter the match.

They do not.

* * *

Entranced with optimism, the Busan players lower their guard. And barely ten minutes into the second half, Lee has his second goal.

The Pride of Pusan are gutted, even more than after his initial equaliser. Once again, Lee's goal is a thing of unusual beauty. But rather than merely being a spectacular effort, Lee's run-up also makes a mockery of Busan's back-line, exposing some Busan defenders as naive footballers still learning how to play the game. The Pride members are perhaps more disappointed with the Busan players' lack of ability than they are bitter at Lee's seemingly unstoppable talent.

Ian Porterfield, the Busan I'cons manager, is visibly dismayed by how easily his squad surrenders to Lee Dong-gook's efforts. Porterfield jumps off the bench and shouts several commands in a thick Dunfermline accent to his players, who undoubtedly aren't able to hear, let alone understand, the instructions. He turns back toward his bench of substitutes with a fleeting moment of eye contact that reveals his disappointment. Rather than throwing his notebook, or cursing and striking out at some inanimate object, Porterfield quietly sits down into his seat, crosses his legs and then folds his arms. He lets out a gentle sigh, and a meek-looking frown forms upon his saddened face.

There he is again. That arrogant bastard, racing up the flank one more time. Dribbling past Busan players as if they are Subbuteo figurines with feet planted firmly into the ground. He dashes forward purposefully, humiliating opponent, after opponent, after opponent. *Come on, somebody stop him!* Put an unsportsmanlike foot into his path. Slide into him with studs showing. Just do *something*!

The Busan supporters can't watch. Most avert their gaze, waiting for the inevitable groan from the home crowd, the collective exhalation of breath tinged acrid with disappointment.

For the first time in the match, a smile finally appears upon the face of Lee Dong-gook, betraying his efforts to keep a cool and unemotional demeanour. The boy has his hat-trick. Busan 2 Gwangju 3.

As feared, Busan I'cons become the first club to lose to the pair of Daegu and Gwangju, the K League's newcomers. Busan are also the first club to lose at home against Gwangju.

Exactly what has former Chelsea manager Ian Porterfield got himself into?

I wandered home and unfolded a newspaper. A *Korea Times* article explained how Korean footballers who were not talented enough to be chosen for Gwangju's K League squad had been intentionally injuring themselves to avoid the mandatory military draft. Ninety-two players had been found guilty of deliberately dislocating their shoulders through excessive weight training, and an orthopaedic surgeon who operated on the players was also convicted in the scam. While most of the players were from amateur leagues, 15 of those found guilty were current or former K League players.

I couldn't help but wonder if prison would be preferable to lacing up for Busan I'cons.

ROUND 8

Busan	**2-3**	**Gwangju**
Daegu	0-1	Jeonbuk
Jeonnam	2-1	Pohang
Anyang	2-1	Bucheon
Ulsan	0-0	Seongnam
Daejeon	2-0	Suwon

K LEAGUE TABLE

Seongnam	22
Daejeon	17
Anyang	16
Jeonbuk	12
Jeonnam	10
Suwon	10
Ulsan	10
Busan	**10**
Gwangju	8
Daegu	7
Pohang	7
Bucheon	1

CHAPTER 6

ALCOHOL – NO; STOLEN MILITARY FLARES – YES

BUSAN I'CONS VS. SUWON SAMSUNG
BLUEWINGS
SUNDAY, 11 MAY 2003
K LEAGUE ROUND 10
BUSAN ASIAD WORLD CUP STADIUM

조족지혈 (鳥足之血), *or* 새발의 피

*– Something insignificant or irrelevant; a weaker
opponent is nothing to be worried about*

(literally, 'a drop of blood from a bird's foot')

SOUTH KOREA'S military dictatorship faced a predicament in
the 1980s: democracy protests were gaining momentum. Citizens
were becoming less fearful of the regime and increasingly daring in
their demands for an end to martial rule. Young men in particular,
with ample energy but few outlets for release, were attracted to the
popular movement in the tens of thousands.

The regime needed a swift conclusion to this trend, but without
spilling any blood. Their solution was ingenious: mass distraction.

The '3S' policy was launched: sex, sports and screens. With
the cynical view that many South Korean citizens were merely
bored and would flock to glamorous entertainment over democracy
marches, restrictions were loosened on adult-themed content. In
fact, this conservative country's leaders expressly encouraged risqué
diversions: in movies, television, books and even comics. Sexually

suggestive cinema became the norm. Television broadcasts were upgraded to colour, broadcast times were expanded and educational programming was replaced with racy fluff. The nightly curfew was also lifted, allowing people to party away their energy every evening.

A similar strategy was engineered for sport. In 1981, South Korea won the hosting rights for the Summer Olympics held later that decade. During the same year, a professional baseball league was launched, with the country's wealthy business conglomerates 'encouraged' to establish and bankroll teams.

Around this time, South Korean football was limited to amateur or semi-pro works teams. But in 1983, the country's first professional football competition was established: the Korea Super League. Arguably Asia's first pro football league (though Hong Kong might dispute that), it began with just five teams – including Daewoo, which eventually became known as Busan I'cons. Two decades later, in 2003, the rebranded K League was in its 21st season and hoped to build upon the excitement of South Korea recently co-hosting the World Cup alongside Japan and advancing to the semi-finals.

* * *

It's an intoxicating feeling as you enter a football ground. An escape from reality, a reprieve from the inanity of daily drudgery. But it's so much more than merely a distraction. I suppose it's the closest emotion many grown adults feel to the excitement of a child overcome with awe entering an amusement park, or waking up ridiculously early on Christmas morning with the anticipation of tearing open presents.

Why does a football ground come to hold such an aura for supposedly mature and rational adults? No matter how poorly our club of allegiance is performing, the journey to the football stadium sends hearts aflutter, makes the sternest of brutes fervent with apprehension, and dares the most pessimistic of grouches to dream of triumph. Simply by placing a foot inside, it is as if we revert from cynical, scowling grown-ups into euphoric youngsters.

It's arguably not the actual football that captivates us. Rather, it's our reawakened imagination, pregnant with belief and brimming with wonder, that enamours us so intensely.

Upon entering Busan Asiad World Cup Stadium, before I could engage in any sort of enamouring, a man in a black suit rushed toward me. I immediately sensed something was amiss. Unlike the fawning over foreigners that Korean hosts occasionally resort to, he presented a stern expression as he delivered a serious message to me. And that was, quite simply, 'No drinking alcohol.'

I was discombobulated by his request – or rather, command – and attempted to figure out the reasoning behind it as I wandered dazedly into the stadium concourse. Sure, the Pride of Pusan members refrained from drinking alcohol during matches, but many other people in the stadium openly consumed beer. In fact, as I scanned the refreshments area of the concourse, I noticed bucket upon bucket, shelf upon shelf of lager for sale. So why had this club staffer specifically singled me out for individual prohibition?

And then it hit me: World Cup stadium 'moats'. Or more specifically, the reason why Koreans installed these architectural ditches for the 2002 tournament: an unfounded fear of drunken Western hooligans rampaging through World Cup venues and across Korean cities, unleashing violence and destruction.

The reality was that Western European football had long since cast aside its ugly hooligan element by the 21st century, replacing it with a bland and money-driven culture that catered to corporates rather than 'casuals'. But I suppose watching grainy, 1970s footage of Millwall ruffians throwing bricks at Leeds supporters armed with broken glass bottles left a lasting impression.

Despite the splendid weather, Busan I'cons were only able to attract a paltry crowd once again: 4,399, which turned out to be the lowest in the K League that weekend. As usual, attendance mimicked results. The recent win over heavyweights Ulsan resulted in more than 10,000 spectators against Gwangju last week, but a loss against the new military team that day dictated today's turnout would be minuscule.

Drew Jarvie, the assistant of manager Ian Porterfield, waves to the Busan faithful before settling into the dugout for the match. The Aberdeen legend is now in his mid-50s and thin, almost to the point of looking gaunt. He's dressed in khaki shorts, a white T-shirt, white trainers and white socks – only the absence of a bum bag prevents him from being mistaken for an American tourist.

Jarvie was raised in Annathill, a tiny coal-mining village in Lanarkshire. The town's men, including Jarvie's father, toiled in a colliery. Similar to Porterfield, Jarvie's parents didn't want him to work down in the pits.

Life was austere for young Jarvie, his family sharing an outdoor toilet with neighbours. According to an interview with *The Scotsman*, there was only one football in the entire village to play with.

Prior to joining Aberdeen, Jarvie only played football part-time, moonlighting as a car electrician. His transfer to the Dons involved the club paying a record fee. Jarvie remained there for a decade, including four seasons under young manager Alex Ferguson, and received several Scotland caps.

Besides football, Jarvie was infamous for his ambitious hair combover – or the amusing result when the wind got the best of it.

'I admit to some vanity: I tried a wee spray to keep the [hair] strands in place but it never worked,' Jarvie told *The Scotsman*. '[Aberdeen team-mate] Neale Cooper used to say, "Drew wasn't offside but his hair was."'

After retirement, Jarvie served as an assistant manager at several Scottish clubs, including St Mirren and Dundee. He rejoined Aberdeen initially as their reserves coach, later becoming the youth manager, but was let go in late 2002. The timing was perfect for Porterfield to invite Jarvie to become his assistant in South Korea.

'A massive challenge lies ahead [for Busan I'cons] but I am very optimistic about achieving our targets,' Jarvie told the *Sunday Mirror*. 'Ian [Porterfield] has worked all over the globe and brings a lot of experience to the managerial post. We have already started identifying European players who are capable of strengthening the team. I have put forward [the names of] a couple of Scots who would do the job.'

* * *

Ten minutes into the match against Suwon, Busan earn a corner. As it's taken, Busan's new Colombian striker, Tommy, races forward. Using his height to his advantage, Tommy lifts off the ground and rises above the gaggle of white Suwon shirts. Korean national team goalkeeper Lee Woon-jae can only watch as the cross falls deftly on to the forehead of Tommy and into the delicate embrace of the net. The converted header is Tommy's second goal of the young season for Busan, now ahead 1-0 against Suwon, one of the strongest opponents in the K League.

Busan and Suwon entered this match level on points, with ten each. A win for Busan would see them leap above Suwon to the dizzying heights of the top half of the K League table – foreign territory for the Pride of Pusan in recent years. And despite impressive accolades in previous seasons, Suwon were currently on poor form. They had won only two of their eight games this season and lost their latest match 2-0 on the road. Could Busan, for all their setbacks, pluck a cheeky win against the would-be league challengers?

It's still early in the match, but the unexpected 1-0 scoreline for Busan means it's time for celebration, if not a display of arrogance and mettle. Many of Busan's normally polite supporters today seem determined to taunt their Suwon equivalents. As I would later learn, these two supporter clubs shared a less-than-cordial history.

Out it came: a flare. Probably the most provocative action that the typically restrained Pride of Pusan members could muster. Magnanimity be damned.

I had seen flares in K League photographs and was aware that supporters of other clubs used them in recent weeks, but this is the first instance of a flare being used here in Busan this young season. The supporter holding it ignites the top of the sphere with a lighter, and after a delay of several seconds, a halo of dark-crimson light bursts out intensely, illuminating the entire stadium section. The poor lad charged with wielding the flare is wearing sunglasses, yet still needs to turn his face away and cover his eyes from the brilliant display. Moments later, the radiance of the flare decreases slightly as a thick cloud of white smoke exudes from its burning top. Many of the Busan supporters, not used to having pyrotechnics in their section, alarmedly cover their mouths and noses with scarves, and some even dart away from the section to avoid breathing in fumes.

The K League had officially banned the use of flares and smoke bombs, technically illegal for South Korean civilians to operate. Since most Korean men begrudgingly spent two years fulfilling mandatory military service, flares and other trivial items tended to go missing from military depots, often ending up in football stadiums.

The precarious 1-0 lead over Suwon survives until half-time. Busan defender Lee Lim-saeng concedes a small grin as he leaves the pitch. With a sturdy frame and a large, square face, Lee had been one of the more formidable defenders in the K League during his prime. Acquired by Busan in the close season when Bucheon's corporate owner cynically cashed in on the club's best players, Lee had represented South Korea at the 1998 World Cup. He was perhaps best known for the famous image of him wearing a bloody head bandage yet insisting on continuing play – similar to the legendary photos of England's Terry Butcher and Paul Ince.

Nicknamed 'The Hammer' for his tough playing style, Lee was declared a K League all-star in four of the past five seasons. However, he was now in the twilight of his playing career. All four of Busan's most-capped defenders this season were already in their 30s, including Lee.

Much like captain Noh Jung-yoon, Lee's signing was a risk for Busan, a club that rarely paid transfer fees. If he were to continue his adept form, he could be a fantastic addition to the beleaguered team. But if Lee were to perform poorly or retire earlier than expected, it would mean Busan squandering some of its limited budget – which the struggling club could not afford to do.

As Lee returns to the dressing room, I notice the large number of Suwon away supporters. They had traversed the five-hour journey – not including the obligatory traffic jams – to the opposite end of the country here in the south-east. There are four or five busloads of them, clad in royal blue replica shirts, gathered at the other end of the stadium. Rather dishearteningly, the travelling Suwonites readily outnumber the local Busan supporters.

The match is soon back underway. Lee Ho, Suwon's manager, must have berated his players for the entire 15-minute interval as they exhibit newfound earnestness. Just four minutes into the second half, Brazilian attacking midfielder Enio Oliveira Junior scores for the visitors. He sveltely glides past several defenders, including the aforementioned Lee Lim-saeng, and into Busan's six-yard box with far too much ease.

The 150-odd members of the Grand Bleu, as the Suwon supporters are known, are galvanised into celebration. Not to be outdone by an inferior Busan opponent, neither on nor off the pitch, the travelling Suwon hardcore light a flare of their own. Then another. And another. Soon, almost a dozen flares bellow smoke and emit bright blue light from the south end of Busan Asiad World Cup Stadium. So much for the Pride of Pusan's earlier swagger.

As much as the equalising goal is a disappointment, it's hardly unexpected. Bankrolled by the mighty Samsung conglomerate, Suwon Bluewings were one of the highest-spending teams in South Korea. Entering the K League in 1996, this was only the young club's eighth season, yet they already boasted 14 pieces of silverware. As the defending Korean FA Cup holders, as well as both the Asian Club Championship and Asian Super Cup winners for the past two years, Suwon were not your ordinary weekend opposition.

The city of Suwon – the club's home – is the capital of Gyeonggi Province, the suburban ring that surrounds Seoul. Its most prominent feature is an old fortress and large wall that today serves as a selfie backdrop for tourists. But Suwon also brandished a unique claim to fame: being the self-proclaimed toilet capital of South Korea.

Yes, you read that correctly: Suwon enthusiastically insisted that it was the bog centre of the country. And they were proud of it. Given this amusing anecdote, I expected supporters of other K League clubs to use this bizarre designation to great effect, producing giants banners of porcelain bogs – perhaps with Suwon Bluewings' club crest submerged in the bowl – at every match. But no. Apparently Suwon's lavatorial swagger was something to indeed brag about.

Desperate to show the world that South Korea was developing, Suwon City Council set up a very serious toilet improvement project. Aiming to produce 'a desirable restroom culture', Suwon's then-mayor, Shim Jae-deok, deployed such slogans as 'Making the Filthiest Place into the Cleanest One!' and 'A Space for Thinking while Resting Comfortably like a Lounge!'

Former mayor Shim, who earned the nickname 'Mr Toilet', even built a grandiose house shaped like a toilet in 2007, garnering worldwide news coverage. Suwon had become the undisputed international King of the Crappers.

* * *

Suwon Bluewings' attacking midfielder, Seo Jung-won, has possession of the ball in the middle of the pitch. Given the nickname *nal-ssaen dori* (or 'speedy'), Seo reportedly turned down a contract offer from Barcelona in his early 20s.

Striding forward toward Busan's goal, Seo makes his way past opposition midfielders and defenders until he's smack in the centre of Busan's 18-yard box. Why bother with intricate passing if you can march straight at goal without even the slightest hint of difficulty? He unleashes a thundering shot with his right foot, which sails past Busan goalkeeper Kim Yong-dae and sets the white goal netting aflutter.

With only a minute left to play, Suwon are ahead 2-1. It's the second consecutive match that Busan have conceded a late goal, and looks like it will also be the second game in a row that Busan lose despite being ahead at half-time. Perhaps more alarming is that both of these collapses have taken place at Busan's supposedly advantageous home ground. The several busloads of travelling Grand Bleu supporters erupt in delight, celebrating that they've probably snatched all three points from Busan. More flares are lit as the din of Suwon chants reverberates throughout Asiad's concrete interior, further agitating the Pride of Pusan members. Annoyed by what they feel is insolent revelry, several male Busan fans let slip colourful phrases. The females look defeated, casting their gaze down to the concrete stairs littered with the remains of confetti and carrier bags, as they grudgingly come to terms with yet another meagre result.

Regardless of club loyalty, you couldn't help but admire the intensity and sheer quantity of the Grand Bleu. Established back in 1995, they were the first formal supporters' club in the K League. Before then, there was no structured football devotion in South Korea.

'The fans were very enthusiastic but there was no organised chanting or other forms of support,' Polish player Tadeusz Świątek, who competed in the K League during the late 1980s and early 1990s, told newspaper *Tygodnika Płockiego*.

Easily the largest supporters' group in Korea, more than 30,000 Suwon faithful had registered on the Grand Bleu's website by 2008. Several thousand of their blue-clad members attended each home match, filling and often spilling over from the north end of the Big Bird Stadium. It was these Suwon hardcore who comprised a large chunk of the early Red Devils, supporters of the South Korean national team. Numerous Grand Bleu songs were coopted for use by the national side, such as the infectiously repetitious '*Dae-Han-*

Min-Guk' chant that captivated worldwide audiences during the 2002 World Cup.

The referee puts his whistle to his lips and ends the match with three brief gusts from his lungs. The blue-shirted supporters are overjoyed and embrace. More flares are lit. Taunts are hurled and – surprisingly – quickly returned by the normally reserved Busan supporters. A couple of the senior Pride of Pusan members attempt to calm their peers, fearful of escalation.

If you asked a Busan supporter which K League club they disliked most – as 'hate' was an awfully strong word for the polite Pride – the answer was almost always Suwon. I was confused by this, as Busan shares a common border with Ulsan and thus I expected a fierce local derby between the two south-eastern clubs. Instead, a historical match between Busan and Suwon created bitterness and resentment that lingers to this day.

Back in 1998, Busan hosted Suwon at the old Gudeok Stadium. Things quickly became testy between the squads and culminated in a mass brawl that cleared both teams' dugouts. As the battle raged, incensed supporters threw objects on to the field and eventually invaded the pitch to take part in the fisticuffs. Players and supporters traded insults and knocks in an enormous skirmish that embarrassed the league.

The eagerness of both clubs' supporters to engage in the brawl was down to one primary reason: alcohol. Both groups were hammered, spurring them to participate in an altercation that initially had only involved players. To prevent such an incident from ever occurring again, the former hard men from Busan imposed a strict alcohol ban upon themselves and removed derogatory chants about opposition clubs from their repertoire. From then on, they would be sober and only participate in positive, uplifting ditties about their team. No booze would be consumed during infuriating losses, nor on monotonous bus trips to cities several hours away. Now that's dedication.

Fast-forward to 2003 and Busan's sober supporters still harboured an intense grudge against Suwon, particularly the Grand Bleu. But now rather than flipping glass bottles or rude gestures at the Suwon supporters, the Pride of Pusan instead flipped open their mobile phones to read other K League scores – mostly expected results that would make bookmakers smile. But hang on:

newcomers Gwangju had beaten fellow south-western club Jeonnam Dragons! This meant that Gwangju, the military club that had joined the K League only weeks ago, were now ahead of Busan on points. The Pride members regarded the updated league table with disbelief. Former behemoths Busan were now third-bottom, with only newcomers Daegu FC and perennial losers Bucheon SK below them.

Welcome to another week in the glamorous life of the Pride of Pusan.

ROUND 9 (postponed due to inclement weather)

ROUND 10

Busan	**1-2**	**Suwon**
Ulsan	3-0	Daejeon
Pohang	2-1	Daegu
Jeonbuk	2-1	Bucheon
Gwangju	2-1	Jeonnam
Anyang	0-3	Seongnam

K LEAGUE TABLE

Seongnam	25
Daejeon	17
Anyang	16
Jeonbuk	15
Ulsan	13
Suwon	13
Gwangju	11
Jeonnam	10
Pohang	10
Busan	**10**
Daegu	7
Bucheon	1

CHAPTER 7

SLEEP-DEPRIVED AND WITHOUT A TOILET

DAEJEON CITIZEN VS. BUSAN I'CONS
SUNDAY, 18 MAY 2003 (RESCHEDULED)
K LEAGUE ROUND 9
DAEJEON WORLD CUP STADIUM (A.K.A. PURPLE ARENA)

울며 겨자 먹기
– Grin and bear it (literally, 'cry while eating mustard seed')

'I've thought about [becoming a football manager] a lot. I'd be silly not to. And one thought that stands out above all others: I want to stay in the game.

'Football is my life. No one can change that. I live and breathe it and therefore it's natural that I shouldn't look beyond it for employment.

'My future lies where it has always been – on the football field.'

– Ian Porterfield (with John Gibson), *The Impossible Dream*, 1973

IT'S SUNDAY, 10am. I'm on a bus with roughly 20 other passengers. I really should be asleep, or at least having a leisurely weekend morning at home. That's what most normal people are doing. But the people I'm sharing this bus with are not normal. They're Busan I'cons Football Club supporters. We're off to Daejeon, some three hours away from Busan if traffic is kind, which in Korea, it rarely is.

As our departing bus approaches the outskirts of Busan, the urban horizon recedes. Towers become edifices, which shrink down to modest houses. The drab grey carpet that smothers Korean cities begins to crack as we enter Yangsan, lush greenery poking through. The bus sails up a motorway, built through a valley of Korea's ubiquitous mountains. Lush fields awash in green dominate the landscape as we enter western Ulsan. The bus soon progresses past a sign stating we've entered rural Gyeongju, the view now pastoral.

Compared to the scorched-earth view when I landed at Incheon Airport just two months ago, the bucolic scenery of the Korean countryside is resplendent by late spring. Hills seem to be everywhere, blanketed by verdant forest, while fields leap with activity. When the sun comes out, the entire world seems to take on an emerald veneer.

One of the Pride of Pusan members gradually progresses up the bus aisle to collect the costs of the trip. ₩10,000 (Korean *won*), or roughly £5. Wow, that's cheap for a round-trip coach ride of some six hours, I remark. But as I pay, I'm also handed a token to exchange for a match ticket. The paltry sum of five quid covers the entire package: bus, game ticket, and return bus. Phenomenal. An away-day package like this would cost at least ten times as much in Britain.

We soon arrived at the city of Daejeon. Known as Korea's technology capital – the self-proclaimed 'Silicon Valley of Asia', although that moniker may cause eyes to roll across much of the continent – Daejeon is South Korea's fifth most populous city. Similar to how 'new towns' were designed in England after the Second World War to alleviate population pressure from London, many South Korea government agencies were relocated from Seoul to Daejeon in the 1990s to ensure that the capital didn't overly dominate the country's economy.

We approached the Daejeon World Cup Stadium, a massive landmark visible from the city's outskirts. Primarily finished with concrete painted white and powder blue, steel beams reached above the venue's sides, providing spectators cover with a structure that appeared dark and ominous from the inside while bright and puffy outside.

The Busan supporters gasped in awe at the large stadium as we approached, tickets in hand. This was where South Korea knocked Italy out of the World Cup less than one year earlier, a golden goal late in extra time. For many of us, including myself, this would be the first time attending a football-specific World Cup venue devoid of an atmosphere-crushing running track. We were keen to enter.

Near the entrance, a banner was emblazoned with perhaps the most dispassionate city slogan in human history: *It's Daejeon*. Other Korean cities tried a bit harder to cast themselves in a grand light with their slogans, often with amusing results:

Cheonan: 'The World's Best City'
Chuncheon: 'The City with Clean Lakes Places for Refresh'
Gongju: 'The Challenge which is Force! Gongju, which is great'
Gumi: 'Yes Gumi. Great Gumi. Brilliant Gumi.'
Iksan: 'Amazing Iksan. The City of Friendly to Women'
Mokpo: 'The city of beauty, Romanticism and Dream!!'
Yangsan: 'Active Yangsan! Nature! Tradition!! Harmonises today!'
Yeosu: 'Oh, Yeosu!'

But there was no pretentious, misleading slogan for Daejeon. For their catchphrase was simply 'It's Daejeon'.

The word Daejeon means 'Great Field', as the region is a large pocket of flat land in a mostly mountainous country. Entering the stadium, it too had the feeling of a deep valley with steep stands surrounding the pitch. Chairs were royal blue in colour, becoming increasing dotted in white toward the top of the stands, as if to mimic a snow-capped mountain. As usual in Korea, the stadium colour scheme didn't reflect the tenant club, given that Daejeon wears a reddish-purple kit. Despite the blue seats, the stadium had the nickname 'Purple Arena' – an act of denial that would make North Koreans proud.

Just as in Busan, there was no merchandise store inside the stadium. Instead, several people who appeared to be Daejeon fans sold a modest assortment of items under a small tent outside the venue. Once inside, there was little sign of activity in the concourse, despite the decent crowd. All of the food stalls were locked shut. There was even a post office in the stadium, but that too was closed.

We made our way behind one of the goals. What a difference it was not to have a gaping running track between the stands and the pitch. With Daejeon Stadium's configuration, we felt not only immediately behind the goal but also high above it, gazing downward.

However, despite the presence of 20,000 spectators and the stadium's lovely architecture, there was no escaping that the venue was still half empty, far too big for most K League matches. Like the majority of stadiums built in South Korea for the 2002 World Cup, it was a white elephant: constructed to make Korea appear impressive to an international audience, but with little consideration for the venue's usage once FIFA's month-long party had ended.

These were Potemkin sporting arenas: gargantuan in size and aspiration, but inappropriate for domestic league football. Even Daejeon's relatively compact, football-specific stadium looked too big. Every vacant chair diluted the atmosphere – something entirely preventable if these stadiums had been more modest in design.

Korea Times referred to the Gwangju and Daegu stadiums as 'soulless, atmosphere-sapping'.

Scottish manager Martin Rennie, who would take charge of a K League club some dozen years after the World Cup, told the *Daily Record*, 'You can have 10,000 [people] there but they could be lost in a 50,000-seat stadium … we're pretty much building a ground within a ground to make it more intimate.'

Some of the venues were too large even for the World Cup. Busan Asiad couldn't achieve half-capacity during the Paraguay vs. South Africa match. Even European powerhouses didn't necessarily fill stadiums: only two-thirds of seats were occupied when Spain played in Jeonju and Gwangju, with a similar attendance when France played in Busan. The stadium on Jeju Island was less than 60 per cent full for a knockout-stage match involving Germany.

The total number of stadiums built for the World Cup was also excessive. Rather than working together, 2002 co-hosts South Korea and Japan were essentially in competition with each other to see who could put on a better show. As a result, 20 stadiums were newly built or heavily renovated – ten in each country, far more than FIFA actually requested. With such a glut of venues, most arenas hosted less than a handful of matches. Grandiose stadiums were also constructed in faraway places such as Seogwipo on Jeju Island – a 42,000-seat venue plonked into an 85,000-population city with no history of professional football.

Perhaps worst of all, half of Korea's ten World Cup stadiums featured running tracks. This was partly due to an archaic Korean law that required most stadiums to be multi-functional, even though athletics is a minor spectator sport in Korea. When K League clubs attempted to rip up running tracks from older stadiums, their requests were usually refused by government.

But on this day, I wasn't complaining. I was excited to be at a new, football-specific venue, albeit wary of how Busan would fare against an opponent enjoying their best-ever start to a season.

This was Daejeon Citizen's seventh year in the K League, and they were on a tear. They had performed poorly since their founding in 1997, finishing in the bottom half of the league every season, and reached a historic low when they won just a single match last year. But inexplicably, Daejeon became one of Korea's hottest football clubs during the close season, tallying more wins by the third matchday this year than from all of last season. With a record of five wins, two draws and two defeats, they stood second in the formative K League table, only behind defending champions Seongnam.

Daejeon were unique in being the K League's first 'citizen' club, meaning they were operated by the local government. Unlike most K League football clubs privately owned and bankrolled by Korea's wealthy *jaebeol* (large, family-owned business conglomerates), Daejeon Citizen were established by Daejeon's city council and received most of their annual budget from the municipality. While this arrangement did present a cost to taxpayers, the upside was that citizen clubs were much more rooted in their local communities.

Daegu FC became the K League's second citizen club in 2003, and numerous others have popped up throughout Korea's football pyramid since then, especially in the lower divisions.

Players emerge from the stadium tunnel. The Pride of Pusan's two drummers begin pounding their instruments, but Daejeon's Purple Crew soon follow, pummelling several bass drums that produce a thunderous boom which echoes throughout the stadium. It seems like an early analogy for which club would likely dominate the upcoming match.

Kick-off. The match starts at a frantic pace. Players from both sides look nervous. Possession is difficult to maintain. Back and forth. Into touch. The ball is cleared upfield in a panic.

A large *tifo* display is unfurled on top of home fans in one of the main stands. This feels like a proper football match. There is passion. Chants from supporters reverberate from the underside of the stadium roof. The venue feels like a cauldron. There is an almost tangible intensity, something completely lacking during most Busan matches at Asiad. Even fans in the main stands take part in the atmosphere, albeit mostly just by clapping along to songs.

The players overcome their nerves; the match takes a more tactical shape. Team formations become evident. Daejeon supporters cycle through their chants, most of which are borrowed from English football tunes and pop songs. To the tune of Culture Club's 'Karma Chameleon':

Dae-jeon Daejeon Daejeon Daejeon Daejeon Daejeon Ci-ti-zen.
Oh Ci-ti-zen; Oh Ci-ti-zen!

With a name like 'Purple Crew', I expected they would be more likely to rip stadium seats out from their foundations than imitate Boy George and hang banners that exclaimed *PERFUME*, but cultural appropriation often results in an odd kettle of contradictions.

Busan are getting hammered. Conceding a goal seems imminent – it's merely a matter of how long we can delay the inevitable.

Daejeon make a deep run and earn a free kick. With the action close to us, the pair of Pride of Pusan percussionists pound on their drums. One of the drumheads bursts, sending a drumstick clattering down the concrete steps. The drummer curses as he fumbles to collect the stick.

Then, the sound of trumpets: the Purple Crew's version of the Sheffield Wednesday Kop band blare out the familiar theme tune to *The Great Escape*. Our single working drum is no match; our group falls mostly silent in capitulation. We are wretched on the pitch, and not much better in the stands. Familiar territory for a Busan supporter.

Up steps a Daejeon midfielder to take the free kick. The shot curls into the upper corner of the goal, beyond even the reach of lanky Busan goalkeeper Kim Yong-dae.

1-0 Daejeon. Busan heads drop. Player heads, supporter heads. Are we about to lose our third successive match?

Busan manager Ian Porterfield throws his hands up in exasperation as if motioning 'I told you so!' to the players looking meekly back at the dugout.

Exactly what magic is Porterfield expected to weave with this inept Busan squad? His FA Cup-winning goal with Sunderland had been a moment of wonder, but surely even he isn't capable of the calibre of sorcery required to make a contender out of this group.

Or is he?

After leading Sunderland to what some called the biggest shock in FA Cup final history in 1973, Porterfield spent four additional seasons at Roker Park. He then finished his 15-year playing career with a brief term at Jack Charlton's Sheffield Wednesday.

Porterfield subsequently moved into management. His first role was at Rotherham United, where he quickly guided the club to the Third Division championship in 1981.

At the end of that season, league opponents and neighbouring rivals Sheffield United went in the opposite direction, as the former top-flight club was relegated to the Fourth Division. Desperate to stop the rot, Sheffield convinced Porterfield to drop two tiers to take over as their manager, a challenge he proved successful at. The Scotsman took the Yorkshire club up two levels, and his final season with the Blades saw them finish in seventh place in the Second Division.

As a young manager who had secured three promotions in a span of just four seasons, Porterfield was in demand. So when renascent Scottish club Aberdeen lost manager Alex Ferguson to Manchester United, the Dons came knocking for Porterfield. He didn't fare too badly at Pittodrie, losing only nine of 71 matches in a spell that saw the club reach a Scottish League Cup final and qualify twice for the UEFA Cup. Porterfield's win percentage remains in the top five of Aberdeen's all-time managers.

Next up was a 15-month stint as an assistant at Chelsea. The players there enjoyed Porterfield's coaching, and the London side went on to win the Second Division title in 1989 with a whopping 99 points, climbing back up to the top flight where they have remained ever since.

Invited back to the London club in 1991, this time as manager, Porterfield's first season in charge was highlighted by the Londoners earning their first win at Liverpool in 56 years. The following season, Chelsea climbed to fourth in the inaugural Premier League table by December and advanced to the FA Cup quarter-finals for the first time in a decade.

It was at this point that the Scottish manager's career would take a distinctly cosmopolitan turn.

'[My wife] knows that my job could take me anywhere,' Porterfield wrote (with John Gibson) in *The Impossible Dream*. 'If someday I was offered the management of Torquay – or even some club abroad – we would be off, providing the kids' education wasn't going to suffer.'

Just two months after Porterfield left Chelsea, the African country of Zambia was struck by tragedy. A military aeroplane carrying its men's national team to a 1994 World Cup qualifier crashed, killing everyone on board. In response, the British government hired Porterfield to rebuild the team. Porterfield was initially wary but came to relish the challenge, his first opportunity to manage a national squad. He took the country to within one point of qualifying for the World Cup, and then to the finals of the African Cup, both within a year of the air disaster. The team rose to an unprecedented 18th in the international rankings, and Porterfield was bestowed with the Freedom of Zambia by the country's government.

'When I left Chelsea in 1993 I'd never worked outside of the UK before and I had no real desire to do so, but the chance came along to go to Zambia because of the tragedy they suffered and it's amazing how things have gone from there,' Porterfield told *The Independent*.

Porterfield would later move to the Caribbean to manage Joe Public FC in Trinidad. Just three months into that assignment, before the season had even started, the Trinidad and Tobago Football Association poached Porterfield to manage its national team. He initially did very well, winning over the Caribbean players with his laid-back attitude. Trinidad finished above favourites Mexico to win their group in the penultimate round of CONCACAF's 2002 World Cup qualifying – leaping to an unprecedented 24th in the international rankings – and lifted the 2001 Caribbean Cup, the last time Trinidad would do so.

With Porterfield once again available for hire in late 2002, job offers poured in from clubs scattered across the globe. One was from Kaizer Chiefs, the most successful club in South Africa. But Porterfield's journeyman ways led him to a new part of the world: East Asia. The struggling Busan I'cons had found their glamorous foreign manager, one whose 24-year management CV boasted leading Chelsea in the Premier League and numerous international exploits. Busan had secured their Guus Hiddink. Surely it was simply a matter of time before Porterfield would have the Korean club back to its rightful place, scrapping with the K League's best – and perhaps even the giants of Asian club football – for silverware and success. The severe cut to the club's playing budget several years earlier was surely just a trivial detail Porterfield could single-handedly overcome.

* * *

Watching Busan play is frustrating. Squad members commit errors one would expect from academy-age players. Passes often miss their target; opponents are left unmarked. Despite lacking the skills to do so, Busan's attacking players attempt to dribble through several defenders rather than pass to open team-mates.

Porterfield has decided to regularly rotate players, due to the gruelling demands of the 2003 season's 44-match schedule. This is to be expected. But the manager's rotation scheme also involves using players out of position. Jang Dae-il, a defender his entire career, is selected by Porterfield to serve as a striker for the entirety of this match. Busan supporters are confused; they quietly mutter comments about managerial decisions.

The assistant referee raises his electronic signboard for a player substitution. Busan's Colombian striker Tommy comes off, replaced by Gwak Kyung-keun.

Gwak is yet another player Busan has taken a significant gamble by signing. Like Lee Lim-saeng, Gwak came to Busan during the recent close season thanks to Bucheon's talent fire-sale. The striker suited up for South Korea at the 1992 Olympics during his university days, and followed Noh Jung-yoon's lead by opting to play professionally in Japan's J.League.

Unfortunately, a previous knee injury from Gwak's university days returned early into his Japan foray, which caused him to return to South Korea. He was chosen first overall by Bucheon in the K League's American-style player draft, where he initially enjoyed a good run of form. Gwak led Bucheon in goals for three seasons and narrowly missed out on a call-up to the 1998 World Cup. But by 2000 and 2001, the striker's scoring prowess had dried up.

When Bucheon decided to get rid of Gwak, he was 30 years old and out of form. Like many of the players Busan targeted in recent years, Gwak was high-risk, but offered potential for high reward: a former national team striker. Bucheon wanted money for him, but not much. Busan's cash-strapped front office couldn't resist, and paid a transfer fee – an increasingly rare act for the south-east club.

Gwak is inserted into today's game, but it makes little difference. He receives scant support from Busan's midfielders. When Gwak does possess the ball, he displays the same disappointing composure that led to his exit from Bucheon.

Busan eventually succumb to Daejeon's superiority – marking Busan's third consecutive K League defeat.

The travelling Pride of Pusan members looked exasperated. Busan's lacklustre start to the season had caused noticeable irritation among the group, but such sentiment was now creeping toward visible indignation.

I wondered how long Porterfield would remain at Busan I'cons. Was he capable of following Daejeon's lead in swiftly converting an impotent squad into league challengers? If not, would Porterfield be pushed out by club management, or perhaps flee to another exotic destination? Or would he stubbornly persist?

'When I came here, we probably had as poor a squad as anybody in the league,' Porterfield would later explain to *Soccerphile*'s John Duerden. 'I don't think that you can snap a magic wand and go from the bottom, where we were, to the top in a short period of time.'

With the match mercifully concluded, the supporters boarded their bus for the journey home. I was not looking forward to this. The meagre rental bus wasn't a problem during the brief trip to Daegu the previous week, but I learned the difficult way on today's longer journey that most Korean buses are not equipped with toilets.

Daejeon to Busan takes at least three hours, and that's if traffic is light. But on Sunday evenings, half the country is headed back to the big urban centres. Traffic grinds to a halt at bottlenecks.

Motorways also offered shockingly few rest stops. Forget the historical Busan–Suwon brawl: now *this* was a legitimate reason not to drink at football! If ever you wanted to test the might of your bladder, a Korean bus is the ultimate trial. Urologists must make a killing here.

The Busan supporters, incredibly voluble earlier in the day, spent most of the ride back to Busan in mournful silence. Either that or they really, really had to pee. Mercifully we did visit one rest area, but the horrendous level of traffic meant we were once again crossing our legs uncomfortably.

At last we arrived back in Busan. The group disembarked from the bus with relief, thrilled to be off the five-hour torture chariot.

Upon our return to civilisation, we checked the football news. Seongnam finally earned their first loss of the season. Over at the Suwon–Anyang match – the most heated derby in all of Korean football – Suwon supporters made a banner of their bluebird mascot getting 'intimate' with a cheetah, Anyang's mascot. Anyang supporters responded by ripping up chairs and chanting abuse for 90 minutes.

And an unexpected development: Bucheon fired their manager mid-season, Turkish Tınaz Tırpan. Unlike in the UK, South Korean clubs tend to refrain from the managerial merry-go-round, usually giving managers several years to achieve their vision. Bucheon hired Tırpan just months earlier, likely hoping he would be as successful as another recent foreign manager: Guus Hiddink, who coached South Korea to the 2002 World Cup semi-finals. But with Bucheon at the bottom of the K League standings and still without their first win of 2003, Tırpan was out.

The cause of Bucheon's malaise, however, was a fundamental rot at the club. The corporate owners, SK, had tightened the club's budget significantly in recent years, forcing the team to sell its best players every season and replace them with untested youth. Poor results meant dwindling crowds at what had been one of the K League's best-supported sides.

This past close-season, Bucheon auctioned off six of their better players, including the transfers of Lee Lim-saeng and Gwak Kyung-keun to Busan. Bucheon fans were furious, derisively referring to the annual sale of their playing talent as the 'Bucheon version'. Tırpan, the club's Turkish manager, had quickly admitted he wouldn't be able to assemble a competitive team under such conditions.

When Bucheon were due to play a series of pre-season friendlies in Turkey, the weaker half of the squad was held back to play matches in China as a cost-savings measure. When the K League season began, players learned that the club would not be running a bus for the team, leaving some players to make their own way to games on public transportation.

Beyond extreme frugality, Bucheon was also accused of transfer falsifications, creating an air of despondency for players and fans alike.

Prior to the 2003 K League season, Bucheon supporters organised a protest in front of SK's corporate headquarters, handing out leaflets that summarised the plight of the club. SK retorted, causing a public slanging match between the fans and the owners, with the club caught in the middle. Bucheon fans escalated at the 2003 season opener – a normally joyous occasion – by unveiling a massive banner that accused SK of damaging the club.

While Bucheon had become a cauldron of negative politics and internal strife, Busan wasn't faring much better. They too had just lost four excellent squad members, replacing them with flashy but older players struggling with injury, poor form, or both. Like at Bucheon, the remainder of Busan's squad was hastily stuffed with university graduates; alarmingly few players were at peak age. A cynic would think Busan was in a race with Bucheon to see how low a K League club could plummet.

The remaining Busan supporters who hadn't already given up were fully aware of what was happening at their once-great club. They were becoming impatient. The discontent was palpable – and intensifying.

ROUND 9 (rescheduled due to inclement weather)

Daejeon	**1-0**	**Busan**
Seongnam	1-2	Jeonnam
Gwangju	2-3	Jeonbuk
Daegu	1-1	Ulsan
Suwon	3-1	Anyang
Bucheon	1-1	Pohang

K LEAGUE TABLE

Seongnam	25
Daejeon	20
Jeonbuk	18
Suwon	16
Anyang	16
Ulsan	14
Jeonnam	13
Pohang	11
Gwangju	11
Busan	**10**
Daegu	8
Bucheon	2

CHAPTER 8

COULD YOU SWITCH OFF THE FLOODLIGHTS? THE AIR FORCE IS CROSS

SEONGNAM ILHWA CHUNMA (PEGASUS) VS. BUSAN I'CONS
WEDNESDAY, 21 MAY 2003
K LEAGUE ROUND 11
SEONGNAM STADIUM (A.K.A. MORAN STADIUM)

백미
– The best (literally, 'white eyebrows')

SEONGNAM ILHWA Chunma Football Club were South Korea's Manchester United, Juventus, or Barcelona. They had won the K League title for the past two seasons, becoming unprecedented five-time national champions. Unsatiated, Seongnam plucked five talented footballers from other Korean clubs and Japan, determined to bolster their squad for the lengthy 2003 K League season and Asian Champions League campaign. They now wielded arguably the greatest squad in the history of South Korean club football.

Despite the menacing opponent, Busan approached the match with a hint of optimism. They looked fondly back at their defeat last month of Ulsan, the club that finished as runners-up for the last two K League seasons. Meanwhile, league leaders Seongnam lost their previous match at home, and had only won once in their last three games.

Seongnam were founded in 1989, and actually started life in Seoul known as Ilhwa Chunma (Ilhwa the corporate benefactor and Chunma a moniker meaning 'Pegasus'). But after the 1995 season, the three clubs based in the capital were evicted by the league, forced to play in other cities as part of a strategy to spread the love for football across the country. None of them moved very far, with Ilhwa Chunma relocating 75km south to the city of Cheonan.

Unfortunately the city-owned Oryang Stadium in Cheonan lacked floodlights, so when the K League later introduced evening games, the club was in a pinch. They were off again, this time back up north to Seongnam, a city to the immediate south-east of Seoul where they remain today.

After another tortuous bus journey, this time across most of the country, we settled in for the match. Kim Do-hoon, a veteran of the 1998 World Cup and arguably Seongnam's highest-profile acquisition of the close season, hammers a shot at Busan's goal, narrowly missing. If Busan I'cons were to have any hope of securing points today, their time-worn back-line would have to frustrate Kim and Seongnam's assembly of stars.

Although Seongnam won the 2002 K League, there were unproven whispers that they may have resorted to match-fixing their final game of the season against Pohang. If true it would certainly be ironic, given that Seongnam were a religious-based club.

Behind Ilhwa Corporation was Moon Sun-myung, leader of the infamous Unification Church. Moon claimed that he was the Messiah and the Second Coming of Christ (as one does) and had 14 children (as one also does). His self-created religion – or perhaps cult is more accurate – became notorious for holding mass wedding ceremonies with participants from around the world. Moon was banned from entering Germany when the government stated that the religion 'endangered the personal and social development of young people', and he would later spend time in an American prison for tax fraud and conspiracy.

Moon's religious activities meant that Seongnam Ilhwa Chunma encountered difficulties maintaining their welcome. The city of Seongnam's abundance of Christian residents were firmly opposed to the team using the council-owned stadium, and roped their mayor – up for re-election and desperate to please – into threatening the football club with eviction. But the dispute would deflate and Seongnam remained in the city.

Seongnam weren't the only religious football club in South Korea. Hallelujah FC were the country's first professional side and won the inaugural K League championship in 1983. The club was comprised of evangelical Christian players who wanted to use the sport to engage in missionary work. Games were often sandwiched with on-pitch team prayers, and occasionally featured a 'worship dance' at half-time.

* * *

Busan have possession and are on the attack. Zoran Urumov wiggles and weaves past Seongnam's midfield, but is smothered by several defenders. The left-footed winger just can't seem to get a clear shot on goal.

Launching a quick counter-attack, a talented player Seongnam plucked from the J.League dashes forward and shoots just wide. The referee blows his whistle for half-time. I pull out my phone and attempt to load the Seongnam website, curious as to this particular player's career background.

But the website doesn't load, and instead comes the message, 'This domain name has expired.' Seongnam, the champions of South Korea, had forgotten to renew their internet domain, knocking their website offline.

During this era, Korean football officials and administrators were regularly criticised by fans for ineptitude. There was no shortage of examples.

Ki Sung-yueng had to delay his international transfer to Celtic when the Korean Football Association's office was closed during the transfer window, postponing Ki's move to Scotland.

Many clubs advertised matches at the wrong venues or times, often with the home and away clubs offering conflicting information.

The lower-division K3 League made the baffling decision to schedule matches during South Korea's 2010 World Cup games. One particular Seoul United match supposedly attracted an attendance of three.

Stadiums sometimes only had one ticket booth open, even during big matches in the country's top flight. Food stalls were frequently closed prior to half-time, or didn't stock enough food.

Obscure match venues and kick-off times were also common. The 2008 Korean FA Cup semis and final were held in a neutral stadium on Jeju Island, the most difficult part of the country to get to. But to make things worse, the matches were staged at Jeju City's old ground with a running track, rather than the football-specific stadium built recently in Seogwipo for the World Cup. Perhaps most perplexing of all, the semi-finals were held on a Thursday morning and afternoon.

The opening ceremony of Changwon's new football-specific stadium, held on a Tuesday afternoon, was perhaps scheduled by the same people.

Additionally, events were often organised or announced at the last minute. The U League, in which university teams compete, was known to release annual fixtures the day before the season opener. And on the occasion of the K League's 20th anniversary, a commemorative logo was unveiled – some five months into the season.

* * *

Seongnam are on the attack again and they look ferocious. Passing the ball with grace and ease, it's obvious why they are forecast to win their third consecutive K League title – a feat the club had already achieved the previous decade.

Newly acquired striker Kim Do-hoon surges forward, comfortably coaxing the ball past Busan midfielders and defenders. The Pride of Pusan members look apprehensive, as if expecting anguish.

Busan defender Jang Dae-il, who has returned to his normal position after being used as a striker last match, runs forward to confront Kim. Colliding in an audible meeting of torsos, Kim is thrust to the ground. Jang acquires the ball and begins to launch a counter-attack, but the referee blows his whistle for a foul.

Jang Dae-il's career began brightly, marked by a call-up to the 1998 World Cup and a contract with Seongnam (then still based in Cheonan). But although travelling to the World Cup put Jang in the spotlight – he was voted by Brazilian football fans as being among the 11 most handsome of the 704 international players – Jang didn't receive any playing time in France. His two years at Seongnam also happened to be when the club uncharacteristically finished bottom of the K League.

Jang was shipped to Busan in 2000, soon after the takeover by Hyundai, and spent much of his career struggling against injury. After playing just twice in 2002, Jang was keen to get his career back on track and impress new manager Ian Porterfield.

In addition to the chiselled face that landed him a coveted spot in *FourFourTwo Korea*'s 'Handsome Perfect XI', Jang was also unique for being the first South Korean international of dual ethnicity. Having a British parent was still a rarity back then in the Hermit Kingdom, especially for someone who represented the country abroad. South Korea was traditionally very homogenous, with the legend of 'one people' (*danil minjok*) from a 'pure Korean race' with 'special DNA' all genetically linked to the mythical progenitor, *Dangun*. Korea was a country dedicated to the maintenance of 'pure bloodlines', and thus a half-Caucasian playing for the national side was quite the novelty.

Jang was a trailblazer in Korean society, but today he was more focused on neutralising the most potent attacking line in Korean football. After smashing down Seongnam striker Kim, Jang looked to the sky, as if asking for divine inspiration.

Seongnam would later be on the move once again, this time to the renovated Tancheon Stadium elsewhere in the city. But wherever Seongnam FC went, stadium problems seemed to follow. The club was informed that their latest ground was within the training range of the South Korean Air Force, and thus they would not be able to use the stadium's floodlights on certain nights of the week during aerial exercises due to safety issues. Yet oddly enough, the government was happy to approve construction of the 123-storey Lotte World Tower – the tallest structure in the entire OECD – just a few kilometres from the airport, despite initial objections from the military that the proximity of the megastructure would prove incredibly dangerous.

Ten minutes remain. Busan are hanging on, although the 0-0 scoreline has been perilously close to rupturing on several occasions. Jang Dae-il and his back-line desperately hack away any ball that comes near the 18-yard box, determined to salvage a point from this foreboding fixture. Jang is surely relieved to return to being a defender, his natural position.

Busan manager Ian Porterfield's rationale for squad experimentation is partly the intense season that involves two league matches most weeks, and possibly some sort of Arsène Wenger-like desire to 'discover' players in different positions. But also at play is that Busan's owners are now resolutely opposed to paying transfer fees to bring in new players. While neighbours Ulsan and other K League powerhouses acquire talent from big Brazilian clubs such as Santos and Flamengo for sizeable transfer fees, Porterfield is only able to reinforce his team with free agents and unattached players rejected by other clubs.

With Busan struggling from lack of talent, Porterfield was doing what he could to make the team as competitive as possible, looking for characteristics in players that might help them to excel beyond their usual roles. It's squad patchwork, primarily out of desperation.

Leo Mendoza, who served as a translator for the club, alleged, 'Ian begged for the [club] to sign some good Korean free agents, but they refused to give him money for [domestic] signings. There were actually quite a lot of good players available, but he got none.'

BBC football pundit Alan Hansen once famously remarked, 'You can't win anything with kids.' Porterfield would perhaps amend that phrase to, 'You can't win anything with kids, retirement holdouts and rejects of other teams.'

Just as it looks as if Seongnam might snatch a late goal, the referee signals for full time. Busan have done it: a draw away to the league's most menacing side. While it's just a single point, the result marks the end to Busan's three-game losing streak. Players and fans alike celebrate. Porterfield looks over toward the Pride of Pusan, waving gleefully as he flashes his trademark toothy smile.

Busan's record was now three wins, two draws and six defeats. Elsewhere, Daegu FC earned an upset win over Daejeon, allowing the novice club to leap above Busan in the league table. We were now second-bottom, with only pitiful Bucheon below us. While this was disappointing, the Busan supporters were happy to be consumed by today's ephemeral triumph, hopeful that it was reflective of improvement to come.

We returned to our bus and looked at more K League news on our phones. Pohang Steelers set an unflattering record for the young season, attracting just 1,320 spectators to their match. It wasn't just Busan that had difficulty attracting fans to their stadium – it was a common woe suffered by many K League clubs.

Reasons for low interest in Korean club football were numerous. Many Koreans preferred to align themselves with a winner; and with the European leagues' ubiquitous hold on television screens around the world, most football fans in the Hermit Kingdom chose between Manchester United or Arsenal, rather than support their local club. The K League was perceived to be inferior, and thus many Koreans opted to support whichever European team their favourite national team player signed for. When glory hunting is combined with the desire for cosmopolitanism, the domestic league suffers.

Even league champions Seongnam had difficulty attracting people to games. The Yonhap News Agency ran a photo from Seongnam's season opener in 2007 that showed just five fans behind the goal.

And don't even think about asking how many South Koreans were fans of domestic lower-division clubs. You're more likely to run into a North Korean secret agent than a scarf-clad Siheung City supporter. Matches often only capture one or two hundred attendees, likely mostly family and friends of the players, in stadiums with up to 50,000 seats.

Turnover of young fans was another obstacle. Most of the dedicated K League club supporters found behind the goals were teenagers, attending matches home and away to cheer their favourite stars – similar to the mania teens develop during their formative years for actors or pop singers they wish to either emulate or fornicate with. But when these fans become young adults and find themselves less interested in hero-worship, often their interest in attending football fades. As such, most K League supporters' groups are populated with an almost entirely new set of faces every few years.

Add poor marketing, the lack of a presence on Korean TV, as well as American-style franchising and club relocation to these problems, and you had a recipe for mass indifference to the K League.

Luckily for Busan fans, an international friendly against glamorous European opposition awaited.

ROUND 11

Seongnam	**0-0**	**Busan**
Daegu	2-1	Daejeon
Suwon	0-0	Ulsan
Gwangju	1-4	Anyang
Bucheon	2-2	Jeonnam
Pohang	1-2	Jeonbuk

K LEAGUE TABLE

Seongnam	26
Jeonbuk	21
Daejeon	20
Anyang	19
Suwon	17
Ulsan	15
Jeonnam	14
Daegu	11
Pohang	11
Gwangju	11
Busan	**11**
Bucheon	3

CHAPTER 9

PLAGUES OF LOCUSTS
AND FLASHY FOREIGNERS

BUSAN I'CONS VS. FEYENOORD
ROTTERDAM
FRIDAY, 6 JUNE 2003
INTERNATIONAL CLUB FRIENDLY
BUSAN ASIAD WORLD CUP STADIUM

종이 호랑이
– *A paper tiger*

TODAY'S FOOTBALL marked a break from typical K League fare: Dutch giants Feyenoord Rotterdam and their promising young striker, Robin van Persie, were on an Asian jaunt. Feyenoord had just signed winger Song Chong-gug from Busan after featuring for South Korea at the 2002 World Cup, and part of the compensation to Busan was to play a friendly in Korea.

Song became a Korean celebrity early in his football career, only spending one and a half seasons with Busan (when he wasn't busy modelling jeans) before being whisked off to grander locales. The defender effectively neutralised Portuguese striker Luis Figo during a World Cup match, drawing interest from European clubs.

Typical for Busan I'cons in their new Hyundai-ownership era, whenever a promising young player showed signs of ability, it wouldn't be long before his departure was announced. Although South Korean national team fans were ecstatic to see their players depart for strong European clubs, for Busan I'cons supporters it meant yet another disappointing *clack-clack* of the talent-exodus turnstile.

But Song left Busan nine months ago, and most fans had already resigned themselves to his exit. Today was to be a joyful farewell.

Porterfield didn't want to leave open the attacking gap created by Song's departure, so the Scot pursued the services of the best player he had managed the previous year at Ghanaian club Kumasi Asante Kotoko: striker Michael Osei. Known affectionately by fans as 'Ember Power', Osei was a key part of Ghana's bronze-winning 1999 FIFA Under-17 World Championship squad, and earned the golden boot at the 2002 African Cup Winners' Cup as Kotoko advanced to the tournament's final.

Shortly after Porterfield left Africa, he convinced Osei to head to South Korea and signed him in time for Busan's pre-season, during which the player thrived. But the deal collapsed, as Osei was unknowingly still under contract back at Kotoko. The Ghanaian club protested to FIFA about illegal player tapping by Busan, and soon Osei – allegedly stitched up by his agent, a lawyer who 15 years later would be temporarily suspended from practising law in Ghana for professional misconduct – returned home embarrassed, facing a four-month playing ban from FIFA.

Porterfield had lost his star signing for the 2003 K League season before a ball had even been kicked.

I entered Asiad Stadium and was pleasantly surprised to see a small spattering of Busan I'cons merchandise for sale – albeit from a fold-away table more befitting of an English non-league ground than a new World Cup stadium. Given the complete absence of merchandise at previous matches and only a feeble collection available today, it seemed that Busan weren't fussed about generating revenue. In the weeks ahead, a British website started offering replica tops for sale, yet the official club website had no such wares to offer.

Kick-off. Against all expectations, Busan dominate. Harry weaves his way with surprising ease past the assortment of visiting superstars.

He notices Urumov tracking his pace up the other side of the field, and arcs the ball over to his team-mate. Urumov takes possession, cavorts beyond two Dutch defenders, and aims for the net. Goal, just minutes in.

Busan are ahead against Feyenoord Rotterdam! Just what sort of witchcraft are we witnessing?

Prior to the match, I perused the Busan I'cons website and was gobsmacked to see they posted the personal email addresses of the club's Korean coaches. Doing such a thing in Europe or South America would likely lead to a torrent of abusive messages from fans of rival clubs. It was endearing that such openness could take place in Korea, but I wondered if the club had thoughtlessly violated the coaches' privacy.

Busan's managerial duo of Ian Porterfield and assistant Drew Jarvie likely didn't have to worry when it came to privacy – most of the Koreans at the club could barely understand a word the pair said. Both spoke in such thick Scottish accents that even the Korean players familiar with English football expressions weren't sure it was English they were hearing. Even Porterfield's Trinidadian wife, Glenda, admitted that deciphering his Scottish burr came with 'great difficulty'.

Regardless, Porterfield continues to shout unintelligible instructions as his squad toils away against the Dutch guests.

Many Koreans were only familiar with the sound of American English. Of the Scottish coaching pair at Busan, Porterfield's accent was far more comprehensible, thanks to a playing career that took him to England as well as managing throughout the UK and overseas. But this was Jarvie's first posting outside Scotland, and his dialect was so indecipherable that even the club's professional translator had difficulty comprehending him.

An early season coaching session involving Jarvie and the Busan squad might have gone something like this:

Jarvie: *Arite, noo we'll practise duntin tae baw eftir heidin it doon.*

Players: (silence)

Jarvie: *Oonerstan'?*

Players: (silence)

Jarvie: (becoming annoyed) *Okay?!?*

Players: *Yes!* (lots of nodding and polite smiling, despite not having the faintest clue what's happening)

English enjoys a revered status in South Korea, thanks to its association with developed economies and its hegemony over international pop culture. In fact, learning English is arguably a national obsession in Korea, where parents spend more than

£11bn each year to send their children to private English tutoring academies. Some fanatical parents even turn to oral surgery to give their children an advantage, hoping that snipping the tissue under the tongue will improve pronunciation.

An entire industry has been built around teaching English in Korea, employing roughly 20,000 foreign workers, mostly from Western countries. English classes often extend late into the evening, even for primary school pupils. The American accent is particularly coveted, due to Korea's intimate relationship with the USA.

Use of English is regularly flaunted in Korea in an attempt to appear educated or trendy – sometimes to humorous effect. K League clubs have been known to give their players odd English nicknames, such as 'Answer', 'Happy Wing', and 'Peter Pan'.

Feyenoord inexplicably had not given their squad cutesy English nicknames. They were already on the second leg of their Asian tour, having played in Japan earlier that week. Overseas playing tours of Asia during the summer have become increasingly common, as larger European football clubs look to expand and cash in on their international fan base.

Asia represented roughly half of the Premier League's overseas television revenue. In reality, friendly matches held against Asian clubs or national teams were merely a sideshow to the commercial activities European clubs engage in during these lucrative tours. With 'financial fair play' encouraging European clubs to generate earned revenue rather than rely on handouts from wealthy benefactors, visits to Asia had become more important than ever.

But the era of European clubs selling out large Asian stadiums has become a relic of the past. When Real Madrid and Manchester United visited Asia in 2005, large swathes of seats were left empty. A Chinese state-run newspaper referred to Real as a 'plague of locusts' for supposedly showing up to extract profit without leaving much benefit for the hosts.

Several of the European players also picked up injuries, including David Beckham and Zinedine Zidane. Beckham told Reuters about the toll that the Asian tour took on the Spanish giants.

'Physically it hasn't been good for the players. We haven't been able to train hard and we're still short of fitness. You finish the games very tired and it takes longer than normal to recover.'

In 2009 when Manchester United decided to visit South Korea – a year after opening a club-themed restaurant in Seoul – they arrogantly announced the dates they would visit the country without first checking if their would-be hosts were available. Furious, a K League official reproached the English giants by telling the media, 'If Manchester United want to play a game in Korea they should look at the schedule of the National League [second division] teams.'

When Liverpool and Tottenham visited Malaysia in 2015 for friendlies against the host country's national team, games were scheduled close to Malaysia's World Cup qualifiers. Enraged locals organised a boycott that led to poor attendances, including a stadium that wasn't even a quarter full for the Spurs match.

Luckily for Busan, a postponed league match and an international calendar window created the perfect interval to entertain a flashy foreign opponent. Feyenoord demonstrated smooth ball movement that was far superior to the usual fare on display in the K League. It was a true spectacle to behold. But for some reason, they weren't scoring.

After a lethargic attempt at goal by Feyenoord, Harry snatches possession. Busan's Colombian enchanter breaks into stride, launching a rapid counter-attack. He spots Urumov rushing ahead and pushes the ball forward through the legs of a Feyenoord defender. Urumov latches on to the through-ball and sends it floating up toward the top corner of the goal. Dutch goalkeeper Edwin Zoetebier barely has the opportunity to move as the ball sibilates the net.

2-0 Busan.

Feyenoord fight back. Argentinean striker Mario Bombarda creates an opportunity to score, as does Robin van Persie, but neither convert. Despite being outclassed for much of the match, Busan are ahead of the Dutch visitors, and in front of a large crowd.

Koreans recently came to hold the Netherlands in high esteem when Dutch football manager Guus Hiddink ostensibly performed a miracle by taking South Korea to the semi-finals of the 2002 World Cup. This was a significant feat, given that the country had never previously won a single match at the international tournament.

Hiddink was declared a national hero and attained cult-like admiration. His image dominated television and newspapers, and plush dolls of the Dutchman were snapped up across South Korea.

After Hiddink was bestowed with honorary Korean citizenship (the only person ever to receive such merit), some locals suggested that he was the reincarnation of legendary naval commander Yi Sun-sin, a beloved historical figure.

Throngs of Korean visitors began travelling to Hiddink's small home village of Varsseveld after the World Cup as part of veritable pilgrimages. Some clipped grass from the local football field to take home, while others surreptitiously scooped sand from Hiddink's childhood house.

So numerous were Korean visitors to the small Dutch town that many slept rough, all in the mere hope of glimpsing something faintly related to Hiddink. Unfortunately, they had nowhere to formally pay their respects.

Thus was born the 'Guuseum', a shrine dedicated to the life of Hiddink. The Guus-themed museum survived for three years until Koreans grew bored of Hiddink and business quickly dried up.

After the World Cup, Hiddink returned to the Netherlands to manage PSV Eindhoven, luring two Korean players abroad with him: Park Ji-sung (later of Manchester United fame) and Lee Young-pyo (subsequently at Tottenham). But Busan's Song Chong-gug joined rivals Feyenoord instead.

Song gallops up the field at Busan Asiad Stadium, although on this occasion for his new Dutch team. Busan's defenders are preoccupied with Feyenoord's swarming strikers; Song, deployed as a right-back for his European club, senses a rare opportunity to score himself. He leans back dramatically as he thwacks at the ball, but the uncomfortable angle causes his shot to lurk considerably wide of goal.

As play restarts, Busan striker Hwang Cheol-min settles the ball and decides to test the Dutch opposition. Despite this being his first appearance of the season due to his peripheral role in the team, Hwang twists the ball beyond Feyenoord's goalkeeper, giving Busan a three-goal lead. He jumps in the air in a celebration infused by both joy and shock, and races over to manager Porterfield for a congratulatory embrace. Hwang's team-mates jump on him, hollering in the delight of humbling a mighty European giant.

The revelry extends into the stands as the Busan supporters clasp each other, then giddily race into formation for the silly bowing dance that brings a smile to everyone's face.

Dušan Šimić controls the ball. The diminutive Serbian midfielder joined Busan for the 2003 season on a one-year loan. Thus far he had played every minute since making his debut back in late March, becoming a staple of Ian Porterfield's squad. Despite possessing a baby face and still just 23 years old, Šimić's brow already featured a permanent furrow.

Busan had the prudent habit of bringing in foreign players in pairs from the same country. Living abroad can be challenging for footballers presented with a different language, culture and customs. But if players have a team-mate from their home country, living in Korea becomes less arduous, increasing their chances of being a success on the pitch as well as off it.

Busan's acquisition of another Serbian was surely deliberate. Forward Radivoje Manić departed during the close season, and Busan likely wanted another Slav to keep Urumov company. Although Šimić hadn't set the K League alight, his workmanlike ability gave Busan's struggling squad some much-needed stability.

But there was one foreign player at the club who didn't have a compatriot. Sitting in the stands in his street clothes watching the Feyenoord friendly was Nigerian winger Emmanuel Amunike. Like several other players at Busan, Amunike's career was blighted by injury and most clubs wouldn't give him the time of day.

But there was something special about Amunike: he boasted a truly world-class footballing CV. The winger had spent four seasons at Barcelona. Even more impressive was his international career for Nigeria: helping them qualify for their first World Cup in 1994 (where he scored against Italy), winning the 1994 Africa Cup of Nations (scoring both of the Super Eagles' goals in the final), being named 1994 African Footballer of the Year, and winning 1996 Olympic gold (scoring the decisive goal in the last match).

Fifteen years before Barcelona midfielder Andrés Iniestia made a surprising move to Japan to join the J.League's Vissel Kobe, former Barça winger Emmanuel Amunike signed with Busan I'cons.

Well, almost.

A long-term knee injury prevented the Nigerian from playing in the 1998 World Cup, and it was still an issue when the Catalonian colossus club released Amunike two years later. His impaired limb would continue to plague him. Busan, however, were very interested, given the club's new policy of not paying transfer fees and readiness to take a chance on talented but risky players.

Amunike's leg required additional physiotherapy and Busan had already filled their foreign-player slots, so the plan was for the Nigerian to train with the squad as he recovered and then hopefully sign him later. As he didn't yet have a contract with Busan, his presence brought little risk yet offered the prospect of tantalisingly high reward.

Unbelievably, Busan are on the attack once again. Lee Jang-kwan, a diminutive but feisty defender who once captained Busan and goes by the nickname 'Bronco', makes a rare run into the opponent's 18-yard box. An inswinging cross bends toward the front of goal, and Lee jumps above Dutch defender Glenn Loovens to head it past goalkeeper Zoetebier.

4-0 Busan. It's been nearly four years since Busan were last ahead by such an emphatic scoreline. Young Dutch marvel Robin van Persie later pulls back a consolation goal for the Dutch visitors from a superb free kick, but it barely marks a notch against Busan's unequivocal victory. The players celebrate – and while their revelry is perhaps partly muted due to the unimportance of this friendly match, it nonetheless represents an important morale boost for the players. Perhaps this will inspirit them to transcend Busan's four-match winless streak in the K League.

Jubilant in victory, Pride of Pusan members light two flares, the largest pyrotechnical display I've witnessed from them. Superstar Song Chong-gug dutifully marches over to his former Busan supporters and chucks his sweaty shirt into the mass of screaming schoolgirls, sparking a polyester and perspiration-induced frenzy.

CHAPTER 10

DEMOCRACY PROTESTERS SUPPORT THE MILITARY TEAM

GWANGJU SANGMU BULSAJO (MILITARY PHOENIX) VS. BUSAN I'CONS
SUNDAY, 15 JUNE 2003
K LEAGUE ROUND 13
GWANGJU WORLD CUP STADIUM (A.K.A. GUUS HIDDINK STADIUM)

하늘이 무너져도 솟아날 구멍이 있다
*– There is a way out of any bad situation
(literally, 'even if the sky falls, there will be a hole
from which to escape')*

Ever the masochist, Sunday morning involved boarding a bus for another cross-country journey. Busan I'cons were due to play away in Gwangju, the largest metropolis in Korea's south-west. A match against one of the K League's weaker sides offered Busan the opportunity to end their four-match winless streak and recalibrate a push for the championship (*cough, snigger*).

It was mid-June. Lush plant life covered the hills of the Korean countryside. Despite Korea's scarcity of natural resources, the trees appeared untouched; in other countries, swathes would be cut bare for timber harvesting.

We soon arrived in Gwangju. Much like in Daegu, a World Cup stadium was built in Gwangju to briefly impress the world, but the US$150m venue found itself without a tenant once the tournament finished. The South Korean military's football club was persuaded to join the K League, and they agreed to play at the new venue. The league was probably also keen to have more member clubs outside Greater Seoul to expand interest across the country.

Unfortunately, Gwangju was a terrible fit for the military team. In 1980, a popular uprising that demanded democratisation and an end to military dictatorship developed out of Gwangju. The army was ordered to suppress the movement with brute force – estimates put the number of citizens killed above 1,000. Many survivors were given criminal records and jailed.

As psychological wounds continued to fester in Gwangju almost a quarter of a century later, someone made the baffling decision that the military football team should play there. As one Western expat who watched the K League put it, the decision was akin to expecting large support for Israeli club Maccabi Haifa in the Gaza Strip. What should have been a cause for celebration – Gwangju finally getting a football club to call its own – instead seemed like provocation for many people.

A group of young soccer fans in Gwangju made the agonising decision to get behind the team, but with distinct reservations. They named their supporters' group '1980', an obvious reference to the Gwangju Uprising (also known as the Gwangju Massacre).

Compounding the south-western city's mistrust of the military team was their decision to retain their clubhouse (really an army barracks) up in Seongnam, some 320km north in the opposite end of the country. Not only was that insulting to the city's residents, but it also made every 'home' match a cross-country journey for the squad, causing unnecessary player fatigue. Busan, the away team in today's match, were actually located closer to Gwangju than the 'home' team's base in Seongnam.

Gwangju's lovely new stadium was the site where South Korea beat Spain on penalties during the World Cup quarter-finals. As part of the resulting Guus Hiddink mania, Gwangju's stadium was renamed after him. Regrettably, the stadium's design included a running track, which just months after its construction was ripped up and replaced with grass, keeping supporters at both ends of the ground well away from the pitch, in seats with scant elevation.

An unfortunate situation was also unfolding in the stadium's toilets. Korea's traditional lavatory plumbing couldn't handle the strain of toilet paper, and thus people were accustomed to putting their used paper into special receptacles located beside toilets rather than flushing it. But there were no such containers in the Gwangju World Cup stadium loos. At a loss for what to do, people simply chucked their used paper into the corner of the toilet stalls, not wanting to cause plumbing problems.

What the stadium administrators failed to communicate was that these new toilets could readily handle toilet paper. So rather than a pristine and modern venue to showcase Korea to the world, Gwangju's stadium washrooms contained mounds of 'utilised' toilet paper. It was now June, with an afternoon temperature well into the 20s. Needless to say, one was hit with an overpowering stench upon entering the stadium's facilities.

But stadium toilets equipped with toilet paper was a relative luxury. During this period, most public toilets in Korea were not stocked with paper, forcing people to carry tissues around with them whenever they ventured outside.

I left the toilets promptly, cherishing the fresh air in the stadium stands. Pride of Pusan members were hanging their assortment of banners, making themselves known to the 5,400 people in attendance. Gwangju was facing a similar predicament as Busan: playing to four-figure crowds that would only occasionally fill ten per cent of their stadium's capacity.

With all four K League clubs immediately above Bucheon in the league table possessing 11 or 12 points, this match between Gwangju and Busan would be a proverbial six-pointer. The sky had become ominously dark prior to our arrival. Like Busan, Gwangju had only amassed three wins thus far. Just what did this foreboding weather portend? Would Busan become the first club to lose twice to the league's military newcomers? That wasn't the sort of record Ian Porterfield – FA Cup medallist and holder of the Freedom of Zambia for his managerial success – had in mind when he agreed to join this South Korean club.

In accordance with American sporting custom, prior to kick-off the stadium play South Korea's national anthem, to which Gwangju's military players all salute.

The first half is uneventful, with both teams cautious about conceding a goal in this important match. Porterfield again resorts to assigning players out of position, moving defender Lee Jang-kwan into midfield while shifting midfielder Lee Jung-hyo to the back-line. Noh Jung-yoon is brought forward to serve as a striker, while Urumov pulls back to midfield.

Half-time entertainment consists of a person waving a sword around in the centre circle like a madman, with both sets of player substitutes warming up alarmingly close by.

Rain begins to fall as the players trot out of the stadium's underbelly for the second half. Busan take possession and thump the ball up the field to Urumov. He swiftly shifts into a sprint, and finds himself beyond two defenders. As he bears down upon the nervous-looking goalkeeper, he selflessly knocks the ball over to the onrushing Harry on the right. Gwangju's goalkeeper darts to cover his near post, lunging toward Harry with one leg out in desperation. But the Colombian is fully composed under pressure, knocking the ball toward the middle of goal, slightly beyond reach of the flailing goalkeeper.

1-0 Busan! The diminutive Colombian jumps into the arms of fellow striker Gwak Kyung-keun. Pride of Pusan members are initially ecstatic, but soon temper their enthusiasm, reminding each other that Busan scored first in their loss to Gwangju earlier this season. At a struggling club like Busan, superstition must be earnestly obeyed.

Like most foreign players in South Korea, Harry came here primarily for the money. Colombia's league ranked well above the K League in quality, but wages in the Liga Águila were low – if they were paid at all. Half a century ago, the league was awash in cash, much of it allegedly drug money, but efforts to clean up the league meant that fiscal restraint was now the name of the game. In contrast, South Korea's *jaebeol* business conglomerates continued to throw ridiculous sums of money at K League clubs. It was tempting for talented South Americans to seek better-paid opportunities in robust overseas economies, such as Korea.

It wasn't an easy decision. Harry had regularly featured for Colombia's national teams at youth and senior level, but by leaving for Asia he annihilated his chance of being capped again. He was also far away from most of his extended family and friends, living in a foreign culture that employed an unfamiliar language.

However, his annual return to Colombia each close season convinced Harry that his Asian adventure was the correct decision. Many of his former team-mates had difficulty acquiring their pay on time, with several clubs teetering on the financial precipice. Colombian players enquired enviously about Harry's experience in Korea, with several asking if he could put in a good word for them.

Harry looks over at the Busan bench after his goal and notices Porterfield's big, toothy smile. Meanwhile, coach Jarvie explains tactical instructions through a translator to striker Ahn Hyo-yeon, who is about to be inserted into the match as a substitute.

Ahn joined Busan just one month earlier, a mid-season addition to the squad. He was expected to become one of the most prominent players in Korean football. As an under-20, Ahn played against the likes of Thierry Henry and David Trezeguet at the 1997 FIFA World Youth Championship. But Ahn would sustain a back injury, one that would never truly heal and kept him from appearing at the 2000 Summer Olympics.

After leading Dangook University to their first national university championship in 30 years and being named the tournament's best player, he opted to launch his professional career in Japan with Kyoto Purple Sanga, alongside future Manchester United midfielder Park Ji-sung. Ahn also played in the 2001 FIFA Confederations Cup as a substitute against France.

However, in a J.League match shortly before he was scheduled to come home to Korea to play in the 2002 World Cup, Ahn aggravated his back injury, which barred him from the tournament. He returned to Japan but was released by Kyoto at the end of his contract.

Similar to new Busan team-mate Gwak Kyung-keun, Ahn initially performed well in Japan but was ultimately cast to the scrapheap due to health issues.

By now you can surely spot the emerging pattern and predict what happened next, dear reader. With most clubs hesitant to offer a contract to the talented but injury-afflicted player, Busan smelled opportunity and swooped in for a bargain signing, hoping that Ahn would overcome his troubles and perform miracles on a low salary. He was particularly worth the risk, because unlike several older players Busan were gambling on, he was still at peak age.

Ahn enters the match with vigour, taking a shot at goal soon after coming on. He's keen to convince Ian Porterfield he still has a good decade of playing time ahead of him. Ahn certainly looks impressive, but whether his questionable body can still handle the demands of professional football will be tested in the months to come.

During a long break in play, a ska band hired by Gwangju attempts to distract the crowd from the lull. After playing several chords, they solicit audience participation.

'You say one, I say two. One!' He points the microphone out toward the crowd, who compliantly respond with a loud 'Two!' despite the mixed-up instructions in English.

Play resumes, and Gwangju have possession. Lee Dong-gook, the same superstar forward who scored a hat-trick against Busan just last month, wants the ball. As he begins to dash toward goal, the ball is struck high in a long, swerving arch. Lee settles the ball with his foot, takes a brief glance upward to locate goal, and strikes the ball.

Ping, whoosh. 1-1. Busan goalkeeper Kim Yong-dae can do little more than watch as the ball smashes against the upper corner of the woodwork, tears at the rear netting and rolls out of the goal, such was its velocity. For the second time in as many months, Busan have given up an early lead against Gwangju.

For Busan, the prospect of losing to Gwangju particularly stings because they represent Jeolla, the south-west region of Korea considered the rival of the south-east. This animosity extends back two millennia when the rival kingdoms of Baekje and Silla fought periodic wars for several centuries. In more recent times, most of South Korea's leaders – including its military dictators – hailed from Gyeongsang and invested very little in Jeolla's development. This, combined with the government's brutal suppression of the Gwangju Uprising in 1980, made Jeolla particularly resentful of the south-east.

Suffice to say many residents of Gwangju and Busan didn't hold each other in very high esteem, adding extra significance to this clash between clubs trying to claw their way up from the bottom end of the K League table.

Gwangju's goalkeeper hurls the ball to the right side of the pitch, launching a quick counter-attack. A midfielder breaks forward, then spots striker Lee Dong-gook near the penalty area. The ball is passed up to Lee.

This is it. Lee has scored four times against Busan in less than two matches for Gwangju. He springs forward and looks up toward goal. You can sense an attempt. Is Lee about to make it five goals in two games, including the match-winners of both?

Everyone is focused on Lee. With the distraction, Gwangju midfielder Kim Byung-chae comes barrelling into the penalty area from the left. Lee taps the ball forward to Kim, surprising all the Busan defenders. On his first touch, Kim blasts the ball at the lower side of the goal, beyond the outstretched arms of Busan goalkeeper Kim Yong-dae.

2-1 Gwangju.

Gwangju players swarm their goalscorer. The home fans leap off their seats, jumping with delight. Busan players' heads slump, with several athletes slinking down to the ground, sulking with disappointment. Ian Porterfield closes his eyes, his face awash with frustration.

* * *

Although Porterfield had attained numerous accomplishments throughout his managerial career, his record was by no means unblemished. Several assignments had ended in disappointment.

At Aberdeen, Porterfield accepted the unenviable challenge of succeeding Alex Ferguson, who had been headhunted by Manchester United. Under Ferguson, Aberdeen won a range of trophies, including three Scottish league championships and the European Cup Winners' Cup. Ferguson had suggested that Aberdeen appoint his assistant to succeed him as manager.

'Instead, they came up with Ian Porterfield – and that amazed me,' Ferguson later told the media.

Expectations were high for Porterfield, but despite inheriting a talented squad, the team was only able to finish fourth in the league on two occasions as well as lose a domestic cup final. Aberdeen's official website included a rather curt description of Porterfield's time at the club, 'He took over from [Alex] Ferguson with little success. He left in 1988.'

To be fair to Porterfield, Aberdeen did twice quality for European competition during his time, and his win percentage remains in the club's all-time top five. But the general consensus was that Ferguson's squad had carried Porterfield. He failed to win any silverware and became known as a draw specialist. Porterfield's player transfers were incredibly poor – shipping out talented individuals and replacing them on the cheap with mediocre journeymen from the English league's lower levels.

It was also during his spell at Aberdeen that Porterfield developed an antagonistic relationship with the news media.

'I feel that some people let me down, the press cut me to ribbons and 90 per cent of it had no foundation,' he said.

Porterfield's next managerial position was at Reading in England's Third Division, but he was unable to improve the team and was sacked after less than 17 months – approximately the same length of time he had lasted at Aberdeen.

He then joined Chelsea in England's top division, where infamous owner Ken Bates had lofty expectations. The London club finished a disappointing 14th during Porterfield's first season, but Bates decided to give him more time to settle. The next year, the inaugural Premier League season, Chelsea were as high as fourth by mid-December. But form soon tanked, and two months later Porterfield assumed the distinction of being the first Premier League manager to be fired.

His sacking was warranted. Porterfield's win percentage was the second-worst among Chelsea's permanent managers in the 35-year period from 1980 to 2015, just slightly better than Glenn Hoddle. Porterfield's naiveté in the transfer market was again evident, with the Scotsman spending £6m on disappointing players while refusing several of Bates' recommendations.

'I had the opportunity to buy Eric Cantona for £1m,' Bates said at a dinner with Chelsea season-ticket holders in 2004, according to *The Telegraph*. 'I asked our then-manager, Ian Porterfield, did he want him? He said, "No, he couldn't play." Eric Cantona was the greatest single contributor to the growth of Manchester United.'

Bates, who had a reputation for being cantankerous, would later tell *The Guardian*, 'Ian Porterfield ... was a great number two [but] a useless number one,' as well as referring to him as a 'pillock' in the *Sunday Mirror*.

Stan Ternent, who served as coach under Porterfield at Chelsea, was scathingly critical of the Scot in his autobiography, *Stan the Man: A Hard Life in Football*.

'I felt I was being used as a skivvy and he seldom discussed tactics, selections or even coaching with me. He preferred to telephone some of his part-time scouts for advice instead of listening to me. I couldn't understand his neglect.

'Porterfield was bankrupt of ideas. On rare occasions when I tried to talk about the playing staff or our tactics, Porterfield could react with abuse.

'... [M]y abiding memory of Chelsea is Porterfield's nonsensical attitude. Working with him, for me, was one of the worst experiences imaginable in football.'

Having lasted less than a couple of years at each of his three most recent managerial jobs, British clubs grew cautious of hiring the Scot – in fact, he would never work in the UK as a number one again. Porterfield would turn his fortunes around with a highly successful spell as Zambia's manager, but this was later followed by a job as Zimbabwe manager that fit his previous pattern of disappointing results and an exit after less than two years.

Porterfield later became manager of Trinidad and Tobago. While they initially flourished, the team flopped to a 7-0 away loss to Mexico in the penultimate round of World Cup qualifying – which remains Trinidad's worst-ever defeat, some two decades later – and tanked during the final round. His spell at the Caribbean nation was also marked by public feuding with English club managers Alex Ferguson (Manchester United) and Harry Redknapp (West Ham) over the call-up of international players. The diplomatic row caused Manchester United striker Dwight Yorke to temporarily quit international football.

Porterfield's relationship with the news media further worsened while at Trinidad. After a World Cup qualifying loss, he snapped at one reporter's question about whether he might be terminated.

'It is an embarrassing question, because this team has played 13 games and lost two, so that is a terrible question,' said Porterfield. 'I don't think Trinidad and Tobago will ever sack me, because if I don't think I can do the job, then I can tell you, I won't be here.'

Prior to the 2003 K League season, Porterfield asked Busan fans for leniency during the initial ten matches and suggested results should improve by June. But it was now June, and Busan were about to earn their fourth loss in five matches, none of them wins.

'*Aisssshhhh*, Porterfield!' curses one of the Pride of Pusan leaders in the away end. Discontent among Busan supporters progressed from quiet muttering to unrestrained criticism over the last few matches.

The referee blows his whistle. We have lost. Busan have realised the ignominy of being the first team to lose twice to newcomers Gwangju.

The trip back to Busan would be a sombre one.

ROUND 12
[Busan vs. Seongnam match postponed due to inclement weather]

Bucheon	1-1	Jeonnam
Ulsan	3-1	Suwon
Jeonbuk	2-2	Pohang
Anyang	0-0	Gwangju
Daejeon	2-0	Daegu

ROUND 13

Gwangju	**2-1**	**Busan**
Suwon	1-2	Daejeon
Bucheon	2-4	Anyang
Pohang	1-2	Jeonnam
Seongnam	1-2	Ulsan
Jeonbuk	1-1	Daegu

K LEAGUE TABLE

Seongnam	26
Daejeon	26
Anyang	23
Jeonbuk	23
Ulsan	21
Jeonnam	18
Suwon	17
Gwangju	15
Daegu	12
Pohang	12
Busan	**11**
Bucheon	4

CHAPTER 11

DEATH BY ELECTRIC FAN (OR, DON'T FORGET TO SMEAR RED BEAN PASTE ON YOUR DOOR)

BUSAN I'CONS VS. DAEJEON CITIZEN
SATURDAY, 21 JUNE 2003
K LEAGUE ROUND 15
BUSAN ASIAD WORLD CUP STADIUM

칠전팔기

*– If at first you don't succeed, try, try again
(literally, 'if you fall down seven times, get
up eight times')*

A CRISIS loomed at the former club champions of Asia. Busan I'cons were winless in their last five K League games. Ian Porterfield had some dry spells in his various managerial stints, but this new job at Busan quickly threatened to become the greatest stain on his entire career. It could jeopardise his current employment, and possibly even alarm potential future employers.

After the loss against newcomers Gwangju, Busan faced an away trip to formidable Suwon Samsung Bluewings, the young but well-funded club awash in silverware. It would be a challenging fixture for Busan to improve their form.

Busan are fortunate to visit Suwon while the hosts are navigating a rough patch, and unexpectedly snatch a point from a 0-0 draw. While it is a good result in isolation, it extends Busan's winless streak to six matches. One more game without a win would equal the club's record over the past nine seasons. Although Busan's performances did seem to be improving, especially against the league's better opponents, Porterfield and assistant Jarvie were desperate for the team to start winning again.

The Scottish coaching duo could definitely do with a bit of luck.

If they were indeed superstitious, Korea offered them a myriad of novel beliefs to adhere to. One of the local urban legends was that using an electric fan in a room with closed windows could cause death. Explanations ranged from suffocation – either due to all the oxygen somehow being sucked out of a room or the air pressure becoming too great – to hypothermia.

As recently as 2006, the Korean government warned the public about the dangers of fans causing asphyxiation. Electric fans in Korea usually came with a warning label that stated, 'Do not use to generate a strong wind close to you in a sealed room. There is a high risk of death if used while sleeping.' Many fans also included an automatic timer to ensure they were not used continuously overnight.

A common superstition that extended to Korean football was to present food offerings to the gods before the start of a new season. Each March there would be footage of teams bowing before a decapitated pig's head.

Another traditional Korean belief was to smear red bean porridge on the front door of a house during winter solstice, the darkest day of the year, to ward off evil spirits. But today was summer solstice, the longest day. With Busan hosting buoyant K League opponents Daejeon, massive red banners were plastered on the upper tier of the Asiad World Cup Stadium. Perhaps the intent was to ward off Daejeon's players as much as encourage our own.

In an effort to bolster attendance at Busan matches, the Pride of Pusan had relocated from behind the goal to the touchline near the stadium's primary entrance. The hope was to get more fans into the spirit of supporting the team, as the Pride's usual location was distant from the main stands.

Having recently played Feyenoord in a friendly, the sports media reported that Busan had signed a Dutch player. It turned out that the mystery newcomer was actually Serbian midfielder Šimić with less grease in his hair than usual, illustrating just how reliable the sports tattlers were.

Busan's starting 11 and their formation was displayed on the stadium's large screen. The Colombian duo of Tommy and Harry would start together for the first time in more than a month, joined up front by Lee Jung-hyo. The problem was that Lee was a defender, yet was being asked by Porterfield to serve as a striker.

Lee was yet another university football standout who somehow ended up at Busan, although he eschewed club custom by becoming injured *after* signing with Busan, rather than before.

Daejeon supporters arrived from their three-hour journey in good number. They marked kick-off mischievously by lighting a flare and setting off several other minor pyrotechnics.

Busan captain Noh Jung-yoon beckons for the ball as the match gets underway. Attempting to resurrect his career in Korea after a decade overseas, the elder player signals he wants possession virtually every time Busan obtain the ball.

Wearing the captain's armband affords a player deference from their peers anywhere in the world. But in South Korea, the reason a player was granted such an honour was remarkably different than in the West.

As a Confucian society, social seniority demands respect. Juniors are expected to obey their seniors. In turn, seniors are presumed to act benevolently and be sagacious in their actions and speech.

When two Koreans are introduced, one of the first questions they will ask is the other person's age, to determine how politely they should address their peer. Younger Koreans are expected to speak to their elders with greater respect.

Even football didn't escape these social customs. Captaincy of a K League team was determined solely by age in most cases: the eldest player was awarded the armband by default. Ability or leadership skills were rarely considered. The older players were virtually guaranteed playing time regardless of form.

When Noh Jung-yoon arrived at Busan in 2003, he was awarded the coveted armband largely because he was the oldest. According to several people at the club, he took the role very seriously off the field, acting as a disciplinarian and keeping younger players submissive. But rather than showing leadership skills on the field, he often berated players whenever a mistake was made during a match.

Team captains in Western countries are expected to communicate tactics, enforce positions, and defend team-mates during skirmishes.

But in South Korea, captains often either wore the armband with complete indifference or expected to be constantly given possession.

Noh Jung-yoon was the latter. Almost every time an attack was mounted, he would anticipate being involved, regardless of where he stood or how many opposing players were marking him. Several players surreptitiously referred to him as the 'customs service', given that most plays would inevitably have to go through him.

A European player who would join Busan I'cons later in 2003 had this to say when asked about cultural differences, 'When I came into Busan's dressing room it was the first time that age was important, not name. It probably helped that I had played in England, but it was first and foremost that I was among the elders that made sure I won respect and trust.'

When Dutch manager Guus Hiddink took over the South Korean national team for the 2002 World Cup, one of his first priorities was to eliminate deference to seniority among the squad, instructing the players to instead treat each other as equals. The request was initially met by stony silence, as the juniors felt uncomfortable speaking disrespectfully to the seniors, while the elder players felt like their high standing was being diminished. However, younger player Kim Nam-il, infamous for cracking jokes, broke the ice by turning to the oldest player, Hong Myung-bo, and blurting out, 'Hey, Myung-bo, let's go eat!' in informal speech. The entire squad burst into laughter, lightening what might have otherwise been a cumbersome transition.

Hiddink also broke Korean tradition by selecting the best players, rather than favouring the oldest. When some players and even coaches protested, they were axed. Hiddink's methods were unorthodox for Korea, but they were undoubtedly effective: he turned a country that had never won a single World Cup match into semi-finalists.

When Busan I'cons hired Ian Porterfield as their manager shortly after Hiddink's unprecedented success with the national team, the club hoped the Scotsman would generate equally impressive results. But Porterfield may have been unaware of the transformation Hiddink orchestrated behind the scenes, arguably a major factor of his success. Noh Jung-yoon was permitted to become Busan captain due to his age. When Noh regularly requested possession during games, Porterfield didn't overrule him.

Could Porterfield hope to transform Busan's results based entirely on tactics, despite the continuation of squad seniority trumping meritocracy within the starting 11? It was possible, but was Porterfield unwittingly making his job more difficult by neglecting to learn from a successful precedent?

Daejeon and Busan jostle for the ball in midfield. Tommy acquires possession and weaves some of the Colombian magic that earned him a coveted foreign-player spot in South Korea, flicking the ball deftly to one side of his opponent while slipping past him on the other. The dumbfounded Daejeon player stands in awe, attempting to comprehend how he had been beaten so adroitly.

The Colombian maven dashes forward with only the resigned-looking goalkeeper ahead of him. As Tommy approaches the 18-yard line, he takes a crack, smashing the ball into the right of goal.

1-0 Busan.

Busan had recently earned surprising away draws at K League leaders Seongnam as well as Suwon, and are now ahead of high-flying Daejeon. It was still too early in the match to assume a win, but I couldn't help but wonder: why were Busan flourishing against the league's tougher opponents yet losing against struggling teams? Were psychological issues at play?

If Busan were to hold on to beat Daejeon, it would be a fabulous result. But with less than 2,500 people in attendance at this 60,000-capacity venue, would many locals even notice? This was the worst weekend attendance figure across the entire league so far this season.

You would be mistaken to assume that Busan residents didn't care about sport. They eagerly attended football during the former Daewoo Royals glory days, while Busan's baseball club was one of the better-supported teams in the Korean baseball league.

Part of the problem was that most Korean football fans hadn't established an emotional connection to the K League. While many Koreans cheered on the national team during major tournaments, it was more out of nationalist zeal than an actual love for football. Meanwhile, Koreans who were connoisseurs of the world's game tended to put their allegiance behind a glamorous foreign club, usually European. Correctly or not, many Koreans assumed the K League lacked quality.

But today I was sharing the stadium with a couple of thousand Busan residents who do care about K League football. The Daejeon players aren't making it easy for Busan as they cynically flop down on to the pitch with the faintest of contact.

Tommy acquires possession of the ball once again. Harry emerges as an option on the right, and Tommy passes to his compatriot. Harry receives the ball shortly before meeting the 18-yard box. As he enters the penalty area he sends a thundering shot to the right side of goal. It rockets above the lowered shoulder of the Daejeon goalkeeper. Enraged by being beaten twice on the same side, the goalkeeper launches a verbal barrage at his back-line. Harry stands with a smirk on his face and motions for his team-mates to join him in celebration.

2-0 Busan.

For the first time that season, the Pride of Pusan unleash a smoke bomb, such is their delight. It may be a banned device at K League grounds, but a two-goal margin against a strong opponent demands more than merely hooting and hollering.

Maybe Busan aren't so bad after all. Perhaps they will become a championship contender. Maybe Ian Porterfield actually *is* the K League version of Guus Hiddink!

Had we all been too harsh on Porterfield by questioning his management ability? Were we too impatient, much like the Korean press had been during the start of Hiddink's time in charge of the national team? Were our expectations unfair given the numerous obstacles to Busan's success?

* * *

While Porterfield had suffered his fair share of failures during his career, perhaps some of it could be excused, considering the adversity he endured over the decades.

Shortly after joining Sunderland as a player, Porterfield was frozen out of the squad for a full season by a disciplinarian manager. Seven years later – the season after Porterfield's much-lauded goal and Sunderland's FA Cup triumph – he was involved in a car accident that shattered his skull and left him with life-threatening injuries. His doctor initially expected Porterfield would be dead within five hours, but the Scot survived surgery and would be ready to resume playing football in less than a month.

Despite a successful rehabilitation, Porterfield rarely saw any playing time as Sunderland were careful not to jeopardise a potential insurance pay-out.

Maltreatment arguably worsened after his transition to management. Porterfield joined Sheffield United and earned the club two promotions, yet faced a reduced playing budget as well as abusive fans envious of bitter derby rivals Sheffield Wednesday prospering in the top flight.

The Scot would take over at Aberdeen, where expectations were immense. The extreme job pressure quickly took its toll on Porterfield's private life. His first marriage ended when his wife left him for a wealthy meat salesman just months after he took the post. Turning to alcohol to stem the stress, Porterfield would soon be convicted of drink-driving.

His next managerial job was at Reading. He fared poorly, and once again turned to alcohol in desperation. His time at the club was cut short by a second drink-driving conviction, which earned him a several-year driving ban. His second marriage began to show signs of strain.

To the surprise of many, Porterfield was then appointed manager of Chelsea – likely because club owner Ken Bates sought to appoint a managerial team on a low budget. When things weren't going well, Bates didn't hesitate to publicly pile on further pressure.

His next job was managing Zambia's national team, perhaps Porterfield's greatest success. But even that ended acrimoniously when he quarrelled with John Fashanu, his Britain-based boss, over salary expectations.

Bolton then beckoned Porterfield back to the Premier League in an assistant role. Four months later, when the club failed to evade relegation, he was found drunk in his car yet again. Porterfield received his third conviction, as well as an eight-year driving ban. He was forced to serve 100 hours of community service in Surrey, and was put on probation for 12 months.

Porterfield would never work in the UK again.

'I'd have liked to have been great [as a British football manager], who knows but for that [alcoholism and drunk-driving convictions],' Porterfield told the *Northern Echo*.

'It's a bit sad, but when you leave the UK the doors seem to get closed to you getting an opportunity back there again,' Porterfield told *The Independent*. 'Why that is I will never know, because if you go overseas you learn so much from the different people and the different cultures. It makes you a better person and a better coach.'

Determined to forge on, Porterfield agreed to manage Zimbabwe's national team. He resigned after 20 months, citing 'too much unwarranted criticism' from national association president Leo Mugabe, nephew of the infamous Robert Mugabe.

Porterfield then became boss of Oman's national team. They were renowned for unrealistic expectations, and when Porterfield couldn't deliver an immediate transformation he was out of a job once again.

Trinidad and Tobago came calling next. After years of being away from home, his second marriage finally collapsed. That same year Porterfield also struck and killed a pedestrian while driving in Trinidad.

Footballing matters didn't start much better on the Caribbean island. His predecessor, Bertille St. Clair, was adored in Trinidad, with both the fans and players furious about St. Clair's sacking. Much like at Aberdeen, Porterfield unwittingly walked into a minefield.

Porterfield eventually won over the players and the team flourished. But Porterfield became depressed, and according to his former Trinidad colleagues, his mood affected the players' performances. A former manager was rehired to replace Porterfield, with the expectation that he would resign. But the Scot's refusal to leave created an acrimonious relationship that soured his eventual departure.

His last position before joining Busan saw a return to Africa, this time at Ghanaian club Kumasi Asante Kotoko, which just the year prior had played a match that resulted in a stadium stampede killing 126 people – the worst disaster in African football history. Porterfield claimed he was not given a copy of his contract and that he was not paid.

Porterfield wrote a detailed account of the treatment he claimed he received at Kotoko, which he publicly released and was published by several news outlets in Ghana. The Scot alleged that CEO Herbert Mensah pinned him against a dressing room wall, punched his arms several times and 'nearly strangled' him when he refused to let Mensah interfere in team tactics. Porterfield alleged that

Mensah shouted, 'You and I cannot work together and I won't pay your salary, so why don't you just fuck off.'

Porterfield also alleged that Mensah verbally threatened the lives of Porterfield and his wife, warning them both to leave Ghana. Porterfield criticised his treatment, saying, 'The incident ... is by far the most disgraceful, embarrassing and shameful flaunting of power I have ever witnessed.'

Just four months into the position, Porterfield was terminated by the club and engaged in a public legal battle. Charges brought by Porterfield included wrongful dismissal, breach of contract, as well as assault and battery.

Porterfield's career had been surprisingly turbulent, with some of his experiences bordering on traumatic – particularly the job immediately before coming to Busan. Knowing this, I was willing to offer the Scot some leniency.

But Porterfield doesn't need to ask for any pity today, as Busan are up by a two-goal margin against a tough league opponent. Full time arrives and the Pride of Pusan members are in celebratory mood, apparently willing to forgive the six-match winless spell that now seems a distant footnote.

Porterfield and Jarvie must have felt relieved. This was the first match Busan had won by more than a single-goal margin all season, and the team had once again earned points from a difficult fixture. While the team's chemistry still wasn't prodigious, their passing had noticeably improved. And goalkeeper Kim Yong-dae was named in the league's unofficial 'best 11' for the week after keeping two consecutive clean sheets.

Busan had leapfrogged newcomers Daegu into tenth spot, now level on points with Gwangju and with a match in hand. But would Porterfield be able to build on today's success?

ROUND 14
Suwon	**0-0**	**Busan**
Daejeon	0-4	Ulsan
Seongnam	3-3	Anyang
Gwangju	1-2	Jeonnam
Bucheon	0-1	Jeonbuk
Daegu	0-1	Pohang

ROUND 15
Busan	**2-0**	**Daejeon**
Pohang	1-0	Bucheon
Ulsan	3-0	Daegu
Jeonbuk	4-2	Gwangju
Seongnam	1-1	Jeonnam
Anyang	2-2	Suwon

K LEAGUE TABLE
Jeonbuk	29
Seongnam	28
Ulsan	27
Daejeon	26
Anyang	25
Jeonnam	22
Suwon	19
Pohang	18
Gwangju	15
Busan	**15**
Daegu	12
Bucheon	4

CHAPTER 12

FOOTBALL? ON A SATURDAY?!? RIDICULOUS!

BUSAN I'CONS VS. DAEGU FC
SATURDAY, 28 JUNE 2003
K LEAGUE ROUND 17
BUSAN ASIAD WORLD CUP STADIUM

'No one goes to football in Busan. It's a city full of Russian hookers; who needs it?'

– A sardonic Daegu FC supporter

SCHEDULING FOOTBALL matches was tricky when such a big chunk of the country still worked on Saturdays. Sunday afternoon was the ideal time, but South Korea's summer heat made afternoon games unbearably hot – for players and fans alike. Sunday evening was too close to the start of the next working week. So with the advent of the intense summer temperatures, Saturday evenings temporarily became the default time for weekend matches.

Busan played away in midweek to Ulsan, the team that finished in second place the previous season, and it ended in a 1-0 loss. Despite the result, I sensed an air of optimism for today's home match against new club Daegu FC. Although Busan had lost away to Daegu earlier in the season, Daegu had since dropped below Busan in the league table, and Busan subsequently earned several impressive results against top opposition.

The primary concern amongst the Pride of Pusan was consistency, or more precisely, whether Busan's squad was motivated to put in the same effort against minnows such as Daegu as they had against the league's stronger clubs.

Daegu's central midfielder Song Jung-hyun makes a deep run down the left, scurrying past Busan's defenders. As he reaches the goal line he pivots toward the net and bear down upon Busan goalkeeper Kim Yong-dae. Kim guards his near post as best he can, but Song flicks the ball back to Daegu striker Gu Dae-ryung in front of the 18-yard box. Gu volleys with his first touch. The ball glides unimpeded across the line.

1-0 Daegu.

After a shaky start, Busan find their composure. Defender Lee Lim-saeng makes a rare foray into their opponents' penalty area. He sees Urumov rushing closer, several yards away and unmarked, and provides him the ball. Urumov takes a couple of brief steps to synchronise his timing as he meets the ball, and thrusts it forward with a powerful shot. The ball sails into the top left of the net.

1-1.

Zoran Urumov is an Eastern European character destined to become part of K League folklore. The Serbian had already earned himself a reputation as a sturdy consumer of alcohol, particularly *soju*, Korea's most popular liquor.

As one Busan staffer put it, 'I spent many nights with the soju-master. I've seen him drive into Saturday morning training coming directly from Texas Street [Busan's sin district], wearing the same rumpled training clothes from the night before, and manage to get through the entire training session without throwing up on the field.

'No one on the team could even [hold] a candle to him.'

The Pride of Pusan were perhaps the only ones in Korean football who abstained from alcohol. K League fans were allowed to consume booze anywhere in the stadium, purchased at dirt-cheap prices in the concourse or brought to the stadium from outside. Some clubs even gave alcohol away for free as part of promotions with large breweries or distilleries.

With the overlapping of economical booze and the stereotypical polite-but-potentially-fiery Korean temperament, it was inevitable things would sometimes get out of hand. One particularly drunk fan, with a collection of empty glass *soju* bottles by his feet, begins to roar with anger. He decides it would be a good idea to launch bottles down on to the running track, and so there they flew, one after another. When match stewards had the gall to look at this gentleman the wrong way, he stood up, inflated his chest, and challenged the nervous-looking lads to a brawl. Off came his shirt, thrown to the ground to signal his macho provocation.

Then the real security arrive. Men dressed in impeccable black suits and ties. I fear the worst for this drunken yob. If people in the USA have to be careful about strangers carrying concealed firearms, here in South Korea you're gambling as to what degree of taekwondo familiarity an unknown person has. Virtually every man in the country has spent upwards of two years conscripted into mandatory military service, and that's just your average Kim on the street. These guys are professional security goons who only emerge from the stadium's shadows when things really kick off. I cringe as they approach their target.

Astonishingly, nothing happens. The man continues to yell and scream, challenging the entire group to a fight. None comply. I had expected that, at best, the drunkard would be ejected from the ground. No such luck. The trepid goons do their best to verbally reason with a drunk who is well beyond rationalism. The man eventually becomes bored and sits down, providing the hired goons with the excuse to scurry away.

Soju is a wicked creation. Much like tequila is famed for messing with the mind, people fare little better when they encounter Korea's potent mix of ethanol and water. Many typically reserved people become temporary sociopaths when on the Hermit Kingdom's embalming fluid.

According to Euromonitor International, South Koreans drank an average of 13.7 shots of hard alcohol every week as of 2014 – more than double the consumption in Russia. Deciding that enough was enough, the Korean government declared that one Monday each month would be officially deemed a 'moderate drinking night'. But the other 29 to 30 days? They were still fair game, of course.

By now our local football yob has fallen asleep in his plastic stadium chair. Down on the pitch, Daegu are awarded a free kick near Busan's arc circle.

Despite Busan's defenders jostling to form the perfect wall ten yards ahead, Daegu's free kick sails perfectly through a gaping hole between the players. It leaves Busan's goalkeeper little opportunity to see the ball's trajectory before it approaches goal.

2-1 Daegu.

Ian Porterfield lifts his head, gazing skyward in exasperation. His facial expression seems to silently scream, 'What the hell have I got myself into?'

Managing a match involving two hopeless K League teams had not been top of Porterfield's career to-do list. The Scot had dreamed, both as a player and a manager, of participating in a World Cup.

Shortly after scoring the winning goal for Sunderland in their 1973 FA Cup Final victory, Porterfield outlined (with John Gibson) in *The Impossible Dream* his desire to play for Scotland's national team.

'I kept harbouring thoughts of perhaps winning a Scottish cap … That longing has never left me since. I still dream of playing for my country although I am now 27 years old … It makes me sick when I see so many players who are automatic choices for their country display such obvious indifference while I'm dying for the honour.'

It seemed that Porterfield's time would soon come. But a car crash in late 1974 that nearly ended Porterfield's life would preclude him from ever receiving a cap from Scotland.

As a manager, Porterfield almost earned a berth in the world's grandest tournament during his first overseas posting. The Scot led Zambia to within one goal of qualifying for their first World Cup.

Two World Cup cycles later, Porterfield would have another chance. He was put in charge of Trinidad and Tobago, who also hoped to advance to the international tournament for the first time. They fared exceptionally well during the penultimate qualifying round, but collapsed during the final stage.

Porterfield had been a football manager for a quarter of a century when he agreed to lead Busan I'cons. It was unclear if he would ever take part in a World Cup. He certainly seemed a world away from any such glamour today, leading a diminished Busan against Daegu's hastily assembled collection of dilapidated veterans and unrefined university graduates, in front of an embarrassingly small crowd.

But the Scot isn't feeling sorry for himself. He's determined to succeed, regardless of challenging circumstances.

Busan midfielder Kim Tae-min is similarly determined to find an equaliser. Kim wasn't expected to feature much this year – at just 20 years of age at the start of the season, he was one of the squad's youngest players. After being Busan's first pick in the 2001 high-school draft, the youth star was shipped to the Netherlands for three months in 2002 as part of Busan's academy programme. When website *OhmyNews* compiled a preview of Busan's 2003 season, it predicted Kim would be peripheral, fighting for a fourth midfield spot. Instead, he became a regular starter under Porterfield.

Given his youthful age, Kim was unpolished and showed occasional flashes of naiveté. Regardless, he continued to see playing time. The supporters joked that Kim must be Porterfield's stepson, as his inclusion in Busan's starting 11 was virtually guaranteed.

But Porterfield's insistence on playing Kim was proving astute. The player's potential was maturing quickly, and there were noises of the South Korean under-23 (Olympic) national team possibly capping Kim.

As the ball comes through to Kim, he immediately volleys it with his right foot, a powerful shot that thunders toward goal. Daegu's goalkeeper correctly guesses where Kim will send the ball, but the velocity of the shot is too great for it to be saved. The diving goalkeeper lands on the pitch, where he remains flat, limbs fully extended and face cast down in frustration at conceding two equalisers – this one in second-half stoppage time.

2-2. As Kim breaks into a celebratory trot, he kisses his wedding ring, pulls it off, then kisses it again repeatedly while struggling not to drop it, such is the youngster's excitement.

The referee signals for full time.

How to judge this Busan performance? Was this a resilient comeback, overcoming a deficit on two occasions to earn an important point? Or was this two dropped points from what should have been one of the easier matches for Busan – playing at home against a lightweight opponent? Were Busan indeed struggling with a lack of motivation when playing the league's weaker teams? If so, surely it was Porterfield's responsibility to conquer such psychological hurdles.

The stadium speakers announced the attendance as 1,283. This was Busan's smallest gate for any 2003 game thus far. Rather displeasingly, it also set the record as the entire league's lowest attendance of the season. This new nadir transpired mere days after Busan had broken its previous smallest weekend crowd figure. Dare we contemplate what attendance Busan would muster next week?

Porterfield was asked by *Soccerphile*'s John Duerden about his opinion on the team's lacklustre crowds. He replied, 'When I first came to Busan and met people, no one knew that there was a football team here.

'I think that one of the reasons that we don't get good gates is that we play in the World Cup Stadium way over outside of town. It's very difficult to get there, no train service and it takes a long time by bus. This is a big disadvantage to the people here. The old stadium, there's been talk about even moving back because the crowds are so poor.

'I certainly agree that if we had a more compact stadium, it would be a big help ... The atmosphere is not there as the people are too far away because we have the running track. Hopefully, one day, I gather [club chairman] Mr Chung is planning our own stadium.'

Busan had been utilising the new Asiad World Cup Stadium for barely three months, yet team officials were already openly contemplating leaving.

But it wasn't just the inappropriately large venue, or lack of subway service, or residents busy working on Saturdays behind Busan's poor attendance. There was also some truth to Porterfield's suggestion that many people in Busan were simply unaware their city had a team.

Marketing of Korean club football, both from the league and individual clubs, was almost non-existent. There were no adverts on television paid for by the clubs – only teasers from the channels themselves hyping the occasional future broadcast. Very little effort was made to let people know about upcoming games.

When Jeonnam Dragons wanted to promote a pending match, rather than shelling out the cost of hiring an advert billboard they instead stuck a group of senior citizens with a banner and a flag near the side of a road and told them to get to it.

Some marketing efforts bordered on the surreal. Busan would later establish a short-lived 'Lady Zone', meant to let female fans enjoy football without the hostility and excessive machismo of male fans. When the club realised women occasionally enjoy spending time with men, the promotion was disbanded.

A decade later, in an attempt to boost crowds, Busan I'cons would allegedly 'encourage' all of their squad members – including Australian international midfielder Matt McKay – to purchase 15 tickets for every match, to either sell on or give away for free, according to a former employee. Who knew football incorporated pyramid schemes?

Match results were, of course, another major reason for Busan's inability to fill even a decent fraction of their stadium. While Busan failed to earn more than one point today against lowly Daegu, fellow strugglers Gwangju won away to basement club Bucheon, allowing the military team to climb two points above Busan. We were now third-bottom.

In the days ahead, rumours swirled that Porterfield was looking to sign some players from the United Kingdom.

'... [M]an management and the careful selection of players will be important,' Porterfield wrote back in 1973, still a player at the time but already contemplating the rigours of football management. 'They will have to be hand-picked not just for skill but for temperament and loyalty as well.'

ROUND 16

Ulsan	**1-0**	**Busan**
Daejeon	1-1	Anyang
Jeonnam	1-2	Suwon
Seongnam	3-2	Jeonbuk
Gwangju	0-1	Pohang
Daegu	0-0	Bucheon

ROUND 17

Busan	**2-2**	**Daegu**
Bucheon	0-2	Gwangju
Pohang	2-0	Seongnam
Jeonbuk	2-2	Suwon
Jeonnam	1-0	Daejeon
Anyang	1-2	Ulsan

K LEAGUE TABLE

Ulsan	33
Seongnam	31
Jeonbuk	30
Daejeon	27
Anyang	26
Jeonnam	25
Pohang	24
Suwon	23
Gwangju	18
Busan	**16**
Daegu	14
Bucheon	5

CHAPTER 13

FRIDAY NAIVETÉ (OR, BUILD, BUILD, BUILD)

BUSAN I'CONS VS. ANYANG LG CHEETAHS
WEDNESDAY, 2 JULY 2003
K LEAGUE ROUND 18
BUSAN ASIAD WORLD CUP STADIUM

JEONNAM DRAGONS VS. BUSAN I'CONS
SUNDAY, 6 JULY 2003
K LEAGUE ROUND 19
GWANGYANG FOOTBALL STADIUM (A.K.A. DRAGON DUNGEON)

용 꿈젰 꾸다

– Dream of dragons (dreams that invoke dragons are said to be omens of positive things to come)

TRAVELLING TO K League away matches can be exhausting. You're cooped up in a bus for hours, at the mercy of Korea's ubiquitous traffic jams and without a toilet. Every time I ventured out on one of these masochistic journeys I ended up deeply regretting it. By the time the bus finally finished trudging home, I always muttered 'never again!' to myself.

And yet, despite how agonising these trips were, the itch to watch live football – and visit new stadiums – kicked in again just days later. The sport is a cerebral anaesthetic, producing just enough dopamine to conceal even fresh psychological trauma. A person in control of their mind should have a visceral reaction to the mere notion of being dragged along on another of these painful treks.

But by late in the week, all of the pain and suffering vanished as if it had never existed. Inexplicably, I found myself once again enthusiastic to attend an away match. The process repeated, ad nauseam, throughout the entire season. I couldn't shake off this inescapable Friday naiveté.

It was now Sunday, and Busan were due to play away to Jeonnam tonight in the southern Jeolla city of Gwangyang. As today's opponents played at one of Korea's older football-specific venues, I was keen to experience their stadium.

South Korea's heavy rains can cause match postponements, especially during the monsoon season each summer. It had been raining all morning, but the weather forecast predicted that it would stop in the Jeolla region around noon, some seven hours prior to kick-off.

Halfway to the away ground, there was a ghastly traffic jam headed in the opposite direction – likely people travelling east to Busan for the day. We were grateful to briskly pass the obstruction, and assured ourselves that the congestion will have cleared up in time for our return journey some five hours later.

After 90 minutes on the motorway, the head of the Pride of Pusan received a phone call. Everyone became tense, knowing what this could mean.

It was a Busan I'cons club official. The match had been postponed.

Cue a long string of expletives.

It had been raining all day (never trust the weather forecast), yet the match officials decided to wait until two hours before kick-off to cancel the game. We had already completed three-quarters of the journey to the stadium, and now had to face the same journey back – with no reward.

Cue further expletives.

After turning around and rejoining the motorway for the ride home, we noticed that traffic wasn't moving very quickly. Oh no. Coming home early meant we had ventured into the peak of the traffic jam.

Cue yet more expletives.

* * *

Three days prior, Busan hosted a midweek match against Anyang Cheetahs, one of the bigger K League clubs, bankrolled by the hundred-billion-dollar LG business conglomerate. Anyang finished top-four during the last three K League seasons. On paper, this would be a formidable challenge for Busan. But Anyang had staggered in recent weeks, failing to earn a win in their last four games.

Anyang supporters have a reputation for being rowdy and enjoy cementing that notion during their travels. They're determined to push the boundaries of what league officials tolerate, lighting a wide assortment of pyro during the match. Two flares are ignited at kick-off, triggering gasps from the Busan faithful. As the match progresses they let off fireworks, some of which bounce off the underside of the stadium's partially enclosed roof.

Despite Busan's ubiquitous squad rotations, Harry and Tommy are paired up front for the fourth consecutive match. Porterfield seems to be taking a shine to the Colombian strike partnership.

Busan win a free kick just outside the penalty area. As rehabilitation project Noh Jung-yoon readies to take it, left-back Yoon Hee-joon creeps forward unnoticed on the left wing. Noh lobs the ball high toward the middle of the penalty area, and Yoon leaps head first toward the ball's destination. He lurches his head back, then whips it forward. The ball springs goalward, passes by the Anyang goalkeeper just inches inside the right post and flutters the net.

1-0 Busan.

As a defender who would score only a handful of goals in a dozen-year career, Yoon was elated to put Busan ahead. His job was to thwart goals, not score them. There was no elaborate, rehearsed goal celebration. Yoon could only muster spontaneous joy.

Despite having his hair bleached a trendy shade of caramel, Yoon Hee-joon's age was now on the wrong side of 30. He had been the captain at Busan prior to Noh's recent arrival. Unlike Noh, Yoon had been a laid-back captain. He hadn't given the position much thought, and certainly didn't attempt to stamp his authority on to the squad's youngsters. Yoon had no interest in ensuring junior players were subservient. He was far keener just to concentrate on his job as a defender.

Forfeiting the armband wasn't the only change for Yoon this season. Manager Ian Porterfield moved the centre-back over to the left side. Yoon transitioned admirably, relishing the opportunity to embark upon an occasional lengthy run down the wing.

Yoon had been with Busan since being picked first by the club in the 1995 K League player draft. He matured into an impressive defender, earning an invitation to Guus Hiddink's first national team training camp to select players for the 2002 World Cup. Although Yoon ultimately wasn't chosen for the global tournament, he received a number of caps for the national team during that period.

With just one minute remaining in the first half, Busan concede an equaliser to Anyang. Several members of the Pride of Pusan curse under their breath, although one of them shouts criticism of Porterfield. It was the first time I heard such unrestrained condemnation. Considering the hefty match opponents, the heckling seemed unfair. Had Busan instead battled back from a 1-0 deficit, would he be just as critical?

The second half begins. Busan press forward, though they find it difficult to penetrate Anyang's back-line. After possession rotates back and forth between the teams, an Anyang midfielder obtains the ball under pressure. Pinched by two Busan players, he retreats the ball backward in favour of safety. It's a momentous error. Busan striker Harry nicks possession and presses toward goal from the left side. Two Anyang defenders approach, but Harry weaves inward. Just as he swerves past the second defender, Harry swings the ball toward the far post. Anyang's goalkeeper looks to have the post covered, but the height on Harry's shot puts the ball beyond the reach of the stopper's padded hands.

2-1 Busan.

We're ahead again! What the Pride of Pusan lack in pyrotechnics, they make up for with the enthusiasm of supporters starving for any excuse to be optimistic. They merge into a sea of bouncing red and white replica tops – well, more of a modest pond, really.

Anyang won the K League in 2000, the same year Busan fell under new ownership and a reduced playing budget. Since then, the clubs headed in opposite directions. But are Busan about to pull off a huge upset today? Will Porterfield redeem himself to the fans?

Not everyone is jubilant. Anyang's goalkeeper is Valeri Sarychev, a 43-year-old from Tajikistan. So talented is Sarychev that Korean football fans nicknamed him '*Shin Eui-son*' – 'Hands of God'.

As K League teams in the 1980s and '90s were only permitted to have three foreign players, most opted for strikers and midfielders. Ilhwa Chunma (the team later based in Seongnam), however, made the unprecedented decision to sign a foreign goalkeeper in 1992. They chose Sarychev, who had more than a decade of experience guarding the net for Moscow clubs. The signing worked brilliantly: after finishing as runners-up in 1992, Ilhwa won the K League three seasons in a row between 1993 and 1995.

Foreign goalkeepers quickly became all the rage in the K League due to Sarychev's success, with most teams signing a non-native custodian. Eventually the Korean Football Association had to intervene, worried that a lack of Koreans serving as goalkeepers would hinder the national team. The amount of games that foreign goalkeepers could play was gradually reduced over several years, and by 1999 they were barred completely.

With the ban in place, the so-called Hands of God found himself out of a job. Anyang came calling, convinced that the Tajik would make a successful goalkeeping coach. But first, they encouraged Sarychev to apply for Korean citizenship as a way to extend his playing career.

By 2000 he was naturalised as a Korean and made a return to playing in the K League with Anyang. In his first season there, the northern club won the K League despite finishing a woeful second-bottom the previous year. Sarychev's powers indeed appeared divine.

Busan are ahead today against Hands of God and his holy team-mates, but their play isn't inspiring. Busan resort to frequent long balls, and constantly give up possession while struggling to gain it back. Meanwhile, Anyang pass the ball fluidly but create surprisingly few goalscoring opportunities.

The 2-1 scoreline holds until full time. Much like Busan's recent victory over Daejeon, we were lucky to win. Several errors by Anyang ultimately allowed the lesser team to prevail.

The Busan players applauded all four ends of the Asiad Stadium, then approach the Pride of Pusan. The squad members lined up and held hands as they bowed deeply to their forgiving supporters, who in turn were happy to serenade them in song and cheer.

As the celebrations wound down and most of the players turned back toward the dressing rooms, Busan striker Zoran Urumov remained behind, still applauding the fans. He wrestled off his shirt and threw it to the crowd.

It struck me as odd that a player who wasn't in a particularly lucrative football league would give away his shirt after a mid-season match. Such footballers often do this at the end of a season, but to do so now seemed strangely premature. However, Harry and Tommy had given away their shirts to fans several weeks ago, so perhaps there wasn't anything more than exhilaration behind the give-away. Maybe it was nothing more than a spontaneous gesture of joy and appreciation.

* * *

The bus carrying Pride of Pusan traversed back through Busan's unnamed streets. After the postponement of the Jeonnam match was capped by getting stuck in a horrendous traffic jam, the group was irritable. It certainly didn't relieve tensions when we learned that games scheduled in Jeolla's two other K League cities, Gwangju and Jeonju, both went ahead.

Gwangju had lost, providing a morsel of consolation to the Busan supporters. We were now above them on points, thanks to the midweek Anyang win. Oh, the euphoria of climbing to the heady heights of fourth-bottom.

On the ride back we also discovered that the north-eastern city of Pyeongchang had failed in its bid to win the hosting rights for the 2010 Winter Olympics. It was a particularly galling loss for the Koreans as they had secured the most support during the initial round of voting.

Strangely, I felt relieved for South Korea. Aware of how much money it recently cost them to build venues for the World Cup, and that many were either unused or on the brink of being abandoned for more modest venues, I was pleased that the country wasn't about to sink billions more pounds into a two-and-a-half-week money pit.

Pouring concrete was practically a national sport in South Korea, a country in which 'build, build, build' seemed to be the motto. Construction accounted for a whopping 18 per cent of the country's gross domestic product.

Although collusion between democratically elected politicians seeking donations and construction companies jockeying for lucrative government contracts was common around the world, the dubious practice was pervasive in South Korea. The country's infamous *jaebeol* business conglomerates gave large financial contributions to politicians, and in return were awarded lofty – and often completely unnecessary – building projects paid for by Korean taxpayers.

'South Korea was a completely different world – every aspect of life was different,' Polish footballer Tadeusz Świątek, who played in the K League during the late 1980s and early 1990s, told news outlet *Tygodnik Płocki*, as translated by Andre Zlotkowski. 'There were [ostentatious] displays of wealth, grand construction projects which you don't see in Europe.'

Publicly funded stadiums became ubiquitous, with South Korea boasting more sporting venues than any other Asian country. In the 1980s, nearly every city in South Korea built a multi-purpose stadium that included a football pitch and an athletics track. Just 15 years later, the country constructed another ten brand-new stadiums for the 2002 World Cup – a record still held by South Korea. Most of these stadiums were far too large for regular usage – their primary intent was simply to show Korea off to international audiences for one month during the World Cup.

Like most of the new venues, Incheon Munhak Stadium's 50,000-seat capacity was far too monstrous for the K League. Although a football club would briefly play there, they would abandon the facility for a smaller, football-specific stadium just eight years later. But when Incheon wanted to host the 2014 Asian Games, the unused Munhak was somehow deemed too small and thus another giant venue was built, this time even larger. In just a dozen years, Incheon had built three new stadiums. Only one of them – the small, football-specific venue that opened in 2012 – would be regularly used.

The city of Cheonan built a stadium in 1983, followed by a replacement in 2001 – just 18 years later. The initial stadium was eventually torn down, and only hosted club football for four seasons during its entire lifespan.

Wasteful construction didn't stop there. New airports were built in rural locations despite negligible demand. The Korean Citizens' Action Network told the BBC that 'hundreds of millions of dollars' were wasted on unnecessary airports, because 'politicians, in order to gain votes, promise their constituents an airport'.

Although some construction projects in South Korea were wasteful, at least these days they were properly built. During the dictatorship era from the 1960s through the 1980s, construction firms were expected to finish projects rapidly. Corners were cut, leading to unsound structures. An apartment building in Seoul was the first to abruptly tumble, killing 32 people in 1970. The city's Sungsoo Bridge collapsed in 1994, just 15 years after it was built, due to structural failure. In 1995, Sampoong Department Store unexpectedly crumpled less than five years after it was constructed, killing approximately 500 people. In the latter case, construction companies were found guilty of a slew of offences, such as using inferior concrete and not reinforcing the structure adequately. City officials in Seoul were found guilty of accepting bribes in exchange for approving unsound construction.

Fast forward to 2003, and some Busan supporters possibly hoped the new Asiad World Cup Stadium would collapse at night when nobody was around, allowing the team to return to their traditional Gudeok Stadium.

The Pride of Pusan's bus approached our drop-off point in Busan city centre. Four hours after venturing on to the motorway, the group finally disembarked from their ill-fated Jeonnam trip. The relief was palpable.

'Never again,' I muttered to myself, not for the first – nor last – time. 'Never again.'

ROUND 18

Busan	**2-1**	**Anyang**
Ulsan	3-2	Jeonnam
Daejeon	2-2	Jeonbuk
Suwon	1-1	Pohang
Seongnam	1-0	Bucheon
Daegu	2-1	Gwangju

ROUND 19

[Jeonnam vs. Busan postponed due to inclement weather]

Bucheon	1-2	Suwon
Pohang	0-0	Daejeon
Gwangju	0-1	Seongnam
Jeonbuk	1-2	Ulsan
Anyang	5-0	Daegu

K LEAGUE TABLE

Ulsan	39
Seongnam	37
Jeonbuk	31
Anyang	29
Daejeon	29
Suwon	27
Pohang	26
Jeonnam	25
Busan	**19**
Gwangju	18
Daegu	17
Bucheon	5

CHAPTER 14

COLGÓ LOS GUAYOS (HANG UP THE FOOTBALL BOOTS)

BUSAN I'CONS VS. JEONBUK
HYUNDAI MOTORS
WEDNESDAY, 9 JULY 2003
K LEAGUE ROUND 20
BUSAN ASIAD WORLD CUP STADIUM

POHANG STEELERS VS. BUSAN I'CONS
SATURDAY, 12 JULY 2003
K LEAGUE ROUND 21
POHANG STEEL YARD (A.K.A. BLAST
FURNACE)

눈 감으면 코 베어먹을 세상
*– It's a dog-eat-dog world (literally, 'it's a world
where people will cut off your nose and eat it if
you close your eyes')*

'WE WILL drink your blood.'

That was the ominous message scrawled across a Pride of Pusan banner hung in Asiad Stadium.

I had my doubts whether the vampiric threat genuinely alarmed any opposition players. Many K League teams consider a match against struggling Busan an assured victory – relinquishing a dollop of blood in return for three points seemed an auspicious exchange.

132

Third-place Jeonbuk would visit Busan midweek, hoping to acquire a win without sacrificing too much haemoglobin. Jeonbuk were performing well this season and were recently finalists in the Asian Cup Winners' Cup. However, Jeonbuk hadn't won much silverware at this point in their existence, finishing in the bottom half of the K League table most years. Although currently in third place, they hadn't won in four matches and a considerable gap was opening between Jeonbuk and the league's top two.

Form-wise, it was an opportune juncture for Busan to snatch a win.

In a desperate bid to increase attendance, Busan I'cons dropped the price of match tickets from ₩7,500 down to just ₩5,000 (roughly £3.50). It made no difference, with Busan once again lowering the season record for poorest league attendance down to a paltry 1,213.

Despite Busan winning their previous match and being undefeated in their last two, Porterfield can't resist the urge to anatomise his squad yet again. Right-back Shim Jae-won, who spent time playing as a defender for a German club as well as the South Korea national team, is moved up front to play as a striker. The Pride of Pusan members are bewildered.

Serbian striker Urumov, who threw his shirt to the fans last match, is absent.

Jeonbuk supporters stand in the away end, many adorned with green necklaces made of large plastic baubles. Their team has a throw-in, deep in their own half. The ball enters play, where the recipient decides to perform a fancy, one-touch flick of the ball to his team-mate. His plan fails. Tommy intercepts the ball, races forward toward goal, and shoots low at the far post. Jeonbuk's goalkeeper dives to his right to thwart the shot but isn't able to stop it.

1-0 Busan.

A light drizzle begins; traumatic memories from last weekend's rainout come storming back. Most Pride of Pusan members unravel and erect umbrellas. Is this a cheeky statement against the recent match postponement? In an instant, the rain intensifies dramatically, my first time experiencing a proper monsoon. Everyone in the stadium not already protected by the semi-open roof flees up the stairs for cover. Within ten seconds, the monsoon diminishes back down to a moderate sprinkle. Self-conscious laughter erupts throughout the venue as people settle into higher seats.

Midway through the second half, Jeonbuk equalise. Five minutes later, Porterfield pulls Tommy out of the match. He's replaced by Doh Hwa-sung, a young midfielder who has only played ten minutes in the last two and a half months. Harry, who started today as an attacking midfielder, is moved up front.

Pride of Pusan members mutter about the substitution. Why take out a proven goalscorer when the score is level? Don't we want to win? Are we consigning ourselves to dragging out a mere draw?

The match ends in a level scoreline. Some Busan supporters were relieved to snatch a single point from an opponent in third place. Others felt we should have left Tommy in and attempted to win against a team struggling with poor form.

The result is typical for Porterfield: a draw. His managerial record at clubs such as Aberdeen showed a preponderance of stalemates. Although the Scot's teams didn't often lose, a draw was closer to a loss than a victory as far as the league table was concerned.

Busan had been fortunate to face the league's top three sides when they were each suffering from wobbly form. We beat Ulsan before they embarked on an eight-match winning tear, and later managed an away draw up north against Seongnam. Today we took a point from Jeonbuk.

But what would the remainder of the season have in store for Busan? If we couldn't climb out of the bottom third of the K League table despite meeting opponents on fortuitous occasions, what would our league position become if our luck ran out? The only way Busan could hope to climb any higher up was to improve their play. They had already maxed out their good luck; the sole remaining option was for Porterfield to employ some of the managerial magic he once sprinkled upon Sheffield United, Zambia and Trinidad.

The reality was that Porterfield stumbled as often as he succeeded as a football manager. Which fate would Busan face from the Scotsman?

As bad as things seemed, it was comforting to remind ourselves that it could always be worse. At the basement of the K League table was lowly Bucheon, who had now strung together a pitiful 19 matches without a win. After a recent match, the Bucheon players trudged over to their supporters to thank them. But as they acknowledged their devotees, several of the players began to weep.

It was as if an emotional dam had burst; tears soon streamed down the faces of almost the entire Bucheon squad. The Bucheon fans, who had equally suffered from the same fruitless spell, were unable to hold back their feelings. Dozens of footballers and fans bawled together for minutes in what must have been an extraordinary event to witness.

* * *

When Busan coach Drew Jarvie was asked by the Scottish media what living in South Korea was like, his first response was about the weather.

'The climate is good although we're right in the middle of the rainy season now,' said Jarvie. 'So it's not much different from Aberdeen. But that doesn't stop me from wandering around in shorts and T-shirts which amuses most of the locals.'

Today was exactly that sort of day: a light drizzle that kept the locals in trousers, yet hot enough to warrant leg exposure from a typical Westerner. We were off to Pohang for one of the closest K League away trips. Luckily the scant precipitation wouldn't be substantial enough to cause another traumatic en route cancellation.

The Pride of Pusan bus departed. Although Busan's 2003 home opener saw them defeat Pohang back in late March, this would prove a tricky match. Pohang were solid, mid-table opponents bankrolled by POSCO, South Korea's largest steel-producing *jaebeol*. They were undefeated in their last seven matches: four wins followed by three draws.

Along with Busan, Pohang were one of the five founding K League clubs from the inaugural 1983 season. The club was previously called POSCO Atoms, named after the Japanese animation character known as Astro Boy in the West (or 'Atom' in South Korea), before tweaking its moniker to 'Steelers' in a nod to their corporate owners.

One hundred years ago, Pohang was little more than a fishing village where the Hyeongsan River emptied into the East Sea. But heavy industry now dominated Pohang, with a large chunk of the city's south devoted to steel mills and shipbuilding yards. Factories overshadowed much of the Yeong-il Bay's inner harbour. Ever-expanding land reclaimed for industry jutted out into the water like a giant claw, a man-made artefact that would serve as the perfect setting for a James Bond villain's lair.

As our bus crossed the bridge into southern Pohang, a dystopian view emerged. Chimneys and blast furnaces belched smoke and steam, obscuring the skyline. Piles of iron ore pellets and coal nestled between industrial buildings. Extensive yellow pipes criss-crossed the terrain, resembling a London Tube map in which the Circle Line had consumed the entire grid.

While most K League stadiums were public facilities, our bus ventured on to unmistakably private land as we turned off from the East Sea Road. Carved into a swathe of urban forest was POSCO's national headquarters, complete with helicopter landing pads and barbed-wire coils that fenced the perimeter.

Our bus approached the Pohang Steel Yard Stadium. Surrounded by trees, the football citadel sat in an enchanting setting. Nicknamed the Blast Furnace, the stadium was encased in a concrete exoskeleton that bulged outwards.

Despite being the oldest football-specific stadium in the country, the Steel Yard remains many people's favourite Korean ground. With a capacity of just over 17,400 and no running track, it's one of the more intimate stadiums in the country. Seating is steep, making for fantastic views but perilous stair-climbing.

Manager Ian Porterfield sauntered over to acknowledge the travelling Busan supporters. I briefly chatted with him through the stadium's metal fencing.

'This team wasn't very good when I inherited it,' he said, apropos of nothing. 'I need more time to improve it.'

I remembered that Porterfield had asked back in pre-season for several months to sort out the team. Those several months had come and gone. Results should have started to improve by last month according to the original timeline he proactively volunteered. But he was now pleading for more time.

Porterfield was intended to be the foreign saviour of Busan I'cons, in the same mould as Guus Hiddink's miraculous performance with the national team. But what many Koreans either forgot or were unaware of was that it took more than a year of patchy performances before Hiddink's team started to impress. Korea lost by an embarrassing 5-0 scoreline against both France and the Czech Republic during the year prior to the World Cup. Hiddink's side then lost four of their first six games in 2002, including a defeat to Canada. The Dutchman was berated by the same Korean news media that would declare him a national hero just months later.

Perhaps Porterfield also deserved more time, but he was undermining himself by proclaiming unreasonable goals. With Busan a former K League juggernaut, staff and fans alike wanted to believe his audacious vision for improvement. They felt the club deserved to reclaim its lofty place in Korean club football. But with Busan's budget severely reduced under new ownership, Porterfield should have been more careful about managing expectations – which he naively inflated.

Switching topics, Porterfield confirmed a rumour that swirled online for nearly a month: Busan I'cons had signed English striker Jamie Cureton, formerly of Norwich City and Reading. Porterfield was also attempting to snare another UK-based forward to join as Cureton's strike partner.

With a limited number of foreign-player spots, how would this revelation affect Urumov, Harry and Tommy, Busan's current goalscorers?

Porterfield became amicable and talkative. When I mentioned his time with Trinidad, he laughed.

'They'll probably be calling for me to go back there!'

Defensive just moments ago, Porterfield was now confident and at ease. My mention of Trinidad could have summoned painful memories of World Cup qualifying failure or being undermined by players and colleagues. But instead he was chipper.

Perhaps it was the reassurance of working for trustworthy club management here at Busan. People who wouldn't interfere in his team selection. People who would provide him with a copy of his contract and always pay him on time. People who, at least thus far, were supportive and patient regardless of early results.

Porterfield's team selection is curious. Urumov doesn't get his kit on for the second consecutive match. He had picked up a yellow card in his last game, which possibly explained his absence from the subsequent Jeonbuk fixture. But why wasn't Urumov playing today? Was there more meaning than just celebration when he threw his shirt to the Pride of Pusan earlier this month?

I spot Urumov in the stands, sitting with his wife and two children. He must still be with the club. There was nothing about him in the media recently. Is he injured? Did he perhaps have a spat with Porterfield?

Tommy is kitted up and on the bench. He and Harry both started the last five matches, but Porterfield opted to leave the taller Colombian as a substitute. Harry would have much to do today.

Busan's performance is tedious. They constantly give away the ball, defend like amateurs, and waste what little possession they do earn by blasting long balls aimlessly up the pitch.

Porterfield may try to blame poor results on a deficient squad, but it's his decision to play a 4-4-2 formation and to smash the ball hopelessly. There is scant ground-level passing between Busan players. Surely Porterfield and assistant Drew Jarvie are culpable if there is a reluctance (or perhaps fear) to move the ball on the pitch.

Pohang are manifestly the superior team. Ushering their back-line is Lee Min-sung, a defender who played for South Korea at the 1998 and 2002 World Cups. His ability to effortlessly brush off Busan's attempts at goal is particularly grating because Pohang lured him away from Busan this past close season.

If Busan had remained under the ownership of Daewoo, Lee would likely still play for them. But the new reality at the club was that players of Lee's ilk didn't hang around Busan for very long. Whether it was a player's ambition to seek a better club, Busan's desire to acquire a transfer fee, or both, in recent years most of Busan's skilled players were soon off to superior teams.

For the Pride of Pusan, encountering star Busan players they had idolised for years now toiling for the opposition must sting. It's one thing to continue supporting a fading club, but it's especially masochistic to pay money to watch your former heroes outstrip your waning team.

Lee rushes up the right flank and takes a shot at Busan's goal from distance, but the ball travels wide. The referee blows for half-time. Busan's supporters dash to the concourse as Pohang's stadium is only furnished with a few food stalls. I don't usually opt for stadium fare, but given the road trip and our early arrival, most of us are famished.

Pohang's regional culinary speciality is *gwamegi* – raw herring semi-dried from several days of exposure to ocean wind. But a football ground in the middle of South Korea's heavy-industry heartland doesn't offer foodie fare. Instead, I opt for *beondaegi*, boiled silkworm pupae cooked in salty beef broth and served in a small paper cup with a toothpick. For the uninitiated, they taste like chestnut-laden red meat, and are absolutely delicious. It's a Korean food that raises eyebrows among foreign visitors, as do *sundae* (blood sausage wrapped with intestines), *gopchang* (barbecued intestines), *dakbal* (chicken feet), *gejang* (raw crab), *hong-eo* (fermented skate fish that smells like ammonia), *sannakji* (fresh octopus legs that wriggle as you eat them), *gaebul* (fresh spoon worms), and last but not least, *boshintang* (dog meat soup). *Bon appétit!*

I had just finished my delectable cup of silkworm pupae and returned to the stands when Brazilian striker Santos (or in full, Rogerio Pinheiro dos Santos) scores for Pohang, only two minutes into the second half. Porterfield rises to his feet and begins pacing in the technical area.

The fourth official raises his substitution board. Tommy is joining the match. The Pride of Pusan members are relieved we'll see more of an attacking threat.

Tommy is a treat to watch. A great work rate, constantly sprinting. By observing both him and Harry, one would expect Tommy to be the target man to provide the ball to Harry, but Tommy is just as enthusiastic to take defenders on and score himself.

Full time nears. Harry adds extra urgency to his play and takes down a Pohang defender while attempting to score. The referee blows the whistle. He rushes toward Harry and flashes a yellow card.

Harry becomes incensed. He leans forward at the referee, aggressively barking his innocence. The referee snarls back. Harry continues his bluster, but the ref has had enough. A second yellow card is shown, this time for dissent. Harry is sent off.

But he isn't going anywhere. Harry roars back at the referee, Lim Jong-ho. Lim stands his ground, staring back at Harry, holding full eye contact. Harry shakes both fists in the air as he remonstrates with the official. Sensing Harry might not be able to control his rage, Leo Mendoza, Busan's Spanish-language translator, enters the playing area and rushes toward the confrontation. Mendoza wraps his arms around Harry, pulling him away. Harry continues to shout abuse at the referee as he's wrestled off the pitch.

As Harry is eventually shepherded toward the dressing room tunnel in the corner of the home end, Pohang supporters begin to throw glass *soju* bottles down at him. One lands squarely on the

Colombian striker's foot. A Busan employee (whom I shall refrain from naming) throws at least one glass bottle back into the crowd in retaliation, supposedly hitting its intended target.

The referee has seen enough. Seconds after play resumes, he signals for full time. Busan lose 1-0.

Today was a disaster for Busan. The club's record dropped to an unenviable five wins, five draws and nine defeats. Harry would surely receive a several-match ban and a fine for his actions. The struggling club certainly didn't need any scurrilous headlines from the sports media, what with attendance already abysmal.

But the media couldn't resist. Several outlets claimed that Harry had actually struck the referee, which both Harry and translator Mendoza vociferously denied. Regardless of the truth, reputational damage had been inflicted.

Even if Harry hadn't hit the referee, his verbal onslaught before and after the second yellow card didn't reflect well on him. Was there a discipline problem in the squad? Was genial Porterfield able to control his players?

A decade earlier at Chelsea, coaches and players alike complained about how lax conditions were with Porterfield in charge.

Tony Cascarino, a striker with Chelsea at the time, told *The Times* that Porterfield 'was so laidback that the players took advantage by turning up late for training and then ignoring the exercises he wanted them to do'. Players who were late were rarely punished, their dubious excuses accepted. The squad also regularly indulged in greasy fry-ups and biscuits.

Cascarino once told one of Porterfield's assistants that the Chelsea atmosphere felt like a 'Christmas club'.

Stan Ternent, who spent a year as coach at Chelsea, described working for Porterfield as being a 'living hell' in which the senior players were really the ones in charge. He referred to Porterfield as 'a walkover'.

'I felt [Porterfield] couldn't handle big-time players,' Ternent wrote in his 2003 book, *Stan the Man: A Hard Life in Football*. 'As a consequence, the most forceful stars felt they could pick the team by committee.'

Former Chelsea scout Gwyn Williams agreed, stating in Ternent's book, 'Porterfield had four players who would pick [the] team.'

'[Porterfield] lacked strength and character,' wrote Ternent. 'If running Chelsea had been a military operation, it would have been classified as a "clusterfuck".'

Porterfield had a similar style while managing Trinidad's national team, his job previous to joining Busan. A writer in the *Trinidad Guardian* called Porterfield 'unassuming' and credited the Scot's laid-back nature as being an 'astute cultural assessment of the local scene'.

But was Porterfield's relaxed style when interacting with the Trinidad squad a shrewd acknowledgement of Caribbean culture, or simply his usual personality? Just prior to his firing, WorldSoccerNews.com mentioned 'increasingly poor discipline in the Trinidad squad'.

Was Harry's tirade today against the referee the first public sign of indiscipline within the Busan squad, or simply a one-off burst of frustration?

After Busan supporters boarded their bus for the trip home, K League news was read aloud. A midweek meeting was scheduled for football executives and Seoul city officials to discuss establishing a new 'Seoul FC'. Seoul's Mayor Lee Myung-bak had promised during his successful election campaign to create such a team. It would certainly make sense for the football-specific Seoul World Cup Stadium to have a tenant. But who would they be?

ROUND 20

Busan	**1-1**	**Jeonbuk**
Anyang	1-1	Jeonnam
Ulsan	0-0	Pohang
Daejeon	1-0	Bucheon
Suwon	1-0	Gwangju
Daegu	2-3	Seongnam

ROUND 21

Pohang	**1-0**	**Busan**
Seongnam	2-1	Suwon
Gwangju	1-1	Daejeon
Bucheon	0-2	Ulsan
Jeonbuk	1-2	Anyang
Daegu	1-2	Jeonnam

K LEAGUE TABLE

Seongnam	43
Ulsan	43
Anyang	33
Daejeon	33
Jeonbuk	32
Pohang	30
Suwon	30
Jeonnam	29
Busan	**20**
Gwangju	19
Daegu	17
Bucheon	5

CHAPTER 15

WE'LL SHOW THOSE NEO-COLONIALIST BASTARDS

MONDAY, 14 JULY 2003
ENGLISH STRIKER JAMIE CURETON SIGNS FOR BUSAN I'CONS

사촌이 밭을 사니 내 배가 아프다·
– Keeping up with the Joneses (literally, 'I have a stomach ache when my cousin buys a field')

IT WASN'T often that Sepp Blatter lamented football becoming too greedy.

In an interview with the *Financial Times*, FIFA's infamous president – who would later be charged with criminal mismanagement and misappropriation – bemoaned the latest threat to the world's game: European clubs plundering poorer countries for talented players. He condemned such wealthy teams for 'neo-colonialist' behaviour, claiming it was tantamount to 'social and economic rape'.

He said, 'I find it unhealthy, if not despicable for rich clubs to send scouts shopping in Africa, South America and Asia to "buy" the most promising players there.

'Europe's leading clubs conduct themselves increasingly as neo-colonialists who don't give a damn about heritage and culture, but engage in social and economic rape by robbing the developing world of its best players.'

Asian Football Confederation (AFC) general secretary Peter Velappan echoed the comments in a statement, lamenting the loss of players from North East Asian countries.

'The AFC is also very disturbed with the actions of these mega clubs who want to buy up all the superstars, and who are concerned more about the commercial benefits than football,' he said. 'I have been watching the scouts coming to Asia to take good players, especially from Korea, Japan and China, purely for commercial reason so they have more income from television and merchandising.'

Velappan's comments – meant to portray Asia as the victim of football's international exploitation – were rather ironic, given the high number of South American players poached by Asian clubs each year. In fact, the day after Velappan made his remarks, Chinese mega club Shanghai Shenhua signed Uruguayan starlet Peter Vera from Nacional Montevideo for a relative pittance of a transfer fee – just US$100,000.

Almost every K League club featured a handful of foreign players from countries with developing economies. Brazilian was the most prevalent foreign nationality, with a spattering from other South American and Eastern European countries.

But under Ian Porterfield, Busan I'cons were now seeking talent from countries more affluent than South Korea. After more than one month of rumours, the club officially announced on its website on 14 July that it had secured English striker Jamie Cureton.

The new arrival was a former England under-18 international and previous Premier League striker with Norwich City. He subsequently spent several successful seasons at Bristol Rovers and most recently Reading, where he helped the Royals win promotion to the First Division (as it was before being rebranded as the Championship in 2004) and contest the play-offs in an unsuccessful push for a spot in the Premier League.

Despite his youthful appearance, Cureton was already 27 years old when unveiled by Busan. He had developed into a fertile striker with Bristol and especially Reading, and looked like an excellent signing for the Korean club. Scottish manager Porterfield beamed during the photoshoot with the English forward.

Cureton would be only the second British player to compete in the K League. Dalian Atkinson, perhaps most widely known for a specular effort with Aston Villa that earned him BBC *Match of the Day*'s award for the best goal of the 1992/93 Premier League season, was Britain's trailblazer in Korean football. Atkinson suited up for Daejeon and Jeonbuk for just five matches in 2001 before promptly retiring – possibly an omen that the K League wouldn't be a cakewalk for Cureton.

But it was nearly Manchester City legend Shaun Goater who became the first player to swap British football for its Korean equivalent. Goater received contract offers from several overseas clubs in 1996, including Suwon Bluewings, then in their first season participating in the K League. Hoping to win the league but finishing a disappointing third place during the initial half of the season, owners Samsung were determined to be victorious in the second half and attempted several splashy foreign player signings. Goater did entertain moving to the Land of the Morning Calm, but ultimately chose to remain in England due to having recently married.

Football first came to South Korea in 1882 when a British Royal Navy vessel, the HMS *Flying Fish*, was docked in the port city of Incheon. Sailors held several impromptu matches near the harbour and explained the game's rules to interested locals.

Some 121 years later, Bristolian striker Jamie Cureton, still very much in the prime of his career, was announced as the intended impetus of a football renaissance at struggling Busan I'cons. Expectations were massive. He had scored goals habitually at his last two English clubs; surely he would prove triumphant in the K League?

Busan manager Porterfield confirmed to the intrigued news media that several other British-based players were also being courted, and mentioned that one had already ventured out to South Korea to scrutinise the club's facilities.

A British revolution was underway at Busan I'cons. Porterfield was about to mould a team that would unquestionably be his creation. But would his new squad return Busan to the apogee of Korean club football, elevating Porterfield as the Guus Hiddink of the K League? Or would he struggle to assemble a coherent team from unattached players mostly spurned by other clubs, inadvertently constructing a dysfunctional motley crew of free agents?

The Pride of Pusan members were running out of patience. Porterfield had to produce results – quickly.

That evening I caught up with K League happenings. The latest Busan I'cons scuttlebutt was that Porterfield was pursuing five additional players from Britain, according to the *GetReading* website. With ITV Digital's collapse in late 2002, Football League clubs were struggling financially and British players whose contracts were up for renewal faced significant pay cuts. Busan, meanwhile, were able to offer relatively large wages and tax-free contracts to overseas players.

Numerous British news media outlets speculated as to who the five targeted players might be. Four names were suggested: Martin Butler, Colin Murdock, Mark Williams and David Zdrilic.

Butler had been Jamie Cureton's strike partner at Reading and utilised the same agent as the new Busan man. Porterfield mentioned that signing a player from one of Cureton's former clubs would help the Bristolian to settle in South Korea, but Butler would ultimately opt to join Rotherham instead. Butler still had one year left on his Reading contract at the end of the 2002/03 English season; was Busan's reluctance to pay transfer fees hindering Porterfield's search for British footballers?

Northern Ireland international Colin Murdock, a former reserve player at Manchester United, was also offered a job in Korea by Porterfield. After being released by Preston North End, the defender flew out to Busan to evaluate the club. Speaking to the *Lancashire Evening Post* about the potential move, PNE manager Craig Brown said, 'Apparently it's very good money out there – and it's tax-free. Who wouldn't be tempted when you consider the financial state of the game over here at the moment?

'I'm sure Colin could be a sensation over there with his height. We all know he is very good in the air and he would cut a very impressive figure in the K League.'

Murdock, however, opted to remain in the UK and signed for Hibernian in Scotland.

One British newspaper incorrectly claimed Butler and Murdock had both signed for Busan, and suggested Busan (which it misspelled as 'Buscan') played at the national stadium (which is actually in Seoul, five hours away) in front of crowds of 50,000 (ahem).

Porterfield also attempted to lure another Northern Ireland international defender to Korea: Mark Williams. The player received a slew of offers, including from Crystal Palace. Williams chose to accept an overseas offer, but on a different continent, signing for Columbus Crew of Major League Soccer. He would only play five matches for the American club before returning to

England, marrying a porn star and appearing on an episode of reality television with her.

Finally, Australian striker David Zdrilic was also made an offer after running down his contract with Walsall, but he preferred to sign for Aberdeen as he reckoned remaining in the UK would be best for his international career with the Socceroos (as this was several years before Australia moved to the Asian Football Confederation).

Names of other players who also spurned offers to join Busan later trickled out, including young Scottish striker Darryl Duffy (who opted instead to warm the bench for Rangers) and defender Jamie McAllister (who ultimately chose Livingston). The Scottish media suggested Porterfield had also chased strikers Steve Lovell and Kris Boyd, although both were mid-contract with Scottish Premier League clubs at the time and would have required significant transfer fees.

Despite the difficulty luring decent British-based footballers to the Land of the Morning Calm, Porterfield was committed to doing so. He didn't have much choice. It was either that or opt for a collection of unknown Brazilians based on the recommendation of a scout, as many K League clubs do.

PNE boss Brown explained to the *Lancashire Evening Post* why some players in Britain might be tempted by Porterfield's offer to play in Korea.

'The stadiums are terrific and the people are football crazy,' he said. 'I'm sure everyone who watched the World Cup on television would have been impressed by the facilities over there.

'The Koreans are very warm people and I'm sure [British players] will be knocked out by the welcome [they get].'

The next day, I was informed of a credible rumour that Urumov had quit Busan I'cons, and that Harry and Tommy were also about to leave. If true, this would mark a profound change for the squad: the trio were Busan's three highest-scoring players. Their departure would create a prominent hole in the struggling squad.

If Porterfield was behind the alleged foreign-player exodus, he would need to recruit replacements at least of an equal ability. But if Busan were to become successful, the newcomers would have to prove even better.

Jamie Cureton hadn't even kicked a ball for Busan, yet expectations had already become gargantuan.

CHAPTER 16

THE CONFRONTATION (OR, EVEN MANCHESTER UNITED TOOK TIME TO BUILD)

BUSAN SUPPORTERS MEET
WITH IAN PORTERFIELD
SATURDAY, 19 JULY 2003
BUSAN I'CONS CLUBHOUSE

첫술에 배부르랴?

*– Rome wasn't built in a day; things take time;
don't be too quick to judge (literally, 'can one's
hunger be satiated with the first spoonful of food?')*

SOUTH KOREANS were renowned for violent protests during the 1970s and '80s, whether opposing ruthless dictators or exploitative employers. Demonstrations were common, and when police stormed in to clear streets, weapons would be utilised by both sides. Bags of rotting shrimp, Molotov cocktails, steel pipes, as well as rocks and bolts fired with slingshots were the arms of choice by citizens; police would resort to batons, the sides of metal shields and the exterior of fire extinguishers.

Tactics substantially softened in subsequent years, but protests still involved large crowds.

Almost three decades after mass protests that resulted in free elections, millions of Koreans took to the streets in 2016 to demand that president Park Geun-hye resign from office over a collusion and coercion scandal.

Ardent supporters of K League clubs could be similarly inclined to engage in protests, especially if their team was underperforming. That was the case as the Pride of Pusan travelled to the city's rural outskirts to visit the new Busan I'cons clubhouse.

The club was kind enough to invite its supporters to tour the new facility, constructed at a cost of £5m (the equivalent of £8.3m in 2020 after inflation). But the primary purpose of the day was to allow increasingly contemptuous Pride of Pusan members to formally meet manager Ian Porterfield for the first time. Club officials hoped that a face-to-face conversation would encourage the supporters to air their grievances constructively, diffusing the temptation to criticise the club publicly. Officials also wanted to give Porterfield the opportunity to convey his vision for the club directly to the supporters in an effort to regain their approval.

The Pride of Pusan, however, regarded the day as an opportunity to interrogate Porterfield, particularly to demand answers as to why the club's top-three scorers – Urumov, Harry and Tommy – were supposedly all leaving. The meeting was bound to be an acrimonious affair, at least during its onset.

The Pride of Pusan's bus departed from Asiad Stadium, venturing westbound on to a motorway that tunnelled between the Baek-yang and Geomjeong mountains. I considered how today's encounter might unfold. Would we witness an initial outpouring of anger, followed by a sympathetic understanding of the difficulties everyone at the club faced, and finally some cordial tears before everyone agrees to persevere united? Or were we about to behold an afternoon of bluster and grandstanding, demands for resignation and possibly a few overturned tables?

The event seemed likely to either repair the fractured relationship between supporters and manager, or irreversibly raze it.

Our bus progressed on to the new Gupo Bridge, transporting us across the width of South Korea's longest waterway, the Nakdong River. After arriving at the shiny new clubhouse and disembarking from the bus, the Pride of Pusan members filed into the foyer and awkwardly awaited their invitation into the building's inner sanctum.

A door opened at the far end of the foyer. Jamie Cureton emerged. Most of the supporters didn't react, likely unaware who he was.

Cureton carried a youthful appearance and a slight smirk. His hair contained bleached highlights and was spiked up.

I introduced myself to Cureton, who was more than eager to share his thoughts. He had now been in Busan for one week, recently joined by his new English girlfriend to live with him in South Korea.

Cureton confirmed the tactical plan: he would serve as a poaching striker, supported by a larger forward acting as a target man. Busan's attack would be built upon providing Cureton possession of the ball deep in the opponent's half. His partner hadn't been signed by Porterfield yet, but the player hunt would focus on attributes complementary to Cureton's playing style.

Cureton revealed he had more options than just coming to Busan, including another overseas offer from the USA.

'D.C. United [in Major League Soccer] was really Mickey Mouse, with coaches arriving late for training and an atmosphere that seemed too laid back,' said Cureton. This comment struck me, as the American club sounded similar to how numerous people had described Chelsea under Ian Porterfield – and now Cureton was coming to play under Porterfield at Busan.

The Bristolian was still living in a hotel with his girlfriend and hoped to get permanent living arrangements sorted out promptly. He noted that he had enjoyed living in South Korea thus far and was surprised how developed the country was.

'I reckon that other British footballers would be keen to play in the K League if they knew what it's like out here,' he said. However, Cureton also mentioned that many Koreans stared at him – a fact of life as a foreigner living in the Hermit Kingdom, a country slowly opening to globalisation.

The Pride of Pusan members were invited beyond the foyer. They were escorted into a large room with tables arranged like a classroom, all facing the front.

Shortly after the supporters made themselves comfortable, Ian Porterfield entered, flanked by coach Drew Jarvie, coach Choi Man-hee, the club's administrative manager, two players and a new translator.

Leo Mendoza had served as the translator up until this point; his absence – and apparent replacement – suggested the rumour of Harry and Tommy's departure was accurate.

After a cursory introduction and explanation about the purpose of the meeting, Busan I'cons supporters were invited to ask questions of Porterfield. Here we go.

Jang Seok-ho, the president of Pride of Pusan, went first.

'Busan has played 19 games and scored 19 goals,' he said. 'Urumov, Tommy and Harry scored the most goals. Why have they all left the club?'

Seok-ho's frustration was understandable. In addition to scoring, Urumov and Harry were also both skilled at creating opportunities. Urumov had the most assists in the entire K League in 2001.

Busan had already lost four of their better players between mid-2002 and the subsequent close season. Now they were also losing their three best goalscorers of the current season – notching the list of departing stars up to seven within one year.

Porterfield replied, 'Urumov never came to me to ask to stay at Busan I'cons. When it became clear that Urumov wanted to leave, I said I would let him go, as long as he didn't sign for another K League club.

'Urumov's contract was up at the end of July. I had various meetings with club officials and administrators. I was told that players can't change clubs within the K League on a free transfer – their rights would have to be sold, even if their contract is up. I was informed that Busan would continue to hold Urumov's K League rights for six months after the end of his contract – so until January 2004.

'I was misinformed. This is an administrative error, not a coaching error.'

I felt my jaw drop. Busan's top goalscorer was leaving the club and joining a K League opponent without any transfer fee because the manager received incorrect information about how intra-league transfers work? Everyone was aware that the club's budget had been reduced since the Hyundai takeover, but now we were to believe that staff incompetence was holding the club back as well.

I was stunned. Porterfield had only been at the club for a number of months yet already found it necessary to go on the defensive, pinning blame on his colleagues at a semi-public forum. He must have felt significant pressure already if he was so quick to accuse a club staffer of failing their duties. Had journeyman manager Porterfield unwittingly stumbled into yet another toxic workplace?

He then attempted to minimise Urumov's accomplishments by noting that two of his goals were merely converted penalties. Several of the Pride of Pusan members audibly scoffed in response.

'As for Harry, he had discipline problems,' said Porterfield. 'He hit a referee on two occasions. It wasn't good for the club.'

Harry and translator Leo Mendoza had both denied accusations that Harry struck the referee at the recent Pohang away match. I wasn't aware of a second alleged incident, but Porterfield supplied this as the primary reason for removing the popular South American from the team.

'Harry was also three and a half weeks late for pre-season training, and received several red cards,' claimed Porterfield. 'Beyond that, I had some other personal problems with him.

'The linguistic barrier was also tough on Harry. He is a talented player, and on a really good team he could play well.

'Ultimately he wasn't interested in the team – he was only interested in the money.'

Coach Choi then explained what actions had been taken against Harry for the more recent alleged referee assault.

'Harry was suspended for eight games and was fined a hefty sum for hitting the referee in Pohang,' said Choi, with assistance from the new translator. 'Even if Harry had remained in the squad, he wouldn't be permitted to play again for more than a month.'

'Tommy was only here on loan for three months, to serve as cover until I could bring some players in from Britain during the summer,' said Porterfield. 'Tommy is a wonderful, fantastic boy, but he's not good enough.'

Porterfield then switched topics, wanting to explain why the club was struggling to win matches.

'When I came here, this team was in a mess,' he said. 'A big mess.'

Although Porterfield tended to quickly earn people's trust with his unassuming temperament and loquaciousness, his personality swiftly changed at this meeting. His voice became increasingly loud, to the point of nearly shouting. He was unable to mask his irritation.

'I watched two games before taking the managerial job here at Busan. I knew it was going to be a tough job,' said Porterfield.

If the purpose of this meeting was to improve relations, such an objective seemed elusive by this point.

'This club is going in the right direction,' said Porterfield, though few in the crowd looked convinced.

Porterfield then explained why several quality players left during the recent close season. The Scot wanted to retain prolific striker Woo Sung-yong, who featured in the 2002 World Cup, but the player fancied a move. Defensive lynchpin Lee Min-sung followed him to Pohang. Additionally, midfielder Kim Jae-hyung picked up a nasty injury in 2002 before Porterfield's arrival, ruling the player out for the entire 2003 season.

The odds seemed stacked against Porterfield before he even arrived at Busan.

But as he was about to naively admit, Porterfield wasn't merely an onlooker regarding the exodus of Busan's talented players. At this point in the meeting, Porterfield made a crucial mistake, revealing that it was his decision not to re-sign two well-respected players from 2002: Serbian striker Radivoje Manić and Brazilian striker Didi. Half the room gasped in shock. Most of the supporters had probably assumed the club was stingy during contract-renewal negotiations and wouldn't offer the players a raise in pay, prompting the pair to seek better offers elsewhere. Instead, Porterfield inadvertently affixed yet another target to himself by confessing that he personally pushed them out.

The mood of the room turned combustible within seconds. Incredulous murmurs between supporters rapidly amplified into derisive remarks. An amicable end to this meeting appeared highly unlikely.

Despite the language barrier, Porterfield could see that the supporters were becoming exasperated. He needed to win them over, and fast, lest this meeting crystallise into permanent antagonism.

Porterfield was previously fired as manager of Sheffield United due to fan hostility despite the team playing well, so he was aware of the importance of keeping the Busan supporters onside.

'You've got to support us. It's not my team, it's your team.' Porterfield leaned over and patted Lee Jang-kwan, the defender he called upon most, squarely on the top of the head in a sign of affection. Several female supporters gasped. Although such gestures would become commonplace in Korean football a dozen years later due to globalisation, at this point it was still highly disrespectful for an adult to pat another adult on the head – an act usually reserved for interacting with children. Porterfield had unknowingly committed a cultural *faux pas*. Lee, the player involved in a brawl against an Ulsan opponent earlier that season, grimaced as his head was touched.

This meeting had quickly become a calamity for Porterfield. The Scot was unknowingly riling up even the few people in the room who did support him.

I noticed that Porterfield referred to the domestic Korean players on his squad as 'Mr [surname]' rather than their full name, or sometimes even just by their squad number. On several occasions, Jarvie had to help him with names. While Korean was a foreign language for Porterfield, the written script is relatively easy to learn – arguably the simplest of any language on Earth – and it serves as a helpful foundation for learning the language. Had he not bothered? Referring to some players only by number – eight months into the job – suggested he was failing to integrate, both in the culture and with the team. If the players had noticed he was still referring to some of them by number, surely they would have found it disrespectful after all this time.

'Look, I'm just starting this job,' said Porterfield. 'When I came here, I knew this was going to be a hard job. How many games did you win last season?' Porterfield was pinning poor results on the squad he inherited from past managers.

The supporters weren't in a forgiving mood. Although Porterfield was arguably providing reasonable justification – trumpeting the club's poor recent seasons and diverting blame in the hope of earning himself more time – he was inadvertently twisting the proverbial knife deeper into the already cantankerous supporters. They wanted to hear how Porterfield would turn things around for the better, but instead were presented with a litany of excuses.

It became evident public relations was not Porterfield's forte.

'[Busan] finished second-bottom last season – is that right or wrong? We don't have the quality in the team to do what you want to do,' said Porterfield.

'I inherited a poor team. One guy left for army duty, another has a broken leg, another has a ligament injury. We really only have three good players. I couldn't sign many players when I came here, because few were available.'

Many of the supporters scoffed. One of the senior females in the Pride of Pusan was livid at Porterfield for blaming the squad for the poor performances.

Porterfield explained his dearth of options by listing the team's better players on a dry-erase board, which elicited nods of agreement from several of the supporters. Perhaps he was gradually winning some of them over.

'In football, you can only work with the material you have,' said Porterfield. 'We want to play entertaining football if it's possible. But unfortunately we don't have the squad to do that at the moment.'

Despite Porterfield's willingness to lay blame on the team, the two players in attendance appeared to endorse their new manager. When one Busan supporter asked a tough question of Porterfield, defender Lee Jang-kwan let out an *'Aiissssshhhh!'* – the Korean equivalent of an abbreviated 'oh for f*** sake'.

The players' backing of Porterfield surprised the Pride of Pusan. The role of supporters is ultimately to get behind their team, so when squad members asked them to give the manager more time, it was hard to ignore such a plea.

'You should also keep in mind that the club is working on a tight budget, which makes it difficult to attract players to join Busan,' added Porterfield.

The Scot then spoke about some of his long-term aspirations for the club, such as moving away from the American model of drafting players already developed by high schools and universities, and instead building a professional youth academy. If Busan were at a competitive disadvantage compared to other K League clubs regarding how much money they received from their corporate owners, being one of the first Korean clubs to launch a world-class youth academy would help restore the competitive balance.

'We need to find better players,' said Porterfield. 'Korean players.'

He then mentioned how Manchester United – greatly adored in South Korea – gradually built a winning team under Alex Ferguson by nurturing youth players through the academy system.

Porterfield boasted that he had advised national football associations how to improve their youth development during his previous stints in Africa, and he had wanted to do the same in Trinidad. He seemed keen to take on this role again here in Busan.

I couldn't help but wonder: was Porterfield in the wrong job? Rather than being a team manager, should he perhaps instead have been an *administrative* manager, offering advice on how to construct youth academies? He looked more passionate and less confrontational when he spoke about this topic. His eyes began to twinkle again.

Would Porterfield be better off chucking in this football management malarkey and instead becoming a football academy consultant? It would certainly come with much less pressure and criticism.

'It takes time to build a team,' said Porterfield. 'Success doesn't come overnight. Four months is not long enough. I need more time.' Again, the supporters responded with muffled jeers.

'You should give us a chance. Give us a chance! Did you have this meeting last year?' Porterfield was playing the victim card, becoming stroppy that he was being personally challenged even though last season's performances under the previous manager were just as poor.

A Pride of Pusan member brought up the newspaper article from pre-season that quoted Porterfield as saying the team would enjoy better results by June.

'I was misquoted,' claimed Porterfield. 'I didn't say that.'

Porterfield's colleagues decided to interject in his defence. The administrative head, a tall chap who was loitering behind the panel of club officials, whimpered a meek 'this hurts us'.

Choi, with an ever-present, beaming smile plastered to his face, said, 'We cannot win all the time.'

Jang Seok-ho, head of the Pride, pointed out that Busan had lost to both of the K League newcomers: Daegu and Gwangju.

'It takes time to build a house,' said Porterfield. 'You lay a foundation, you put a roof on it. It takes time.

'Who's been the most successful coach in Korea? Hiddink. And is he Korean?' Porterfield felt his nationality was perhaps partly to blame for the Busan supporters turning on him so quickly.

'Hiddink took 15 months to sort things out. In two years' time when I leave here, your club will be better than when I arrived. There will be an improvement. You won't be second-bottom.'

Porterfield noted that his contract runs for two years, but hinted he would really need three years to fully rectify the team. Coach Drew Jarvie then finally joined the conversation.

'The team has improved in terms of work rate, organisation and club morale,' he said. 'There is a great attitude from players here. You'll see a big improvement during the second half of the season with the three new players from Britain.'

Porterfield spoke about efforts to attract quality foreign players.

'Lots of new players arrived for try-outs in January, including a Dutch player, but none of them were very good and they were sent home,' he said. 'But now, with the season ending in Britain, there will be a lot of players available on free transfer.'

Many of the Busan supporters had been unaware that the club essentially refused to pay transfer fees and would only approach out-of-contract players. The revelation perhaps earned Porterfield greater empathy.

The door at the side of the room opened and Jamie Cureton walked in, flashing a smile at the supporters as he entered. A few of the younger female supporters audibly inhaled at the sight of Busan's new Western import.

'Jamie Cureton can do what Tommy did,' Porterfield said as Cureton joined the panel at the front of the room. 'Given time, Cureton will score more goals than anyone in this country,' the manager continued, pausing to look specifically at me, 'and that's a quote for you.'

No pressure then, Jamie.

Porterfield stated the club had already secured the signatures of two Britain-based players, and that a third would arrive in the city tonight to sign a contract. Cureton was then asked to say a few words.

'My aim is to do well for the team, help the team to improve, score lots of goals, and make you lot happy,' he said.

Porterfield smiled and patted Cureton on the top of his head, pushing down on the English striker's spiked hairdo. Like Lee, Cureton grimaced.

'We also have ambitions to put another two or three [domestic] players into place,' said Porterfield. 'We have no room for attitude or cockiness – we want fighters and workhorses only.'

Porterfield claimed he was devoting all his energies to the job of Busan manager.

'You won't see me at the Paradise Hotel, as I work 24 hours a day for this club,' he said.

'I've got a dream. Only if you try, can you succeed. Please give us a chance. Support us, and we can build something. I've got a dream to make Busan I'cons the best.'

Porterfield, a former Chelsea manager from the admired Premier League, unexpectedly found himself pleading for – or perhaps demanding – leniency from supporters of a club he had likely never heard of just one year earlier.

I began to wonder what initially attracted Porterfield to the chaotic career of football management. As a player he had been thwarted by tempestuous managers.

In *The Impossible Dream*, the short autobiography Porterfield wrote (with John Gibson) shortly after winning the FA Cup with Sunderland in 1973, the Scot's explanation for being attracted to management seemed nebulous at best.

'I'm a deep thinker about the game,' wrote Porterfield. 'I've played it at a high level and I can communicate with people. I've been ambitious as a player. I've always aimed at the top. And for that very reason I want to be a manager. The number one guy.'

Had Porterfield unwittingly stumbled into a career field without appreciating the brutal antagonism that so frequently accompanies it? Did the Scot really possess the interpersonal skills to win over people both on and off the field?

After three gruelling hours, the meeting finally wrapped up. The Pride of Pusan members were invited to enjoy a complimentary meal in the players' canteen and visit the new training pitches adjacent to the clubhouse (in previous years, the squad had to be transported to other cities to be able to train, as no appropriate facilities had existed in South Korea's second-largest city).

'You're welcome to come anytime,' Porterfield said to the Busan supporters.

Although Porterfield was affable and portrayed a captivating vision, one impediment he faced was the inability to mask his emotions. While attempting to win over the supporters with his words during the meeting, his body language was tense and often hostile. If Porterfield had learned to grit his teeth and flash that toothy smile even when annoyed, he could have become one of the most persuasive men in football.

Exhibiting friendly body language is particularly important when trying to overcome linguistic barriers and relying upon the assistance of the translator. As Porterfield was speaking, most of the Koreans were unable to immediately understand his words, amplifying how he physically carried himself. His face repeatedly conveyed irritation, and he regularly crossed his arms in what could have been interpreted as a gesture of defiance.

My impression from the three-hour session was that Porterfield was a decent person who harboured ambitious plans for Busan I'cons, although perhaps he should have been more thorough when evaluating the club's financial status prior to accepting the managerial job.

Some of the supporters, perhaps a minority, were successfully convinced to give Porterfield more time. Having a couple of the players advocate for the Scot clearly helped. So too did the explanation that the squad was ineffectual and required a drastic overhaul – a process that requires time. It was also tempting to believe that the pending trio of players arriving from British football would produce an immediate improvement.

Unfortunately, a considerable number of the Pride of Pusan members weren't feeling magnanimous. That may have stemmed from pent-up frustration at the club's struggles, simmering since the 2000 season. In that regard, Porterfield was an innocent scapegoat. It wasn't he who had caused the Asian financial crisis that bankrupted former club owner Daewoo, nor was he responsible for the club's reduced budget or reluctance to pay transfer fees. In fact, Porterfield's private views on this subject were almost identical to the fans.

The Scot's foreign status in Korea may have been partly responsible for the degree of scorn he was receiving. Dutchman Guus Hiddink, who had been brought in to manage South Korea, faced regular condemnation from the Korean media prior to the unexpected 2002 World Cup success. Were the Busan fans less forgiving of a manager who wasn't Korean? Or was Porterfield's mistake not being able to immediately emulate the success that fellow European Hiddink eventually found after more than a year of struggle? Was Porterfield the foreign saviour who was failing to instantly deliver?

While that was a possibility, it was certain some of the supporters had become weary of Porterfield's British-style long balls and his old-fashioned 4-4-2 formation. Had the Scot instead utilised a 'tiki taka' style of possession and controlled passing on the ground, would the Pride of Pusan have been willing to tolerate poor results longer?

Factor in Porterfield's penchant for pushing out some of the club's better players, and the Scot was having difficulty winning over the supporters. It would be interesting to observe the Pride of Pusan during the next few matches to see if today's meeting would blunt or amplify their criticism.

As the meeting concluded, I spoke with Porterfield privately in a corridor.

'This is the hardest job that I've ever taken,' he admitted. This from a man who worked for the Mugabes in Zimbabwe, served under the infamous Ken Bates at Chelsea, and was allegedly choked and punched by a club chairman in Ghana.

He continued, 'The budget here at Busan is a mere fraction of most other K League clubs.

'I had the choice of three jobs before I came here. Kaizer Chiefs in South Africa was one. The other was in Dubai. Ultimately I chose Busan because I had a good feeling.

'I believe we'll come stronger in the second half of the season.'

Porterfield would later supply *Soccerphile*'s John Duerden with more detail about why he chose to work in South Korea.

'Mr Chung, [the chairman], was looking for a coach to come to Busan I'cons and I think he'd gone to five different countries,' said Porterfield. 'I couldn't meet him in London but suddenly I managed to come out here and speak to him. I was so impressed with the man and the type of person he was. I saw the club and I came [to Haeundae Beach], I was absolutely amazed at what I'd seen. Well, I was sure that my wife would enjoy it here.'

And what about Urumov's unexpected transfer to a K League rival?

'Urumov is now making twice the money at Suwon,' Porterfield told me privately in the clubhouse corridor. 'I was lied to. There have been a lot of envelopes passed around behind the scenes over this.'

Porterfield was confiding in me – a near-stranger – that Urumov's transfer to Suwon was not the 'administrative error' he had suggested just minutes ago to the supporters, but instead a surreptitious manoeuvre that allegedly padded the pocket of several recipients. However, Porterfield did not provide any evidence to support his assertions.

The Serbian attacker had moved to Suwon via free transfer, and received a three-year contract that would earn him US$120,000 each year, as well as a US$350,000 signing bonus. After three more years of kicking a ball, Urumov would be set for life.

'I'll never bring in any more Yugoslavs to this club,' said Porterfield. 'Only English-speaking people.'

Porterfield rattled off a long list of players from Britain he was courting, name-dropping their clubs, such as Southampton and Birmingham. He then swiftly changed topics again, more than happy to carry the conversation all on his own.

'It originally took me three years to adjust to life in England,' said the Scot, 'so I don't think I'll be bothered by culture shock here in Korea.'

Although Porterfield was confident both about adapting to life in a foreign country as well as his prospects of improving Busan I'cons, history wasn't on his side. Ominously for the Scot, the club's three previous non-Korean managers each lasted only one season.

Busan I'cons weren't just impatient with foreign managers. In the decade prior to Porterfield's arrival, Kim Ho-gon was the only manager, Korean or otherwise, to last longer than a single season. Of the 15 Busan managers who preceded Porterfield, only three remained employed for consecutive seasons. Busan's rapid rate of turnover was highly unusual by K League standards.

With such foreboding history lingering above Porterfield's appointment, a fair chunk of the Busan supporters were baying for blood. Nothing less than a return to winning ways reminiscent of the Daewoo Royals glory days would satiate them.

Success for Porterfield could only be acquired through the hasty assembly of out-of-contract players on wages lower than what most of Busan's K League opponents paid. Perhaps the Scot's suggestion that this was the most difficult job of his quarter-century career in football management wasn't an exaggeration.

CHAPTER 17

CURETON'S DEBUT (OR, BUSAN'S TREBLE OF EMBARRASSMENT)

BUSAN I'CONS VS. BUCHEON SK
SATURDAY, 26 JULY 2003
K LEAGUE ROUND 22
BUSAN ASIAD WORLD CUP STADIUM
작은 고추가 맵다
– Good things come in small packages (literally, 'though it is small, the pepper is hot')

BUSAN I'CONS continued to slog through the 2003 K League season, unprecedented in length at 44 matches. Today marked round 22, the halfway point.

This weekend's match was at home against lowly Bucheon, who hadn't yet won a single game all season. If Busan's form had been disappointing, Bucheon's was absolutely dire. What better timing for Porterfield to grind out a win to placate the rapacious Pride of Pusan members?

The Busan I'cons players emerged on to Asiad Stadium's playing surface. Judging by his gelled-up and highlighted hair, Jamie Cureton was an advocate for self-preening. Noticeably absent from the collection of players warming up were fellow imports Urumov, Harry and Tommy.

This was to be Cureton's debut. Porterfield's future at the club was dependent on the English striker's performance.

* * *

Jamie Cureton grew up in a council estate in the Bristol neighbourhood of Eastville. He began life as a footballer with Bristol Rovers under-tens, inflating his age by a couple of years to meet eligibility requirements. Cureton soon moved to Norwich City's academy, leaving home at the age of 15, but swiftly caught the attention of Manchester United manager Alex Ferguson. After a week's trial, Cureton was offered a four-year deal by the famed club: a two-year apprenticeship and two-year professional contract. Despite personally supporting United as a child, Cureton felt settled at Norwich and was wary of United's reputation for underutilising youth players. Speaking with the *TNC Podcast*, he said, 'At the time, United were buying loads of players and going through a period where they weren't winning a lot ... Norwich were obviously at the time ... a top Premier League team, they were finishing second, they were pushing for titles, they were breaking into Europe, but they were bringing young kids through as well.'

Cureton decided Manchester United might not be his best development path, famously turning down Ferguson and opting to remain at Norwich. Without realising it, Cureton had declined to suit up alongside such future stars as David Beckham, Ryan Giggs and Paul Scholes, who would become Manchester's famed Class of '92 and global megastars. Speaking with the *Back of the Net* online video channel, Cureton said, 'They obviously won the Youth Cup, and seven of their players went on to become established Man United and England [internationals]. It gets brought up a lot, because within the group, they didn't have a centre-forward, and obviously at the time I was hotly tipped around England. ... I often sit dreaming that I would have become a big star like the rest of them, but you never know, I suppose.'

Cureton quickly ascended to Norwich's senior team, being an unused substitute against Inter Milan at the San Siro in the 1993/94 UEFA Cup, before making his professional debut in the Premier League the following season. He would be written into Norwich City lore for wearing green hair dye during an Old Farm derby away to Ipswich Town in which he scored.

Cureton naively assumed that he would spend his entire career in the top flight, but relegation loomed for the East Anglian club.

After Norwich dropped that May, never again would Cureton play in the Premier League.

He then moved to hometown club Bristol Rovers, where he enjoyed excellent form for several seasons.

'It's where I made my name and started scoring,' Cureton told the BBC. The young striker took the club close to promotion on two occasions and personally developed into a prolific goalscorer, enjoying 31- and 29-goal seasons. His feats included scoring four goals during a memorable 6-0 away win at Reading – the first hat-trick scored at the Madejski Stadium. With Cureton paired up front alongside Jason Roberts (later of Wigan fame), the Gas looked destined for promotion, but after two failed attempts Cureton handed in a transfer request in 2000 with the hope of moving to a Premier League team.

Instead, Cureton ended up at Reading, another third-tier club with ambitions of promotion.

'They were probably the best three years on the trot that I've had in my career,' he told *GetReading*. Cureton's goalscoring rate at the Berkshire club was even more prolific than at Bristol. Partnering the front line with equally fruitful striker Martin Butler, Cureton scored 28 goals overall in his first season at Reading, including knocking one in at the Second Division play-off final. It was perhaps the best season of his entire career.

The next year, Cureton scored the game-winning goal for Reading against Brentford in the final league match of the season that would fatefully decide which club earned automatic promotion to the second tier of English football. The much-celebrated goal prompted Reading's supporters' trust to have a newly discovered star in the Perseus constellation named after him.

Although Cureton had climbed closer to the Premier League, his playing time with Reading decreased each subsequent season. Cureton's contract would expire in the summer of 2003, after his third year with the Royals. The general situation was also grim for professional footballers in England at the time as the ITV Digital collapse left many clubs scrambling to avoid financial administration. Contract offers were modest during this rare period of fiscal austerity.

'It would be nice to get an offer,' Cureton told the *Reading Evening Post*. 'It's not the best of times not to have a longer contract behind you because of the financial situation in football.'

As summer loomed, Reading offered Cureton a one-year extension, but he desired a longer contract and was worried about a lack of playing time. Manager Alan Pardew's formation often involved only one striker, yet Cureton – as a traditional centre-forward – was most comfortable as part of an attacking duo and expected to be fed the ball by a target man. As a result, Cureton's playing time had dwindled.

Cureton wasn't even included in the squad for a match in March 2003 and received no explanation from Pardew, which angered the striker.

'If I'm not even making the bench then maybe it does push me closer to the exit door,' he told the *Reading Evening Post*. 'All I want to do is play football.'

Cureton also received contract offers from several third-tier clubs, including Queens Park Rangers and Bristol City.

'Then from nowhere my agent rings me and says, "Look, you've got [offers from] South Korea and America,"' Cureton told BBC Radio Berkshire's Reading FC podcast. Both D.C. United of Major League Soccer and Busan I'cons of South Korea's K League were interested in the Bristolian. With English football in a perilous financial situation, the overseas offers were particularly appealing.

'I was invited [to Busan] by the manager, Ian Porterfield, a former Reading boss,' Cureton told Reading FC's website.

'[Busan I'cons] flew me and my agent out first-class,' Cureton said to the *Non League Nosh* podcast. 'We spent five days out there.'

'It was a completely new experience, but I was really impressed,' Cureton said to Sky Sports. 'They've got an excellent stadium, which was built specially for the World Cup, and the training ground is new as well. It's hard to find any faults – it's a lovely area, the facilities are first-class and it helps that they've got a British manager.'

After spending time visiting both overseas clubs, Cureton decided to take the plunge and move to North East Asia.

'I'm sad to leave [Reading], it's a massive wrench and I've thoroughly enjoyed my three years. It's been a really tough decision,' read his statement on the club's website.

'I just felt it was the right time to make a change, so why not make a change in a big way and go to Korea? The timing was right on all fronts, it will be a completely new experience and I am looking forward to it.'

Pardew was disappointed to see Cureton leave and stated, 'I can't deny it's a fantastic opportunity for him, and a challenge which is possibly too good to turn down. The footballing world is getting smaller, it is now a world market and we've lost a player to the new frontier.

'On behalf of everybody, especially the fans, I wish him all the very best for his new life in South Korea.'

Just as English football was tightening its financial belt, Cureton would earn US$350,000 over two years, tax-free, at Busan I'cons. He received a large chunk of his contracted salary up front as a signing bonus.

The diminutive striker did seem a peculiar choice of player for Ian Porterfield, who was reputed to have disliked 'compact' players and released several such individuals during his time as Aberdeen manager.

Shortly after his arrival, Cureton seemed to cherish his new life in South Korea.

'I really enjoyed the place,' he would later tell *The Guardian*. 'The training facilities and the set-up were great.' The club also accommodated Cureton and his new girlfriend in a waterfront flat in the trendy Haeundae area.

'I was in an apartment overlooking a beach,' he would recollect to *The Independent* a dozen years after his arrival. Cureton was referring to Haeundae Beach, the most popular beach in South Korea which attracts people from across the country and beyond. With his housing taken care of, Cureton was expected to be able to focus entirely on football.

* * *

Noh Jung-yoon wins a corner for Busan. As he squares up to take the kick, a din of boos echoes down from above. It was Hermes, Bucheon's supporter group, standing in the upper tier of the away end. Although less than 30 in number, Hermes draped most of the stadium end in banners, doing their best to create some atmosphere in Busan's vacuous bowl of a venue.

Noh's kick bounces across the top of the 18-yard box, with all 22 players comically looking on. After a sloppy back-and-forth of possession, Bucheon try to clear the ball away, but it falls to a

Busan player. He leaps into the air and heads the ball forward to Busan striker Gwak Kyung-keun, loitering on the edge of Bucheon's penalty area. Rather than attempting to head the ball into goal himself, Gwak instead selflessly heads the high pass down to the feet of the awaiting Cureton, standing just a few yards to the left. Cureton immediately smacks the ball at goal. It deflects off the right post, lands in front of the goal line, but then curls into the goal near the left post due to the strange spin on the ball.

It's an awkward debut goal, but Cureton will take it. He charges away in confident celebration, his arms extended from his sides in his usual fashion, with his index fingers jutting skyward.

1-0 Busan. This is exactly what Ian Porterfield has been planning for months. He may have only just signed Cureton, but the Scottish manager's scheme to acquire the best available players from Britain to run riot in the K League already seems adroit. Busan are on track to pick up their first win since the beginning of the month. Porterfield hopes to silence his doubters among the Busan supporters and intimidate the club's opponents.

Or so Porterfield might have thought. Instead, Bucheon's second-half substitute – striker Lee Won-shik, who featured at the 1996 Olympics – scores one minute after entering the match, then doubles his tally just five minutes later. Wretched Bucheon are in the lead.

Porterfield would make only one substitution during the remaining half-hour of the match – his sole change of the entire game. Bizarrely, he removes striker Gwak and replaces him with young midfielder Doh Hwa-sung, despite Busan trailing and needing to find at least an equaliser.

The Pride of Pusan members are incensed and holler derision at Porterfield. As full time approaches and the Busan players realise they are about to lose at home to the league's laughing stock, tempers fray. Attention turns to the referee, who makes for a convenient scapegoat.

Foul throws are rarely called here in South Korea, but the referee whistles against Busan for such an infringement late in the match. The Busan players are incredulous and swarm the official to dispute the decision.

Football is perhaps the sport most tolerant of referee abuse, but being a match official is an especially masochistic job in South

Korea. Many players here view refs with disdain, showing little restraint when arguing decisions.

The explanation is simple: Korean referees previously tainted their reputation when many accepted bribes on a frequent basis. The profession today has been largely cleaned up, but the stigma of the past lingers on.

If a referee makes a call that affects the outcome of a match, they can expect to be surrounded by insolent players. It's even common for managers and coaches to stray on to the pitch to have a go at the official; club staff being restrained by colleagues from giving the referee a lumping was once a regular spectacle in South Korea.

According to the *Korea Times*, Ulsan manager Kim Jung-nam slapped a referee in August 2002 after disagreeing with a decision.

Park Jong-hwan, the manager of new club Daegu FC, received an 18-match suspension in the late 1980s for aggressively disputing a referee's decision. The *Korea Times* stated that two weeks later he barged into a stadium and kicked the referee, earning himself a one-year ban. Ironic, given that Park had himself served as an international referee during most of the 1970s.

The K League aggravated the issue of referee abuse by being lenient against the abusers, frequently reducing fines or match bans that were appealed.

Unfortunately, a minority of domestic referees continued to accept bribes, causing players to keep them in low regard.

Deep distrust of domestic referees led the K League to hire foreign officials for important league and play-off matches for much of the 2000s.

Referee Park Jong-kyu blows his whistle to signal for full time. After months of agony, Bucheon's ragtag collection of players had finally won, and done so in an away match! They shouted with joy and leapt into the air, congratulating each other as if they had just won the league.

As always in football, celebrations were zero-sum. One team's ecstasy marked the other's ignominy. Most of the Busan players fell to their knees. Embarrassment would be a gross understatement. Losing to Bucheon was an absolute calamity.

While Cureton (or 'Curo' as he's sometimes colloquially known) enjoyed a promising debut, today's pitiful result was Busan's lowest ebb since the Hyundai takeover in 2000. This was all that Ian

Porterfield's team could muster after the showdown meeting with the Pride of Pusan – from what should perhaps have been the easiest fixture of the entire season.

Porterfield may have been able to enthuse his team prior to matches against K League giants, but when it came to playing against minnows, the Busan squad simply couldn't be bothered.

A silence descended over the Busan supporters, astounded by the result. Having scorned Porterfield late in the match, they were now in mute disbelief at how low their club could sink.

Not only had Busan become the first club to lose to newcomers Daegu, as well as the first team to lose to both newcomers – Daegu and Gwangju – but now they also faced the humiliation of being the side that ended Bucheon's record-setting winless streak.

Barely four months into the 2003 K League season, Busan had succumbed to a treble of embarrassment.

The Pride of Pusan members made scant eye contact as they filed silently out of the stadium. I surmised that today's taciturn reaction would be followed in the days ahead by a deafening roar.

Luckily for Busan, they were in no danger of relegation. The K League, as with all of South Korea's professional sports leagues, emulated the franchise system common in the USA. At the end of the season, no clubs would descend to the second division.

The K League would attempt to implement a promotion system for the 2006 season. The winner of the second-tier National League was meant to climb up, but there was no incentive for them to do so. Television rights for Korean football weren't lucrative, and the K League expected the promoted team to purchase a league franchise at the price of roughly US$1m. The cost just to transition a squad from part-time to full-time was prohibitive enough, but asking a small club to pay a million-dollar fee on top of that was ludicrous. Predictably, Goyang KB declined promotion in 2006, as did Ulsan Mipo Dockyard in 2007. The extortionate promotion system was quietly scrapped.

It wasn't until the K League expanded to two tiers in 2013 that promotion and relegation was finally adopted – but only within the K League, excluding the country's lower divisions.

While Busan needed not fear the drop in 2003, they were desperate to finish above newcomers Daegu and Gwangju – and definitely ahead of woeful Bucheon.

The supporters were despondent, but Porterfield was confident that his unfolding plan would come to fruition. Busan I'cons were about to unveil the signings of English striker Andy Cooke from Stoke City and Norwegian defender Jon Olav Hjelde from Nottingham Forest.

ROUND 22

Busan	**1-2**	**Bucheon**
Daegu	1-2	Suwon
Ulsan	2-0	Gwangju
Jeonnam	1-1	Jeonbuk
Anyang	1-1	Pohang
Daejeon	2-3	Seongnam

K LEAGUE TABLE

Ulsan	46
Seongnam	46
Anyang	34
Jeonbuk	33
Suwon	33
Daejeon	33
Pohang	31
Jeonnam	30
Busan	**20**
Gwangju	19
Daegu	17
Bucheon	8

CHAPTER 18

THE BRITISH REVOLUTION

BUSAN I'CONS VS. POHANG STEELERS
WEDNESDAY, 30 JULY 2003
K LEAGUE ROUND 23
BUSAN ASIAD WORLD CUP STADIUM
사서 고생한다
– You make the bed you lie in; you're asking for
trouble (literally, 'buy and so suffer')

IAN PORTERFIELD emerged from the dressing room with
noticeable swagger. Although typically unassuming in manner,
today the Scot exuded confidence. Busan may have lapsed into a
three-match winless skid, but Porterfield's enthusiasm conveyed his
expectation that things were about to change at the Korean club.
Jamie Cureton scored on his debut; and after months of waiting,
the full trio of players imported from British football had arrived.

It was a Wednesday evening under the floodlights at the Asiad
World Cup Stadium, where Busan I'cons were hosting Pohang
Steelers, the club they had lost away to just two rounds earlier.

While Porterfield trusted that his trio of imports would swiftly
dominate the K League, Pohang were undefeated in nine matches
and intended to make it ten against hapless Busan.

Andrew Roy Cooke was a 6ft 1in centre-forward at 29 years of
age. Allowed to sever the remaining year of his contract at Stoke
City, he left England for a lucrative opportunity in South Korea
where we would link up with Cureton. He had previously played
against Cureton, but not yet actually met him.

Jon Olav Hjelde was a 6ft 2in central defender, just days shy of his 31st birthday. After being released by Nottingham Forest, the Norwegian was snapped up by Porterfield on a free transfer in the hope of solidifying Busan's porous back-line.

The pair were admittedly straying into the twilight of their careers, utilised with less frequency by their former clubs before parting ways. But both had been impressive grafters in England's Football League, and considering they were signed by Busan without transfer fees, they looked a promising catch by Porterfield. As with Cureton, Cooke and Hjelde would both earn US$350,000 over two years.

The match against Pohang begins, and it's quickly evident that Cookie – as he was fondly referred to back in England by fans – is intended to be the target man. His role is to receive the ball from midfielders, muscle his way past opposing defenders, and supply possession to poaching striker Cureton.

The Pride of Pusan members are tense, watching to determine whether the trio from Britain can supplant Busan's departed Serbian and Colombians.

Porterfield had earlier confided to me that Urumov's departure was allegedly 'irregular', but he elaborated further in recent days. The Serbian had scored frequently for Busan, earning the attention of the K League's wealthier clubs. As his Busan contract neared its end, Suwon made him a significant salary offer. Busan could have retained Urumov if they were willing to exceed Suwon's offer, but Busan officials allegedly didn't want to pay such high wages.

Nor did they fancy a bidding war against Suwon owners Samsung Electronics, one of South Korea's richest *jaebeol* business conglomerates, according to Porterfield.

If true, this message was never made public, as the club likely didn't want to concede they were being stingy, and nor was Porterfield willing to embarrass his employers by pointing the finger unreservedly at them.

Porterfield insisted privately that Busan officials wanted Urumov out. Rather than an innocent mix-up or incompetence, the Scot alleged that club officials intentionally misled him about Busan's ownership of Urumov to ensure the Serbian's departure. Porterfield also alleged that 'stuffed envelopes' changed hands during the supposed conspiracy, although he did not offer any evidence to back his assertion.

Although Porterfield no longer had to tiptoe around dictators or avoid being choked by chairmen in his current managerial role, perhaps joining Busan meant operating within circumstances more challenging than he originally anticipated.

But was Porterfield's private portrayal of this episode accurate? Were Busan's funds for re-signing Urumov simply relocated to Porterfield's Britain-based trio? Was Porterfield perhaps afraid of taking responsibility for dumping popular foreign players and replacing them with alternatives who may not pan out?

As an aside, one of the more interesting things gleaned from this affair was the prominent role signing bonuses played in the K League. If a player switched clubs, the new club would generally offer a signing bonus in addition to a salary. The bonus could be just as large as the actual salary.

If that player instead opted to re-sign with their current club, they generally were not offered a signing bonus. The result was that in-demand players who grasped this financial situation intentionally sought short-term contracts in the hope of regularly changing clubs, aiming to collect as many signing bonuses as possible throughout their career. Every year or two, coveted players joined the highest bidder, eschewing long-term contracts.

This preference for short-term contracts and signing bonuses from the K League's better players – domestics and foreign imports alike – made it almost impossible for a small club like Busan to retain any promising young players they developed. With little incentive to groom youth, smaller K League clubs often neglected youth development.

Instead, Busan tended to splash money only on their top foreign players. Under Porterfield, this meant his trio of imports from British football.

Andy Cooke appears to be enjoying the change of scenery and new career challenge. Muscling past two Pohang midfielders, Cookie barrels forward with the ball, determined to make a positive start in South Korea. With team-mate Cureton attracting two defenders, Cookie makes an attempt at goal from distance early in the match. The shot has tremendous velocity, but is parried wide by Pohang's goalkeeper.

Minutes later, the ball makes two lunging bounces across Pohang's 18-yard box before anyone can claim it. Cookie races forward. In close pursuit is Rogério Pinheiro dos Santos, Pohang's Brazilian defender, who would later be named in the K League's 'best 11' for the 2003 season. As the ball approaches, Santos sticks his foot out toward the ball's trajectory.

Fortunately for Cookie, Santos's timing is slightly off. The Brazilian commits too early, leaving the ball just beyond his reach. Cookie continues a further half-step toward goal before jabbing at the ball with his unfavoured left foot. The Englishman's timing is also premature, allowing the ball to bounce past his extended limb. But Cookie's other leg, tucked partly underneath for support, is fortuitously right where the ball lands. Sensing this just before contact, Cookie awkwardly stretches his right leg out. He's only able to flick upward at the falling ball, but inelegant contact is sufficient. The ball ricochets dramatically upward and into the top of the net, much to the surprise of Pohang's goalkeeper.

1-0 Busan.

Just 24 minutes into his Busan career, Cookie scores for the struggling club. Porterfield bounds out of the dugout and pumps his fist in the air triumphantly. Cookie's debut K League goal is just as crude as Cureton's from four days earlier, but nobody minds. It's a Busan goal!

The Pride of Pusan's celebrations are noticeably muted. Several hop up and down, many applaud, and a couple of streamers are thrown. But I sensed that the hardcore supporters still weren't convinced – that it wasn't going to be easy for Porterfield and his trio to win over a group hardened with cynicism.

Porterfield's intention was for Cookie to serve as the burly target man who would win the ball and provide it to speedy Cureton – that was the role the Salopian had become known for at Burnley and Stoke City. But if Cookie is able to whack goals in himself, all the better.

After playing for Shrewsbury Town and Telford United during his youth, Andy Cooke began his senior career with semi-professional Newtown. He became a prolific striker at the modest League of Wales team, attracting attention from much bigger clubs. Cookie was surprised how prominent his suitors were, but was truly shocked when Burnley offered him his first full-time contract.

Cookie was a crowd favourite during his five-and-a-half seasons at Burnley, where he scored more than 50 goals. In 1997/98, he helped the Lancastrians avoid relegation and led the team in goals, including a memorable brace scored during the last match of the season. Two years later, occasionally paired up front with former England international Ian Wright, Cookie orchestrated arguably the season's biggest FA Cup upset by scoring the away goal that eliminated top-flight Derby County. By then converted to a target man, Cookie's role was to feed prolific goalscorer Andy Payton, the two forming a 35-goal partnership that earned Burnley promotion to the second tier. Cookie was an 'automatic choice' during his first four seasons at the club according to the *Lancashire Evening Telegraph*, but his playing time eventually dwindled.

When Stoke City – the club that Cookie personally supported – made a mid-season offer for him, he readily accepted. Cookie was keen to increase his playing time, even if it meant moving back down a division to join the Potters. Stoke was an ambitious (and suddenly wealthy) club embarking upon its 'Icelandic revolution'. Cookie helped the club gain promotion during his first full season there, and he led the squad in league goals the following year. But a season of struggle for Stoke and change of manager forced him to look for employment elsewhere.

Cue a phone call from Ian Porterfield. Just weeks later, Cookie was wearing the red and white of Busan rather than Stoke.

Back at Asiad Stadium, Pohang midfielder Kim Gi-dong weaves past a Busan midfielder and defender, approaches the top of Busan's 18-yard box and takes a shot at goal. But Jon Olav Hjelde is there to extinguish the threat. Busan's new Norwegian defender strides in front of Kim, towering over him.

Hjelde began his career at his small hometown club, Vuku, before being abruptly propelled to the top of Norwegian football with giants Rosenborg. It was a massive jump, and Hjelde was not a regular starter during his three seasons there. But he featured in UEFA Champions League matches, earning attention from clubs overseas.

The Norwegian was soon snatched by Nottingham Forest, where he remained for six years – including one season in the illustrious Premier League. His time in English football would make him one of the most recognisable athletes in Norway.

When Forest opted not to renew Hjelde's contract, he was courted by new Stoke manager Tony Pulis – ironically the same person behind Cookie leaving the club. Hjelde had a brief trial and both parties were progressing toward a contract. Portsmouth and SK Brann also expressed interest. But Busan manager Ian Porterfield swooped in with a lucrative offer toward the end of the transfer window, leaving Hjelde with a difficult decision.

'This transfer happened very quickly. I had to make a fast decision,' Hjelde told *Trønder-Avisa*. 'The manager of Busan I'cons, Ian Porterfield, called me. He asked me to come to South Korea to look at the situation over the weekend. I travelled as soon as I could. The transfer window in South Korea [would close soon]. I had to give a yes or no [within two days].'

Given the urgency, Hjelde signed for the club during his initial visit to Korea.

'I would have probably not said yes to this offer if there weren't any English-speaking players at the club,' Hjelde told *Trønder-Avisa*. 'I like the place. Their stadium was used during the World Cup last year and takes in 80,000 spectators.'

That was the maximum capacity; the usual capacity was roughly 53,000. But Busan's attendances often ebbed at a lowly five per cent of the latter figure. Hjelde had obviously seen these new stadiums full to capacity (or thereabouts) during the World Cup, but was he under the impression that Busan attracts crowds anywhere near 80,000 for K League matches? Had the Norwegian been told a fib about the atmosphere generated at Busan's K League games?

Porterfield informed Hjelde that the playing level was 'good' in South Korea; otherwise, the Norwegian had no idea as to the K League's quality. Hjelde mentioned being impressed by the performance of the South Korean national team at the 2002 World Cup.

And why did the Norwegian decide to leave England? Was money the allure?

Hjelde told the *#innspark* podcast that Busan's wage offer was roughly the same as what Stoke City had offered him.

'But I've been offered a fair deal,' Hjelde said to *Trønder-Avisa*. 'The money is not the driving force for going to South Korea. I was getting a little tired of the English style, and want to try something completely new.'

Oh dear. Porterfield's kick-and-rush tactics under a 4-4-2 formation at Busan weren't a radical departure from English football. But those were the sorts of important details overlooked when making a rushed decision.

Regardless of what convincing claims Hjelde was told, he was now here, locked into a two-year contract. His job was to shore up Busan's leaky back-line. How would the Norwegian take to living in Busan – a city that contained a larger population than the entire country of Norway?

Andy Cooke is once again on the attack for Busan. Out-manoeuvring several Pohang players, the barrel-chested forward feigns a pass to an unmarked Jamie Cureton. The sly gesture convinces a defender guarding Pohang's near post to rush toward the diminutive Bristolian. Seeing an opening, Cookie thrusts the ball toward goal. But Kim Byung-ji, Pohang's goalkeeper, is an astute veteran of the game of football. He shifts prudently toward the near post as his defender leaves, easily catching Cookie's brisk shot.

Kim Byung-ji was one of the K League's more eccentric characters. Typically sporting a dyed mullet – usually blonde or some other loud colour – Kim was a larger-than-life presence during his quarter-century career that spanned more than 700 games. He was an adventurous player who regularly strayed far beyond his 18-yard box, becoming the first goalkeeper to score from open play in the K League.

Kim was initially rejected by K League clubs during a late 1980s player draft because he hadn't attended a school with a prestigious football programme. Instead, he became a journeyman welder at construction sites. But, much like Andy Cooke, he would worm his way into the professional game after succeeding at the semi-professional level. Kim eventually became the league's highest-paid player, and in 2000 became the first goalkeeper named as the K League's 'most valuable player'. He would also feature in goal for South Korea's national team on more than 60 occasions.

After thwarting Cookie's effort at goal, Pohang pushed the ball up to striker Woo Sung-yong. Woo was a formidable opponent who featured regularly for the national team and led the K League in goals in 2002. He would go on to break the record for career K League goals in 2008.

Woo's presence today at Asiad Stadium stung the Pride of Pusan. Between 1996 and 2002, he was an attacking stalwart for Busan. But like most of Busan's better players since 2000 – when Hyundai Development Company began funding the team on a reduced budget – Woo eventually moved to a stronger team. He left the club around the time Ian Porterfield was hired as manager, reducing the chances of the Scot succeeding in the near-term.

Woo's departure to a rival K League club was especially irksome. Despite leaving, he remained close by – seemingly within reach, yet agonisingly elusive; impossible to recapture. Woo personified the bountiful former Daewoo Royals era: tantalisingly fresh in the memory, but a gradually fading reminiscence as a stark new reality emerged for the club.

As any football sadist would expect, Woo scores against his former club, inflicting the dagger of cynicism and despondency even deeper into Busan's last few-dozen remaining supporters. By now they bled a putrid blend of enmity and resignation. Woo's shot is taken just several yards from goal, cruelly illustrating how deeply Busan's foes can penetrate.

1-1. Cookie's go-ahead goal is nullified by Pohang's equaliser. In the dugout, Porterfield's face reveals his apprehension. The game carries a cruel symmetry that has become characteristic of Busan's performances under the Scottish manager: scoring in the first half but conceding during the second.

The referee blows his whistle, concluding the match as a draw. Porterfield's British trio fail to earn a win from their collective debut. Busan are now winless in four games, including two matches since Porterfield attempted to assuage supporters' fears regarding the club's progress.

The Pride of Pusan reacted to another day of dropped points fairly quietly once again, with most of the replica kit-clad supporters swiftly fleeing the venue. But a few delayed their departure, chatting about whether the imports from Britain were any improvement over the departed Serb and South Americans. Others expressed doubt whether Porterfield would be able to turn the team around, due to factors both within and beyond his control.

I later read a story on the BBC Sport website that explored why talented South American footballers often flop in the Premier League. Writer Tim Vickery attributed part of the blame to the level of social support that South Americans expect but usually fail to receive from English clubs. Vickery argued that people from Latin cultures rely upon their social support structure more than independent-minded British do. When they find such support usually lacking in the UK, compounded by having to deal with a foreign language and culture on a daily basis, it can lead to feelings of alienation and depression for South American players away from home.

Naturally my thoughts turned to how Cureton, Cookie and Hjelde would fare living in North East Asia, or for that matter, the much older Porterfield and Jarvie. Porterfield, despite his nonsensical comment that experience living in England as a Scot had somehow equipped him for the vast differences of Asia, had admittedly lived in three African countries – but English was an official language in all of them. Porterfield also worked twice in the Middle East where Arabic is most prominent, but he only spent brief time in these positions.

For Drew Jarvie, this was the 54-year-old's first time working outside of Scotland, never mind overseas. His age and lack of international experience made him vulnerable to homesickness.

Cureton, Cookie and Hjelde were in their late 20s and very early 30s, a life stage more conducive to adapting to alien surroundings. The biggest complication for the three players, however, was how their families would fare living in North East Asia. All three had partners. One already had children, while the other two had just signed for Busan while their partners were pregnant – one in her first trimester, the other in her final one. Would the pressures of family commitments prove the biggest obstacle to Porterfield's European trio successfully settling overseas?

Another issue was how well the three Westerners would integrate with their new Korean team-mates. Prior to the trio's arrival, foreign players at Busan I'cons were from countries with poorer economies than South Korea. For them, playing in Korea meant 'moving up' to a higher-paying league, even if the football might not have been as good. The players were grateful for the opportunity.

Porterfield's British imports, however, had come from the sport's birthplace. Two had played in the Premier League and one had been pitted against world-class opposition in the UEFA Champions

League. Perhaps more importantly, they also hailed from Western European countries with developed economies. Might they be prone to looking down upon South Korea – both in footballing and other terms – or would they be mature and cosmopolitan enough to enthusiastically embrace living in a different part of the world? Would they make an effort to form bonds with their Korean team-mates and even try to learn some of the local language? Or would the presence of an English-speaking manager, coach and team-mates make it tempting for the trio to fortify themselves within a British bubble rather than interact with the local players?

Squad fissures can generally be overlooked when a football club is doing well, but Busan were struggling. It would be prudent for the European trio to integrate themselves with their new team-mates – but would they?

ROUND 23

Busan	**1-1**	**Pohang**
Suwon	2-1	Seongnam
Daejeon	3-1	Gwangju
Ulsan	0-0	Bucheon
Anyang	2-4	Jeonbuk
Jeonnam	4-3	Daegu

K LEAGUE TABLE

Ulsan	47
Seongnam	46
Jeonbuk	36
Suwon	36
Daejeon	36
Anyang	34
Jeonnam	33
Pohang	32
Busan	**21**
Gwangju	19
Daegu	17
Bucheon	9

CHAPTER 19

SQUAD SQUABBLES AND EMPTY WORLD CUP STADIUMS

BUCHEON SK VS. BUSAN I'CONS
SATURDAY, 2 AUGUST 2003
K LEAGUE ROUND 24
BUCHEON STADIUM

모로 가도 서울만 가면 된다
*– The end justifies the means; achieving a goal
is more important than how it is accomplished
(literally, 'it doesn't matter how you go, as long as
you go to Seoul')*

THE K LEAGUE had become embroiled in a copyright battle. Two of its clubs, Daejeon Citizen and Bucheon SK, were being sued for playing the South Korean national anthem prior to league matches.

South Koreans adopted the strange American habit of playing the national anthem immediately before domestic league games. The only problem was that in South Korea, the national anthem wasn't in the public domain. Instead, 'Aegukga' (Patriotic Song) was owned by the composer's family, who expected to be paid royalties every time the tune was played. K League clubs Daejeon and Bucheon were accused of not paying up in 2003, and a lawsuit was launched.

That South Korea's anthem once commanded royalties is ironic, given it is said to be heavily inspired by 'O Dobrujanski Krai', a Bulgarian folk song and official anthem of the city of Dobrich.

When Bulgarian conductor Peter Nikolov visited the Seoul International Music Festival in 1964 and heard South Korea's national anthem, he indirectly accused its composer, Ahn Ik-tae, of plagiarism.

'If Bulgarian singers came to Korea and sang "O Dobrujanski Krai", Korean audiences would stand up!' Nikolov is credited to have said.

Today we were travelling to one of the two K League clubs sued for daring to play the national anthem, although our trip didn't involve litigious purposes. Busan I'cons were embarking on a two-match away trip to Gyeonggi, the doughnut-shaped province that surrounds Seoul. Busan and their new European trio would play away to basement-dwellers Bucheon and mid-table Anyang, with Busan manager Ian Porterfield desperate to end the club's four-match winless streak. It was also an opportunity for Busan to temper the embarrassment of their recent loss to lowly Bucheon by exacting revenge on the league's worst team.

South Korea's Capital Area – which comprises the cities of Seoul and Incheon as well as the surrounding Gyeonggi Province – swarms with people. South Korea is a small country to begin with, and much of its terrain is dominated by uninhabitable mountains. Of what little land is suitable for settlement, just one region – the Capital Area – contains more than half of the country's population. This single part of South Korea accommodates more people than the Netherlands and Austria combined.

Much like how London dominates both the economy and politics of the United Kingdom, South Korea's Capital Area emits an immense gravity that lures people from across the country. As such, most other regions have a stagnant or decreasing population, including Busan, where in 2003 the birth rate was the lowest in the nation and the number of inhabitants had been slowly shrinking since the late 1980s.

The Seoul Capital Area had become obsessed with accumulating wealth and flaunting material riches – as parodied in the 2012 'Gangnam Style' music video that poked fun at South Korea's *nouveau riche*. By contrast, the country's football supporters bucked the trend by embracing altruism, community service and collectivism.

When you factored in the time, money, effort and dedication they sacrificed to their adopted team, football supporters were more like unpaid employees than passive spectators. Their encouragement was so animated that they perspired almost as much as the players.

Even at weekday evening away matches held up in the capital area, some five hours away, there would usually be at least a small gaggle of travelling Busan supporters. The most zealous Pride of Pusan members probably put more effort into supporting the club than the salaried staff.

The Pride members were as much match participants as the actual players. These supporters subscribed to the mythology of the '12th man' – that vocal fans have a tangible impact upon matches, affecting outcomes. That might be true when 10,000 ultras in a European cauldron hiss derisively at opponents or unleash flame and smoke, but I doubted whether 25 Busan supporters committed exclusively to positive chanting genuinely boosted their team's fortunes.

Regardless of which country they may live in, football's most committed supporters tend to be social outcasts in need of a tribe. The Pride of Pusan members were no different, comprised of a disparate assortment who appeared to be at the margins of Korean society.

Everyone who watches sport does so as a form of escapism, but the most passionate of supporters construct a considerable portion of their identity upon what to most people is merely ephemeral entertainment. Away matches at the furthest grounds were an opportunity to discover who among the group were the most obsessive in their mania for their hapless local football club.

Although I considered taking the supporters' bus to distant away games to be a punishing ordeal, such journeys were a self-imposed obligation for the group's inner core. Was the staggering amount of energy expended by supporting Busan I'cons – particularly at remote away matches – really worth it? Was there any evidence that attending most games as a fan during a gruelling, 44-match season produced a measurable performance improvement for the team?

I doubted whether the most enthusiastic supporters even considered this. They inexplicably decided that supporting their team at every possible opportunity had become their personal responsibility. They manufactured a sense of belonging, meaning and purpose by supporting their football club, although it was questionable whether the players felt even a fraction of such affection for the supporters in return.

Did the hardcore Pride of Pusan members care whether the players considered them to be essential allies, devoted servants or sycophantic losers? Would they dare even ponder such an existential question about their unique identity?

After arriving and navigating a venue concourse ostensibly designed to befuddle visitors, we eventually emerged into the stands of Bucheon Stadium. Despite opening in 2001, Bucheon's new ground was curiously not used as a venue for the 2002 World Cup. Much like Busan Asiad, Bucheon Stadium contained a massive running track, which helped to ensure that fans remained as far from the pitch as possible and that matchday atmosphere was deflated.

Bucheon pulled in large crowds during its opening season at the new stadium in 2001, but club owner SK Energy's efforts to cut costs had reduced crowds to pitifully low figures. Several dozen members of Hermes – Bucheon's supporter group – were huddled together today, but most of the stadium was vacant other than a few hundred scattered chairs dusted with spectators.

My first sight – other than row upon row of vacant, powder-blue seats – was a massive banner than spanned several sections in the home end. 'WHAT'S YOUR PRIDE? OUR PRIDE OF REDS! UH~', the banner exclaimed. I was admittedly perplexed as to the meaning of the 'UH~' at the end. The sound of confusion? The onomatopoeia of an orgasm? Clearly I still had much to learn.

Most K League teams associated Bucheon with three easy points, but the calamitous northern club recently showed signs of improvement. After winning away to Busan, Bucheon unexpectedly earned a point at current league leaders Ulsan.

As the day slips into evening, the scorching heat begins to relent. Cookie wins possession and attempts to negotiate his way past two Bucheon defenders. After the shot goes wide, Cureton looks over at Cookie in frustration. Cureton points to the space in front of him to suggest that he was not being marked and should have received the ball. Cookie apologises with a slight wave of his hand.

Busan soon launch another attack. A midfielder awards Cureton possession of the ball shortly past the halfway line. Cureton looks up, as if seeking assistance from his barrelling strike partner. But Cookie is on the other side of the pitch, in a position suggesting he would rather launch an attack by himself again than support Cureton.

Isolated, Cureton drops his head and marches forward with the ball. Two Bucheon defenders approach, the first dispossessing him. Cureton looks up in frustration, then over at Cookie. He throws up his hands in dissatisfaction and shakes his head.

It's obvious the two aren't playing collaboratively. Cureton was accustomed to being supplied the ball frequently by Martin Butler at Reading, but such service wasn't forthcoming yet from Cookie here at Busan. Was this a normal teething problem of unfamiliar players brought together, likely to be overcome with time? Or did early signs suggest that the two English strikers might not be compatible?

Andy Cooke had just spent two and a half seasons at Stoke City, coinciding with owner Gunnar Gíslason's 'Icelandic revolution' while the paint was still radiant at the new Britannia Stadium. During Cookie's initial half-season at the club, Stoke qualified for the play-offs for the second consecutive year but were eliminated. The following season, 2001/02, Stoke finally won the play-offs and earned promotion back to English football's second tier.

During Cookie's earlier time at Burnley, he was converted from a goalscorer to a target man, a role in which he would win possession and provide the ball to his strike partner. Stoke had expected Cookie to perform that same role.

'I didn't score a great deal of goals really for a centre-forward, but I would always be a decent foil for any striker I played with,' Cookie told *Duck Magazine*, a Stoke fanzine.

Despite Stoke earning promotion, Icelandic manager Gudjon Thordarson was fired. His replacement, Tony Pulis, didn't think much of Cookie. The striker's playing time was significantly curtailed, yet he still finished the 2002/03 season as Stoke's leading scorer.

Cookie arrived for Stoke's pre-season camp in the summer of 2003, but a brief chat on a golf course with Pulis about the manager's plans convinced Cookie to seek employment elsewhere. His contract was terminated one year early by mutual consent, allowing Ian Porterfield to make an offer to the unattached player.

Stoke fans who learned about Cookie's move to South Korea remarked that the striker was an unyielding ball winner and a skilled provider, but wasn't a prolific scorer. A cheeky chant at the Britannia

Stadium set to the tune of 'That's Amore' went something like, 'When we're on the attack and the ball gets passed back, that's a Cookie.' Stoke fans apparently had no idea that their former striker was an abundant goalscorer at Newtown and during his early period at Burnley.

Porterfield signed Cookie specifically to serve as a target man to complement Jamie Cureton. But from his short playing time with Busan thus far, Cookie's play suggested he might be more interested in resurrecting his former goalscoring prowess.

Despite expecting a defensive encounter from Bucheon, the unfancied home side launch wave after wave of attacks against Busan's back-line. It's evident Bucheon are striving for a win, hoping to earn a double over Busan within a single week. Jon Hjelde and Porterfield's three favourite domestic defenders – Lee Jang-kwan, Yoon Hee-joon and Lee Lim-saeng – are barely keeping Bucheon at bay. Shot after shot is on target, ensuring Busan goalkeeper Kim Yong-dae is uncomfortably engrossed.

The whistle is blown for half-time. The relief on the faces of the Busan squad is palpable. Once again, the match isn't unfolding according to Porterfield's plan.

Before Busan supporters can mutter their first obscenities, the brooding clouds above hit critical mass and dump a torrent of monsoon rains without notice. The fans flee for cover up the stairwells. For the first time that day, many Pride of Pusan members crack a smile. They gleefully rush for shelter, laughter reverberating off the venue's concrete frame. It's an all-too-rare moment when being in a stadium brings joy for Busan supporters.

* * *

The second half begins and Busan start well. Cookie sends the ball to Cureton. Twisting and turning, the diminutive striker makes a break for goal but his shot is well wide.

Cureton's head drops. Some Busan supporters cluck their tongues derisively in that distinctly Korean way; others mutter mild curses.

Elder captain Noh Jung-yoon, despite being a midfielder, is in an attacking position and wants the ball from Cookie. His body language hurls silent criticism at the English pair. Neither notice.

Earlier that week, a troubling rumour was prominently splashed across online message boards: Busan's Korean players allegedly felt they were being ignored by the new foreign trio. I speak with Busan supporters about this, who suggest the domestic players haven't integrated well with the recent European arrivals. The gossip is that it feels like two distinct groups within the dressing room.

If true, this doesn't bode well for Porterfield's British revolution.

'Learn all your team-mates' names.' That was one piece of advice in 'My 5 tips for surviving Asian football', an article on A-League. com.au written by Australian defender Robert Cornthwaite, who spent four seasons in the K League.

Porterfield had referred to his Korean players solely by their surname (or sometimes merely by their number) at his recent meeting with Busan supporters. That was eight months after he became manager. If Porterfield hadn't bothered to learn their full names (or even surnames) by then, would the new Western trio of players bother to?

'The [foreign] players who have the most success in Asia are the ones who adapt the best,' Cornthwaite continued in his article. 'Many foreigners tend to stick together from the various countries they're from, and as such can isolate themselves from the local players.'

The fourth official raises the substitute board in the 66th minute. Third striker Ahn Hyo-yeon is replaced by Lee Jung-hyo, a defender. With 24 minutes plus stoppage time still to play in this scoreless match against the league's worst side, Porterfield is taking off an attacking player and replacing him with a defender. Is he conceding that the most his team can muster from this encounter is a mere draw? Busan striker Gwak, sitting on the bench, looks up to the heavens, as if seeking either instruction or solace.

The Busan supporters are livid, releasing a maelstrom of abuse toward Porterfield. Luckily for the Scot, the dugout shields his ears from the outcry.

Bucheon continue to dominate, but can't quite get past Busan's defences. With just one minute left to play, a second Busan striker, Jamie Cureton, is brought off in favour of a midfielder.

Tempers fray among the Pride of Pusan. Objects are thrown to the ground in scathing anger.

'You're useless, Porterfield!' one supporter shouts with disdain.

The match ends in a 0-0 stalemate. Busan's poor marking was exploited, allowing their opponents too much time and space on the ball. Lowly Bucheon had out-shot Busan by a 2:1 ratio.

Bucheon earned an elusive point, their tenth of the season, and were three games undefeated. Busan, however, were now five matches without a win – and two of those were against the worst team in the league.

As today's result illustrated, stopping your opponent from scoring was not sufficient to win matches. Porterfield needed to get his new English strikers to score consistently.

The one noticeable improvement was Hjelde helping to prevent second-half goals, a frequent Busan weakness.

The big Norwegian had rebuffed offers from other English clubs to come to Korea. Did he make a mistake? What would two years of playing for a luckless club in Asia do to his future career prospects?

Just over four years ago, Hjelde featured in England's Premier League. Now he was playing in a motley mixture of near-empty World Cup stadiums and crumbling concrete venues, turning out for one of the worst top-flight clubs in North East Asia.

As Hjelde explained to Norwegian media, he had fancied a change, much like Jamie Cureton. After his six years at Nottingham Forest was capped by bombing out of the promotion play-offs, he was cut free. He could have remained in England with a different club (Stoke or Portsmouth), gone back to Norway (SK Brann), or ventured out to South Korea. Busan was obviously the unconventional choice, but with a salary of more than one-third-of-a-million dollars over two years, completely tax-free, it was incredibly tempting. Hjelde claimed that money was not the main driving force – supposedly less than he made while briefly in the Premier League several years ago – but Busan's offer was no worse than any of his European suitors were prepared to pay.

Hjelde ventured out to South Korea alone, as his wife Vivi was pregnant with their first child, due in September. Already in her third trimester, she wasn't able to fly. She would have to remain back home in England for the remainder of the pregnancy and begin life as a new family in South Korea after the delivery.

This undoubtedly would have made the decision to sign for Busan all the more difficult for Hjelde. Although it would be more comfortable for Hjelde's wife to deliver their child in an English hospital due to linguistic and cultural familiarity, for the pair to be separated during most of the third trimester of her pregnancy could prove arduous. Vivi would have the support of friends, but most of her family lived in Norway – and even if they had all lived in England, it wouldn't be quite the same as having her partner soothe her each day.

For Hjelde, transitioning to an alien living environment would be more difficult without his wife. He would miss her and perhaps feel guilty about being absent during her time of need.

Hjelde did receive permission from Busan I'cons to quickly sneak back to England during the planned delivery period, but what if the baby arrived early?

Elsewhere in the K League this weekend, Gwangju inexplicably won 2-0 against league leaders Ulsan, allowing Gwangju to leapfrog Busan in the league table, thanks to goal difference. Daegu also earned an away draw, allowing both new clubs to come within uncomfortable proximity.

The morning after the Bucheon match, I stumbled upon a dozen Bucheon supporters in Myeong-dong, one of Seoul's more popular shopping districts where streets are a sea of competing neon signs. The Bucheon hardcore were collecting signatures for a petition in support of the creation of a K League club in Seoul. They were of the opinion that having a tenant in the new Seoul World Cup Stadium made sense, and that another rival for their team in the capital region would be a positive development for the league.

But in the days ahead, northern matters would turn ugly again. Bucheon supporters would publicly denounce SK, the club's corporate owners. Such actions were perhaps harsh, as Bucheon would follow their draw against Busan by only narrowly losing a high-scoring thriller against championship contenders Seongnam, and that result came after the basement club went three matches undefeated.

South Korea had become a country of high expectations, and its citizens felt increasingly justified in venting their frustrations. With Bucheon supporters baying for ownership blood despite on-pitch improvements, what would become of their beleaguered club?

More importantly, what did the future hold for Busan I'cons? With Ian Porterfield once again dragging this team through five straight matches without a win, was his tenure at the club in jeopardy?

Would corporate owners Hyundai Development Company remain committed to funding the club, even if they became the target of public derision from Busan supporters?

Before returning to Busan, I paid a quick visit to the new Seoul World Cup Stadium. It was the largest football-specific venue in Asia, where Senegal upset France during the opening match of the 2002 World Cup. Built at a cost of US$185m and located near central Seoul, surely it would only be a matter of time before this facility hosted a K League club?

ROUND 24

Bucheon	**0-0**	**Busan**
Pohang	4-4	Anyang
Gwangju	2-0	Ulsan
Suwon	0-0	Daegu
Jeonbuk	1-1	Jeonnam
Seongnam	2-0	Daejeon

K LEAGUE TABLE

Seongnam	49
Ulsan	47
Jeonbuk	37
Suwon	37
Daejeon	36
Anyang	35
Jeonnam	34
Pohang	33
Gwangju	22
Busan	**22**
Daegu	18
Bucheon	10

CHAPTER 20

AIRING DIRTY LAUNDRY IN THE NEWSPAPERS

BUSAN I'CONS VS. JEONNAM DRAGONS
SATURDAY, 9 AUGUST 2003
K LEAGUE ROUND 26
BUSAN ASIAD WORLD CUP STADIUM
쇠가 쇠를 먹고 살이 살을 먹는다
*– Groups bicker among themselves (literally, 'cows
eat cows and rice eats rice')*

MUCH LIKE how Southampton and its large port lie at the base of southern England, Gwangyang wields a similar position on the Korean peninsula. As the industrial heart of the south-west, Gwangyang is home to a huge POSCO steel-smelting complex that dominates the city, as well as a K League club owned by POSCO: Jeonnam Dragons.

Jeonnam were due to visit Busan today. The mediocre side languished in eighth place, yet were a dozen points ahead of tenth-place Busan I'cons.

Ian Porterfield and assistant Drew Jarvie were under pressure. A loss today would result in seven Busan matches without a win, eclipsing the six-match streak set two months ago and equalled this past Wednesday.

Rumours circulated of a scheme to dump the Scottish pair and promote coach Choi Man-hee, the man with the ceaseless grin. Choi had served as a coach for the South Korean national team when they won the Asian Under-19 Championship in 1990, defeating the North on penalties. Years later he briefly coached the senior national team, then spent several years as manager at K League side Jeonbuk Motors. In 2002 he joined Busan I'cons, returning to a coaching role.

I scanned the TV listings. Tonight's match wasn't due to be broadcast. Again.

I couldn't believe it. How was the K League expected to reach new audiences and expand interest if it only garnered negligible media coverage?

Sports broadcasts on Korean TV prioritised baseball. On occasions that club football was shown, it tended to be either glamorous European leagues or overseas teams that featured a Korean star. TV broadcasts of South Korea's domestic football league were minimal and sporadic. K League ratings were low: less than one year after the 2002 World Cup, KBS and SBS chose to halt their K League coverage, despite paying for broadcast rights.

When K League matches were broadcast, they were often incomplete. Busan station PSB showed the first half of I'cons matches live on Wednesday evenings, but delayed the second half until late in the evening, often several hours afterward. Broadcasts were truncated if matches ran longer than expected or if a TV station decided to air a brief newscast at the end of the hour.

The 2003 Korean FA Cup Final would be locked in a 2-2 stalemate at the end of regulation time. With golden goal extra time imminent, broadcaster KBS instead chose to cut away to show a pre-scheduled documentary about firefighting.

Several channels would air the same baseball game simultaneously, and at its conclusion all would switch to the same already-in-progress football match. Would it not have made more sense for at least one of the channels to prioritise the football and show the match in its entirety?

But unlike most Busan residents, I would actually attend today's Busan–Jeonnam match, so I wasn't too put out.

Prior to matchday, I was warned that Jeonnam's presence would turn Asiad Stadium into a veritable shrine for one player: Kim Nam-il.

The 2002 World Cup transformed the South Korean men's national football team from perennial duds who had never won a single match into semi-finalists, and made superstars out of formerly anonymous and modestly paid players.

Subsequently, football fans who prised themselves away from fancy European league broadcasts and actually attended local K League matches often did so out of devotion to a particular star player rather than their local club. One recipient of such adoration was Kim Nam-il, who just two years earlier was completely unheard of.

Unlike most celebrity footballers, Kim only boasted mediocre looks, yet he managed to send female hearts aflutter wherever he went. So why were hordes of young Korean women swooning after Kim?

His informality. In South Korea, social formalities could be suffocating. People were expected to act deferentially to elders, be respectful of people in authority, and avoid behaviour that would bring embarrassment to one's peers.

But societies evolve. As the 2002 World Cup approached, globalisation tantalised young Koreans with individualism and indifference to traditional social expectations. While most still wouldn't dare defy their family or other authority figures, many couldn't help but admire the coolness of a rebellious icon.

Enter Kim Nam-il. He initially turned heads for his match performances, and unwittingly came to personify Korea standing up against the imperialist West when he injured French megastar Zinedine Zidane during a pre-World Cup friendly. Later he confronted the rugged play of the American team, often marking several larger opponents simultaneously. Over the course of the tournament he earned the nickname 'Vacuum Cleaner' for his abilities as a holding midfielder.

But it was his antics outside matches that drew mass admiration. South Korea manager Guus Hiddink created an awkward moment for the national squad by demanding players forgo traditional deference to seniority and treat each other as equals. Kim, one of the youngest players, ruptured the tension by crudely hollering out, 'Hey, Myung-bo, let's go eat!' in informal language to the eldest player, causing the entire team to burst out laughing.

Another light moment came before a match against Uruguay. The South American players lined up by the centre circle as a gorgeous actress gave each Uruguayan player a kiss on the cheek to wish them luck. The Korean players looked on enviously. But Kim, never the wallflower, stealthily made his way to the end of the line of Uruguay players. After the last Uruguay player had received a peck, Kim beamed at the actress, turned his face sideways, and extended his cheek toward her. His Korean team-mates howled with delight.

It was Kim's display of fearless determination against supposedly superior opponents, combined with a penchant for tomfoolery and refreshing informality that won him mass admiration, particularly from young Korean women.

With the 2002 World Cup making stars of South Korean football players, many young women who previously idolised pop music performers instead shifted their attention to footballers. Yonsei University cultural anthropology professor Kim Hyun-mee, who specialised in gender and feminist issues, asserted in academic journal *Inter-Asia Cultural Studies* that the World Cup was the first opportunity for Korean women to publicly display fondness for males in a mainstream and socially accepted way. Among the points raised (and translated by Hong Sung-hee) were:

'Women transformed the soccer games into a space where they could project their "sexual desires" ... [W]omen in stadiums, on the streets, and in front of the TV screens enjoyed imaginary and direct "heterosexual" romance with the male soccer players.

'... [A] new collective experience of pleasure by women as viewers of men's bodies and not as objects of men's gaze.

'... [T]he craze of girl fans over the stars provides a rich opportunity for them to openly display their enormous sexual energy. ... To these women, showing their enthusiasm for male stars is a "safe" way to express their socially oppressed desires. It is an "exciting" experience for young women to project their burgeoning sexual fantasies on male objects.

'... [W]omen evaluated the soccer players' bodies and projected their own desires upon them, as if they were potential buyers looking through an exhibit.

'As women's sexual desires became a part of "public discourse", they gained a rapid infectious effect, and Korean women, regardless of marital status, age or region, came to share an experience of collective sexualisation.

'This World Cup was an opportunity for women to let out their sexual energy in a "healthy way".'

Right, then: today's match was really about ogling Jeonnam Dragons midfielder Kim Nam-il. Pity I had just taken my binoculars to the shop for repair.

Fans painted placards with suggestive messages for Kim such as 'Turn off the lights, Nam-il' or 'Let's only have three children, Nam-il' to display at his matches.

Each of South Korea's World Cup stars acquired a loyal following of young women, but none more than Kim Nam-il. There were hordes of women at the stadium today, including many away supporters. These travelling Jeonnam fans hung two banners, both paying homage specifically to Kim rather than to the club they reputedly supported. Many wore Jeonnam replica shirts personalised with Kim's name and number, some bearing his autograph. Several were draped in customised Kim Nam-il scarves. Two held binoculars affixed in the direction of the players' tunnel, eager to see Kim emerge. One even clutched a large camcorder, so important was the occasion.

The majority of Kim Nam-il fans in attendance were not replica shirt-clad Jeonnam travellers, but Busan locals interested in catching a glimpse of their newly famous idol. They certainly weren't at the Busan Asiad World Cup Stadium to support their local football club.

Beyond the celebrity hysteria, a match was to be played. Busan desperately needed a win. Although Jeonnam were in the bottom half of the table, they were undefeated in their last six matches. Busan hadn't won in six matches. I sensed a long 90 minutes ahead.

Busan's best 11 players were decent, but the club was starved of depth. Ryu Byung-hoon, a peripheral squad member now in his ninth year at Busan, was named as a starting defender today despite not having played in more than a month. Two of the six substitutes on the bench were raw debutants, ages 17 and 18.

Just five minutes into the match, Jeonnam take the lead. Brazilian striker Itamar Batista da Silva, in his first season in South Korea, snatches the first goal for the visitors against the run of play. Despite previously labouring for such hefty Brazilian clubs as Palmeiras, São Paulo and Cruzeiro, the offer to play in South Korea – and particularly the ample paycheque from Jeonnam owners POSCO – was too alluring to resist.

The majority of foreign players in the K League were from Brazil, with a decent supplement from other South American countries and Eastern Europe. South Korea's post-war economic growth was so impressive that K League clubs were able to pay such foreign players higher wages than they could ever hope to earn in their native countries. Wealthy football leagues in Western Europe have long plundered South America for talent – think Lionel Messi, Neymar, Luis Suárez or Ronaldinho – but South Korea and other North East Asian leagues similarly came to rely upon the southern hemisphere for reinforcements.

Most of the K League's imported players were treated like relative kings, compared to the low-paid lifestyle they would endure back home. Polish player Tadeusz Świątek relished his 1989–91 stint in Korea, according to an interview in *Tygodnik Płocki*, as translated by Andre Zlotkowski:

'There was a banquet after the [championship] match in a very elegant, luxurious hotel,' said Świątek. 'The banquet was for the club's 40 players and administrators and each was given a female companion who would light cigarettes and put food on the plates.

'We had no living costs as everything was provided for us. Though things were completely different to the way they were in Poland, I have to admit that this was the most wonderful period of my and my family's life. It was a great time for me on the field as well. They even made a TV programme about me.

'Returning to Poland was one of my life's biggest mistakes.'

Today's Busan–Jeonnam match is unusually fierce, with an abundance of tackles harder than normally witnessed in the K League. Cookie relishes the feistiness that gives this match the feel of England's Football League, and responds with hard, swift tackles that make the crowd cringe. The domestic Jeonnam players illustrate their thespian prowess, rolling on the ground in mock agony.

Cookie receives a precise cross in Jeonnam's penalty area and heads it toward the bottom corner of goal, but Jeonnam's goalkeeper makes a superb save.

Meanwhile, Cureton fumbles and errs throughout the match. The poor chap is desperately out of form, but visibly criticises his midfield team-mates for not feeding him the ball when and where he expects it.

In Busan's previous match – a 2-1 away loss at Anyang – Cureton and Cookie still weren't working as a partnership. Cureton spent the game attempting to dance past several defenders on his own but was repeatedly shut down.

The English striker was substituted out of that game with 20 minutes and stoppage time still to play, treatment he was unaccustomed to.

Just as Cureton is provided an excellent through ball today against Jeonnam, he narrowly misses the attempt at goal. The Pride of Pusan respond viciously: a cacophony of moans, groans, face palms, eye rolls, and bitter expletives washes over the Busan supporters' end.

But this time it's different. The abuse is not just one or two casual expletives uttered meekly toward the sky. Instead, it's several sentences of nasty vitriol that specifically single out Cureton. The Busan supporters scowl directly at him throughout their tirade. They want him gone.

A rather frosty welcome for someone in only their fifth match for Busan. But as the supporters have mostly all turned against Porterfield, so too are they quick to lash out at 'his' players who underperform. Cureton's name has already become mud, mostly down to association. Had Cureton been brought in by a previous manager, the supporters would almost certainly be more forgiving and patient.

The Pride of Pusan want Harry back, and they have no qualms about saying so.

Interestingly enough, Spanish translator Leo had been spotted with Busan I'cons officials earlier that day. With Harry and Tommy both gone, why would their translator still be around? Was the club charitably keeping him on until the end of his contract, or was something still unfolding behind the scenes?

Twenty minutes into the second half, an indirect free kick for Busan strikes the crossbar. Shortly afterwards, Busan again fail to convert a set piece. Moments later, Cookie barely misses with a high chip of the ball, as Jeonnam's goalkeeper palms it over the bar.

Busan just can't seem to score.

Jeonnam striker Itamar receives the ball and quickly advances beyond Busan's back-line. After an agonising play that seems to unfold in slow motion as he bears down on goal, the Brazilian scores. Cartwheels and a mid-air somersault mark the brace. Jeonnam are up 2-0 away to Busan.

In frustration, defender Jon Hjelde allows his head to fall forward. His neck appears to carry the psychological burden of Busan's plight. Hjelde's *vertebra prominens* juts upward like a cat arching its back in distress. It seems to reach for the gaping hole of Busan Asiad Stadium's roof, as if Hjelde would prefer to just climb out of the venue and scurry away. The tall Norwegian eventually musters some enthusiasm, erecting his stance and sauntering forward.

Less than a decade earlier, Hjelde joined his first professional club, Rosenborg (a team nicknamed 'The Troll Children', which tells you everything you need to know about Norway). The team had turned pro and went on a 13-season domestic championship run in the Tippeligaen (Norwegian Premier League). The highlight was a successful foray in the 1996/97 UEFA Champions League, in which the Norwegian side – a minnow compared to their European opponents – won away to AC Milan and drew at home against Juventus. The Rosenborg squad became known as 'the heroes of Milan', with the Norwegian Broadcasting Corporation heralding the victory as 'perhaps the best Trøndelag [central Norway] football achievement ever'.

Although Hjelde was a peripheral player at Rosenborg, he featured in both noted Champions League matches, drawing attention from overseas scouts. The large blond nearly concluded a transfer to southern Italian club Bari, then newly promoted to Serie A, when Nottingham Forest instead plucked him away to England.

Forest were enduring a turbulent period when Hjelde arrived. With the storied Brian Clough era concluded, the club was bouncing up and down between the top two tiers of English football. Hjelde joined in 1997 with the club having just suffered its second relegation in five seasons. But it would be another quick rebound upward, with Hjelde helping lead Forest back to the top flight of English football after being crowned champions of the Football League.

The 1998/99 season would be Hjelde's only one in the Premier League – it ended disastrously for Nottingham Forest. The East Midlands club went on a 19-match winless streak, and later conceded eight goals at home against Manchester United. It concluded with Forest's second relegation in just three seasons, and marked the first occasion since the 1927/28 season that the winners of England's second tier would go on to finish dead last in their subsequent top-flight appearance.

Although ultimately unsuccessful, Hjelde's sole season in the Premier League was a heady one, playing alongside the likes of Carlton Palmer (capped 18 times for England) and Dave Beasant (in goal for Wimbledon during their shock 1988 FA Cup win). It was a reasonably strong Forest squad. Despite winning just twice in a run of 32 matches, their back-line was robust.

Before the K League match resumes with Jeonnam in a 2-0 away lead, Hjelde gazes into the stands to observe the sparse Busan crowd: just 4,128 people in attendance at this giant World Cup stadium. His facial expression betrays him, admitting a sombre thought along the lines of 'What have I done?'

Just as the referee is about to whistle for full time, Jeonnam score a third. It's poster boy Kim Nam-il who puts it in. The stadium goes nuts, or at least as loud as a sub-5,000 crowd can be in a gaping venue. At least half of the paltry attendance is here just to watch him.

The Jeonnam supporters light a flare. The Pride of Pusan go silent.

The whistle blows. Seven matches in a row without a win for Busan, including five since Porterfield's 'have faith in me' plea to the supporters. How much more leniency would Porterfield be given?

Judging by the local newspapers, not much. An article titled 'Busan: internal discord' headlined the *Sports Chosun* the following Wednesday. It suggested the playing squad may have already turned against Porterfield.

According to the article, Porterfield had publicly blamed Busan's players for the poor results, comments that the squad became aware of.

'I am the best coach for our team, but the Busan players are short on ability,' the newspaper quoted Porterfield as saying. 'They even finished ninth [second-bottom] in the league last year.'

According to the article, the players were offended by the comments and wanted to protest to Porterfield, but decided to disregard the slight for the time being. However, things later escalated.

'One of the players suggested Porterfield doesn't have tactics – only an attachment to his ego,' one of the players reportedly told *Sports Chosun* during an interview on the condition of anonymity.

'The player said the squad doesn't have confidence in Porterfield anymore.

'I can't understand why he blamed the team's failures on the players,' the unidentified player was quoted as saying.

According to the article, a separate Busan player recently relegated to the bench claimed his demoted status was a reprisal for appealing to Porterfield for changes.

'I've been benched for a couple of games simply because I stood up to him once,' the second unnamed player was quoted to have said. He claimed he intended to leave Busan I'cons on loan to complete his mandatory national military service, ostensibly timed to avoid playing under Porterfield.

'I'll be joining [Gwangju] Sangmu next season.'

Although this second player was never identified, by deduction it was likely Shim Jae-won. Shim was a talented defender who had featured for South Korea at the Asian Games, Summer Olympics and Under-20 World Cup. He was only narrowly overlooked by Guus Hiddink for inclusion at the 2002 World Cup.

Shim joined Busan as their first pick in the 2000 K League draft. He initially showed great promise but lacked consistency. After helping Busan to a runners-up finish in the 2001 League Cup, Shim joined Eintracht Frankfurt in Germany on loan for one season. A clause in the loan contract stated that the German side would have to pay Busan US$1m if they wanted to permanently keep the player. The sum was far too large, and despite Shim begging Busan to lower their demand, they refused.

Gutted at not being able to remain in Europe, Shim returned to Busan in mid-2002. Soon after, a long-term shoulder injury required him to undergo orthopaedic surgery. Healed in time for the 2003 season and reaching his peak age, many pundits expected him to be one of the top domestic players for Busan under Ian Porterfield. Yet instead of featuring as a regular centre-back, Shim was often demoted to the dugout.

The ignominy of returning to Asia and now being benched by one of the K League's worst sides likely increased Shim's willingness to speak with the media, assuming it was indeed him.

There was a startling contrast in team morale between the FA Cup-winning Sunderland side Porterfield once played for and the pitiful Busan squad he was now managing.

'Our team spirit was so high, the bond between us so strong, that no ordinary mortal could break it,' gushed Porterfield in *The Impossible Dream*.

Compare that previous level of affinity to Porterfield's current playing squad calling him out publicly in the news media.

It's possible that Porterfield's managerial style shifted as he aged. Early in his career, he seemed to emulate the philosophy of his favourite former manager, Bob Stokoe: a friendly and laid-back man who won over his players by listening, incorporating their ideas into tactics, and treating them with respect.

'[Stokoe] was actually asking *us*. We were being allowed our say in the running of the team,' wrote Porterfield. 'Stokoe was different in another way, too. We were to be treated like men. Like adults, not naughty boys.'

This seemed to be the attitude Porterfield applied earlier while manager at Chelsea, although arguably he took it too far by being excessively slack with his players.

But Porterfield had also been influenced by a manager he came to despise: Alan 'Bomber' Brown, the man who controlled Sunderland with an iron fist prior to Stokoe's successful reign.

'Alan Brown cost me one full year of an already short career,' grumbled Porterfield in *The Impossible Dream*. 'That's the length of time the Bomber coldly and deliberately put me out of the game because we'd had a blow-up.'

Porterfield explained in his short book how he fell out with Brown.

'All the boys were fed up with the tactics,' wrote Porterfield, 'but when [Brown] asked if anyone had anything to say I was the one who spoke up. Speaking my mind was disastrous, of course. ... I had a feeling that the knife was in to me. But I never dreamed how far the Bomber was prepared to go.

'I was out on my neck. Colin Symm had my job in the first team and I was playing on the left wing for the reserves on a local ground in the area ... I even started to get substituted in those games.

'There was no explanation. Nothing.

'Looking back on those days I feel that I was made an example by Brown to show others what would happen if they stood up for themselves.

'Brown always wanted total obedience and no questions asked.'

So it was ironic that the managerial style Porterfield complained about in a book back in 1973 was eerily similar to the approach his current squad was accusing him of employing almost 30 years later. Parallels could also be seen in Colombian striker Harry's banishment from the club.

Had Porterfield unwittingly become more like Sunderland's 'Iron Man' (Brown) than its 'Messiah' (Stokoe)? Had the traumas and tribulations of Porterfield's 24 years as a manager – including a decade as a global journeyman – twisted Porterfield's personality into something that the younger version of himself would scantly recognise and possibly even abhor?

'I set high standards,' Porterfield would tell the *Northern Echo*. 'I demand certain things and I expect certain things, but most of all I want my players to want to get out of bed in the morning, to enjoy themselves.'

ROUND 25

Anyang	**2-1**	**Busan**
Jeonnam	1-1	Ulsan
Jeonbuk	1-1	Daejeon
Pohang	1-0	Suwon
Bucheon	3-5	Seongnam
Gwangju	1-0	Daegu

ROUND 26

Busan	**0-3**	**Jeonnam**
Seongnam	1-0	Gwangju
Suwon	4-3	Bucheon
Daejeon	0-0	Pohang
Ulsan	2-0	Jeonbuk
Anyang	3-1	Daegu

K LEAGUE TABLE

Seongnam	55
Ulsan	51
Anyang	41
Suwon	40
Jeonnam	38
Jeonbuk	38
Daejeon	38
Pohang	37
Gwangju	25
Busan	**22**
Daegu	18
Bucheon	10

CHAPTER 21

BEST MATES WITH LOCAL DERBY RIVALS

BUSAN I'CONS VS. ULSAN HYUNDAI HORANG-I (TIGERS)
WEDNESDAY, 20 AUGUST 2003
K LEAGUE ROUND 27
BUSAN ASIAD WORLD CUP STADIUM

호랑이에게 물려가도 정신만 차리면 산다
– Even if you're cornered by a tiger, if you remain cool you can survive

THE DAY began with blusterous thunderstorms. Despite the locals insisting that the rainy season was now complete, the weather forecast called for heavy storms for nine of the next ten days. In this part of the world, the rainy season occurs during the summer rather than winter, with deluges of precipitation that make British winters look like gentle sprinkles.

Luckily the clouds subsided by 1pm. With nothing to obstruct the sun, summer rays seared the puddles, causing steam to writhe up through humid air. The temperature quickly soared above 30°C. The air felt like a sauna; walking at a leisurely stride became uncomfortable. I couldn't imagine playing football in this weather for 90 minutes.

Busan's starting line-up was announced on the stadium screen. As usual, there was significant turnover from the previous match, despite a league break for the league all-star game. The two teens who debuted last match were absent. Peripheral striker Kim Chang-oh, who hadn't dressed in almost four months, sat excitedly on the bench.

Intriguingly, Shim Jae-won – who I assumed was the anonymous critic of Porterfield in the news article, complaining about being benched for speaking his mind – was in his kit for the first time in several matches.

I was resisting the urge to assume today would result in eight consecutive matches without a win for beleaguered Busan I'cons. Ulsan were a foreboding opponent. Bankrolled by Hyundai Heavy Industries – one of Korea's wealthiest conglomerate giants – Ulsan's squad was one of the most expensive in the K League. In second place – a whopping ten points ahead of third-place Anyang – Ulsan was nipping at the heels of league-leaders Seongnam.

Today was not the likeliest of fixtures for Busan to finally conquer a mounting winless streak.

Kick-off. Thirty minutes in, Andy Cooke breaks toward goal. Ulsan's ponytailed goalkeeper charges aggressively at him. Realising Cookie will reach a crossed ball before he does, the goalkeeper attempts to discombobulate the English striker by waving his arms. However, Cookie is an old hand at foiling such chicanery; he jumps into the air, gently taps the high ball downward toward ground, and watches as it falls below the custodian and bounces into Ulsan's goal.

1-0 Busan. Fireworks roar toward the white roof of the Busan Asiad Stadium, filling the venue's partly confined air with white smoke. Uncharacteristically, the Pride of Pusan members refrain from performing the silly bowing dance as celebration. Muted applause is their terse response.

For what should be a local derby, this match lacks any semblance of passion from the supporters. In the rest of the world, a game between two neighbouring clubs would be a fierce rivalry. Yet this Busan–Ulsan match has less 'heat' than an average league game.

After asking around about this, I'm startled by the answer. Not only were Busan and Ulsan not considered derby rivals – their supporters actually had a friendly relationship and even occasionally collaborated. The two groups shared possession of an anti-Suwon banner, and often drank together after matches.

A bit of passion makes derbies the most memorable of matches, but drinking beverages together is surely preferable to smashing bottles over each other's skulls.

It's the 39th minute. Busan midfielder Kim Tae-min – being utilised as a striker – takes possession in Ulsan's half. A composed cross meets Jamie Cureton at the left side of goal, who heads the ball downward and across to the right goalpost. Ulsan's ponytailed goalkeeper, having committed to the left post, remains stranded as the ball bounces into goal.

2-0 Busan. Cureton leaps into the air in celebration, finally scoring his second goal for the club. The Pride of Pusan's punitive reticence begins to crack: one waves a sign, another a scarf, while a third throws shredded newspaper confetti into the air. Up by a two-goal margin over a vastly superior opponent, even the most bull-headed supporters are dragged into the silly bowing dance, betraying their cool by revealing grins and – shock, horror – perhaps even revelling in a modicum of joy.

What is happening!

Cureton looks relieved. After scoring on his Busan debut, the diminutive Englishman went four matches without a goal. Although it's normal to expect an incoming player to take time before settling, manager Ian Porterfield publicly announced that he expected a plenitude of goals from Cureton.

If eight years earlier you had suggested to Cureton that he would end up playing in South Korea, he likely would have thought you were deranged. As a promising youngster who turned down Alex Ferguson's approaches, Cureton assumed he was destined to play out his entire career in the Premier League. However, the combination of playing for a club destined for relegation and a lack of discipline as a youngster condemned the Bristolian to a career primarily in the lower divisions instead.

'I got in a fair bit of trouble when I was young,' Cureton told BBC Sport. 'In the '90s, there was a drinking culture and being a young lad you wanted to be in that.

'Sometimes I'd turn up at training in the same clothes as the night before. I wanted to be one of the boys, so sometimes I did stuff just to impress them.

'After every game I'd be out with friends and didn't concentrate on the football. I just turned up on the training ground and knew I could do the business.'

Cureton would later remark that if he had had someone like Ferguson to closely mentor him during his academy days –

specifically, watching out for him and injecting a bit of discipline into the wayward youngster – it might have improved his professionalism and helped him remain at the top of English football. Instead, at Norwich City, Cureton received a lack of off-pitch guidance. Largely left to his own devices, his unchecked youthful rebelliousness undermined any plans for a long run in the Premier League.

Rejecting Manchester United's contract offer not only meant waiving the opportunity to play for a huge club – perhaps more importantly, Cureton would never receive Ferguson's infamous 'hairdryer treatment', a brand of discipline the young Bristolian might have benefitted from.

But it wasn't indiscipline that would cause Cureton to leave England for North East Asia. Instead, it was other matters – personal matters – that made escaping to another continent enticing enough to seriously consider.

First, Cureton was going through a separation from his partner, the mother of his two young children.

'I was going through a relationship break-up at the time … it seemed an ideal time to get away,' Cureton told *QPRnet.*

Second, Cureton had been the victim of unfounded online libel several years earlier. When the striker left Bristol Rovers for Reading in 2000, Cureton was at the peak of his career and scoring plentifully. Gas fans were devastated by his departure – the modest transfer fee probably didn't help – and a small minority took to the internet to smear him. Their fabricated accusations were abominable: that Cureton had supposedly had relations with an underage girl and fled Bristol due to threats from the girl's family. The malicious rumour was completely false, but like most defamation, it had a serious impact on its intended victim. According to the *Reading Evening Post*, Cureton moved house due to the emotional ordeal.

'We can't go anywhere without people asking us if the rumours are true,' Cureton told the *Reading Chronicle*. 'It's unbelievable and I want it all to stop so that we can go back to living a normal life.

'Someone has put it on the internet and now everyone in Reading has started to believe it.'

After leaving Bristol Rovers for Reading, a small section of Gas fans would abuse him with the 'cheeky smile' chant whenever the two clubs met. Eventually knowledge of the chant spread and supporters of other clubs would taunt Cureton with it.

'I was going a bit crazy,' Cureton told the *TNC Podcast*. 'My head was a bit all over the shop.'

Considering his broken relationship and the slanderous abuse that stubbornly persisted – along with the Football League's financial chill that led to reduced contract offers in England – it's easy to understand why Cureton opted for a temporary move abroad.

'I was in a position where I wasn't in a great sort of space [regarding] family and football and stuff, so I thought, "Shall I just get away?"' Cureton told the *GasCast* podcast.

'I had three or four days at both clubs [Busan and D.C. United],' Cureton told *The Guardian*. 'Both contracts were on the table. I came home and … had offers to stay at Reading and in England, but because of what had happened with my family I didn't really think about it and just thought "let's get away" and chose South Korea.'

Busan's offer of a tax-free salary and signing-on bonus undoubtedly sweetened the deal.

'Money was a lot better than [in England] as well, and I thought, I'm in a situation where I'm probably going to need more money, you know, from having two kids to support,' Cureton told the *Back of the Net* online video channel.

'I said to my agent, "Let's just go for it,"' Cureton told the *Non League Nosh* podcast.

'It surprised everyone,' Cureton said to the *GasCast* podcast. 'My mum was upset, and I had two young kids at the time.'

'I just wanted to get out of [the UK],' Cureton told the *TNC Podcast*.

* * *

Jamie Cureton is hungry to score Busan's third. A perfect pass is gifted to him, but the referee whistles for offside. Half-time soon arrives.

Despite the lack of atmosphere in the stands, the match is scintillating entertainment. Ulsan are clearly the better team, creating the majority of shots on goal, but Busan pluckily eke out several chances. Cureton dramatically heads the ball off the post in the 53rd minute, while Cookie nearly scores on the rebound. Busan continue to push, attempting shot after shot against an increasingly rattled Ulsan.

Are Ian Porterfield's boys finally about to break their winless streak?

Cureton is fed the ball and manages to slot it into Ulsan's net – but the attempt is flagged for offside. Howls of indignation reverberate from the Pride of Pusan.

In the 83rd minute, Ulsan's Brazilian substitute Dodô scores. 2-1 Busan. The visiting supporters fervently wave a massive *Bandeira Auriverde*, the national flag of Brazil. In an instant, the semi-miraculous prospect of Busan ending their prolonged winless run against a league powerhouse dissipates into pessimism, a much more familiar sentiment. What seemed a padded, comfortable lead shrivels into an uncomfortably thin buffer. The Pride of Pusan members grow nervous, restless.

Are Busan about to squander a victory within the final ten minutes? Or even worse – lose?

An onslaught commences. Wave after wave of Ulsan attacks hammer Busan. Chucking away the win begins to feel inevitable. A few of the Pride of Pusan members cover their eyes in apprehension.

The clock reaches 90 minutes. Stoppage time begins.

Ulsan win a corner. Their ponytailed goalkeeper surges forward to assist. For them, a loss would mean much more than just the embarrassment of losing to lowly Busan – it would dent their league title aspirations. They only narrowly trail leaders Seongnam.

The corner is volleyed at goal, but Busan goalkeeper Kim Yong-dae parries the ball away. Again and again the ball falls to the feet of an Ulsan player, followed by a quick shot, a save, and another attempt. Observing this barrage is nerve-wracking for the Busan hardcore.

After enduring agony for what seems like perpetuity, the whistle sounds. The Ulsan players drop to the pitch like stones while their Busan counterparts leap into the air as if they have won a championship.

Busan's winless streak is finally vanquished! It's yet another victory against a superior opponent, marking a home double against Ulsan. Today was also the first instance of Busan beating the same team twice this season – after all, it was only their sixth win of the year, despite now being in the latter half of the season. How odd that Busan obtained most of their wins against strong adversaries, while struggling against the league's minnows. Was Porterfield failing to rouse his squad for smaller encounters, or were the league's goliaths not taking Busan seriously enough? The team would face newcomers Daegu on Saturday, which should help settle the question.

With the rare win, I decided to make an even rarer venture down on to the pitch after the match. The players were warming down with coach Drew Jarvie. I noticed Ian Porterfield looking at me, but he was uncharacteristically holding back from talking.

'Nice result,' I said to him.

He returned my gaze with great intensity. Instead of responding with a commensurate thank you or polite greeting, he became unfriendly.

'My daughter has informed me that someone is attacking me online, posting libel about me on an internet message board,' he said. 'I'll be contacting my legal advisers if I can find out who it is.'

Months earlier, I had created an English-language forum for Busan fans to discuss club matters. As it was the only such place on the internet to discuss Korean football in English, K League fans from across the country congregated there. A Scottish expat based in Seoul posted several unsavoury quips about Porterfield, which had come to his attention. His hostility suggested that he assumed the perpetrator was me.

It was quite the assumption, given that the message board had more than 80 registered users at the time.

He abruptly began talking about his most recent divorce, referring to some of the unflattering comments that were posted online, 'Okay, it was a bad period in my life, but I moved on.'

Although Porterfield kept his composure, he was visibly upset as he defended himself against the online gossip. He remarked that he had feared for his life during his previous posting in Ghana, claiming that people were out to kill him and that he resorted to securing police protection.

It was a deer-in-headlights moment for me – not just because he quickly became talkative again, but also due to my unfamiliarity with the accusations he was referring to.

As I struggled to make sense of what he was saying, the topic quickly shifted to his previous battles with alcoholism. He was gradually becoming riled up, so I felt it necessary to step in to assuage his assumptions.

'It wasn't me posting those comments online,' I said.

He continued rambling, but less than a minute later he was visibly calmer, soon becoming his usual jolly self. He continued to talk my ear off, much like I expect he did during his successful job interview some nine months prior. It was half socialising, half sales pitch, and came completely naturally to him.

Just then, Busan's trio of recent imports walked by. Hjelde gave me a hefty pat on the back with his bear-like hands, while Curo shot the same cheeky grin he flashed at me before the showdown meeting just one month earlier. Cookie didn't make eye contact, instead sporting a downward scowl as he passed. I wondered if it was due to the high boot to the face he endured late in the game, or whether it had to do with him removing his boots almost immediately after the match.

Porterfield gave a broad smile to the three players as they went by, then quickly returned to delivering his monologue to me. He mentioned that coach Choi Man-hee, the most senior of the Koreans on his coaching staff, had been moved 'upstairs' to work on securing a new, football-specific stadium for the club.

This flabbergasted me, for two reasons. First, Busan I'cons had only been playing in this monstrosity of a venue for less than half of a year, yet the club was already planning to leave. It cost the government a mere £157m (or almost £258m in 2020 after inflation) to construct it, yet it was already being written off as impractical by its sole tenant.

Then consider that such an exorbitant cost covered just one of ten new Korean stadiums constructed for the month-long party known as the 2002 World Cup, and you begin to appreciate just how absurd this stadium's creation – not to mention co-hosting the FIFA tournament – truly was.

The second thing that struck me was how quickly Porterfield's most senior Korean coach had left for a completely unrelated role at the club. I immediately thought of Stan Ternent, who described serving as a coach for Ian Porterfield at Chelsea as a 'living hell'.

'Working for [Porterfield], for me, was one of the worst experiences imaginable in football,' Ternent wrote in his autobiography, *Stan the Man: A Hard Life in Football.* Ternent dedicated an entire chapter of the book to his stint working under Porterfield, delicately titled 'I Dreamed of Killing Him'.

According to Ternent, Porterfield rarely discussed tactics with him, frequently ignored his suggestions, and regularly undermined him in front of the Chelsea playing squad.

'… Porterfield had made it clear to me he wouldn't piss in my mouth if my teeth were on fire,' wrote Ternent. 'I regarded Porterfield as a waste of space.'

Had coach Choi Man-hee been subjected to similar treatment? And what about Aberdeen legend Drew Jarvie, the elder Scot currently serving as Porterfield's number two?

Porterfield continued to talk my ear off. He still didn't seem acclimatised to the Korean summer, towelling sweat off his forehead every 30 seconds.

'Hot enough for you?' I quipped, trying to interrupt his stream-of-consciousness barrage before he could launch into the next topic, hoping to glean a concluding smile from him before ending the conversation. No chance. My comment didn't even register. He was immediately on to the next topic, continuing to yap my ear off. I wasn't sure whether he enjoyed the sound of his own voice and didn't realise how one-sided this conversation was, or if this was a deliberate attempt to win me onside and disarm me from being a future antagonist against him.

Porterfield then claimed he had improved every team he had ever been involved with, which even I knew was a rather selective reading of his career history.

My greatest impression from our conversation was that Porterfield was a psychologically wounded man. While he was naturally gregarious, he seemed to drag around a tremendous amount of unresolved emotional baggage, and was quick to be set off. That he felt the need to verbally defend himself to a near-stranger unprompted was incredibly odd.

I could sense that Porterfield's journeyman career and the myriad employers he came to depend upon had made him vulnerable, almost to the point of neurosis and paranoia. While he was still chatty and amicable with strangers, he was quick to talk himself up, as if afraid that people would naturally form opinions against him.

Rather than feeling antagonised by the encounter, I actually pitied Porterfield. Clearly he loved the game of football – you could see the sparkle in his eyes when he discussed it. But one unfortunate aspect of football management was dealing with the drama of autocratic bosses, insolent players, insatiable supporters and hostile news media. Perhaps he never quite figured out how handle it all.

Here was a man who had been crossed and betrayed on numerous occasions, who would quickly put up defences – if not engage in barely contained hostility – when faced with any sort of opposition. Maybe that's why Porterfield froze out one of his Busan players for speaking up – the same action he himself once fell victim to as a player.

Porterfield's new translator approached, clipboard in hand, and read off the day's K League scores. Gwangju lost, meaning Busan had leapfrogged them into ninth place, albeit only on goal difference. As a reward for defeating mighty Ulsan, the players were heading off to a celebratory shindig tonight, Porterfield mentioned before heading back to the dressing room.

Again, I couldn't help but notice the parallels to Porterfield's time at Chelsea, where players would imbibe at the pub after matches. Busan had troubles motivating themselves for games against weaker K League opponents, yet the players were off to 'celebrate' less than 72 hours ahead of a match against lowly Daegu.

After two previous encounters, Busan had yet to win against newcomers Daegu, earning only one point from a possible six. Finally slaying Busan's seven-match winless streak today would keep the vultures at bay, but what would a third failure to win against feeble Daegu do to Porterfield's reputation?

Was today's victory simply a lucky break, or the sign of a change in fortunes for hapless Busan?

Much would be at stake on Saturday.

ROUND 27

Busan	**2-1**	**Ulsan**
Anyang	1-2	Daejeon
Jeonnam	0-0	Suwon
Jeonbuk	0-1	Seongnam
Pohang	1-0	Gwangju
Bucheon	0-0	Daegu

K LEAGUE TABLE

Seongnam	58
Ulsan	51
Anyang	41
Suwon	41
Daejeon	41
Pohang	40
Jeonnam	39
Jeonbuk	38
Busan	**25**
Gwangju	25
Daegu	19
Bucheon	11

CHAPTER 22

DOG INJURES PLAYER (OR, PREGNANCIES APLENTY)

BUSAN I'CONS VS. DAEGU FC
SATURDAY, 23 AUGUST 2003
K LEAGUE ROUND 28
BUSAN ASIAD WORLD CUP STADIUM
백지장도 맞들면 낫다
*– Many hands make light work; two heads are better
than one (literally, 'it is better to work together, even
when merely lifting a sheet of paper')*

'DOG INJURES Footballer at Anyang Match.'

Long before the era of online clickbait, such an outlandish headline was sufficient to earn my attention.

At Anyang's midweek match, the half-time show consisted of several dogs performing tricks, such as walking erect on their hind legs and fetching objects. Not exactly scintillating entertainment at an initial glance, but the largest dog unexpectedly collided with a substitute player who was warming up. The sheepdog had been tossed a Frisbee by its handler and rushed forward at full gallop in chase, craning its neck upward to watch the disc descend. It had no idea it was rushing directly toward an oncoming footballer, who was also unaware of his surroundings as he chased a football.

Thwack.

The pair collided at high speed, cartwheeled over each other, and collapsed in a heap. Neither moved for several seconds. The dog began to stir, but the footballer remained motionless for what felt

215

like minutes. He was eventually roused but remained on his backside and held his ankle with an expression of agony, as if fishing for a penalty from a dupable match official.

The substitute eventually walked away from the incident, and should consider himself lucky. A similar incident occurred in England back in 1970, in which a terrier ran on to the pitch during a match and collided with Brentford goalkeeper Chic Brodie. Although the dog appeared relatively small, it crashed directly into Brodie's left knee, damaging ligaments and effectively ending his professional career.

Tonight offered an evening K League contest between Busan I'cons and Daegu FC. It would be an intriguing test of Porterfield's ability to motivate his squad against a lacklustre opponent. After four matches, Busan still hadn't eked out a win against the league's two newcomers, Daegu (today's opponent) and Gwangju.

Today's fixture would serve as a consequential fork in the road for Busan's turbulent 2003 season. A loss for Busan would mean becoming the first team to lose twice to Daegu, while a win would mark the first instance this season of consecutive victories for Busan and an opportunity for Porterfield to stave off increasingly vocal criticism.

Busan start ferociously, creating numerous chances. Jamie Cureton, fresh off of scoring in an upset win over a larger opponent, shows signs of confidence. As he approaches the Daegu back-line, he attempts to nutmeg Daegu's Brazilian defender, Rogerio Prateat, but fails to slot the ball through the tall player's legs. Howls of derision emit from the Pride of Pusan. The supporters kick the empty chairs in front of them in frustration, letting off a few choice expletives. If there was any question whether a single win over Ulsan would satiate the Busan supporters, there was our answer.

The referee whistles for half-time, the match in a scoreless deadlock. Although not being able to score against woeful Daegu is demoralising, Busan are creating opportunities and a rare feeling of optimism permeates into the break. Perhaps most noticeable to fans masochistic enough to endure a season of Busan I'cons matches is that they're finally winning headers. Although the K League wasn't an overly physical competition during this era, Busan players had been particularly hesitant to fully commit to hard challenges. No more. They are now winning almost three-quarters of contested headers. Was this thanks to Ian Porterfield's coaching?

The second half begins. Shim Jae-won – likely the anonymous player who criticised Porterfield in the news media – steps foot on the pitch for the first time in almost six weeks.

Cookie finds himself with another scoring opportunity, but he attempts to take on several defenders and is stripped of possession. Porterfield had signed Cooke primarily to supply the ball to Cureton, but that partnership was not materialising. Both players were resorting to mounting attacks on their own. Was Porterfield pleased with Cookie for showing more goalscoring prowess than expected, or frustrated that Cureton wasn't getting enough possession from him?

That morning I was surprised by player movement news. First, former Barcelona winger and Olympic gold medallist Emmanuel Amunike, who was attempting to rehabilitate several serious injuries in the hope of being offered a playing contract by Busan, had decided to leave the club. This was likely due to the arrival of Cureton, Cooke and Hjelde maxing out the club's foreign player spots.

But the real bombshell was translator Leo Mendoza revealing that Colombian striker Harry Castillo was still under contract with Busan. Porterfield had stated at the 'showdown' meeting with supporters last month that Harry's contract had been terminated, but Mendoza now claimed that the player's contract was still valid through December.

Mendoza also denied Porterfield's earlier assertion that Harry displayed behavioural problems, referring to the claim as 'a lie'. Mendoza wrote that Porterfield had been telling various people, including the news media, about Harry's supposed behavioural problems, which caused Harry to opt to sit out the remainder of the K League season and return to Colombia, with the objective of moving to a different K League club during the close season.

Although it's difficult to know what the truth was, that Porterfield would get into a public slanging match against one of his foreign players and then be criticised publicly in the media allegedly by his domestic players suggested the Scot might not enjoy a long tenure at the Korean club.

78th minute. A long ball is heaved up the pitch and eventually settles at the feet of Cureton. Rather than his normal tactic of going for goal himself, he makes the unusual decision to assist someone else. Cureton looks across the pitch and sees two attacking team-mates: young striker Ahn Hyo-yeon and Cookie. He crosses the ball. It's not the best of passes – the ball looks as if it will fall short of Cookie and instead be intercepted by a pair of Daegu defenders. But young Ahn rushes forward, leaps into the air above his opponents, and flicks the ball toward Cookie.

A third Daegu defender rushes in. It looks like Cookie's pending effort will be contained, but the tall Englishman casually brushes the ball slightly to the right, then takes a stiff shot at goal. By this point the Daegu goalkeeper is also charging down upon Cookie. But the ball's trajectory is perfectly angled, sailing through the narrow gap between the third defender and the approaching goalkeeper. Daegu's net rustles.

1-0 Busan.

Keeping with his strong but unassuming nature, Cookie's celebration is muted despite the vast importance of his goal. He jogs toward the Pride of Pusan and simply raises his right index finger in celebration. His team-mates are much more expressive with their joy: veteran Noh Jung-yoon and Cureton embrace Cookie in celebration. Noh turns to the supporters, who are already bouncing with far more delight than usual, and motions with his hands for them to be even louder.

The goal is Cookie's fourth in six games. Not bad for a guy who was signed to essentially serve as a big brute to win the ball and supply it to someone else.

After severing his playing contract early with Stoke City, Cooke became a free man that summer, entertaining offers from prospective clubs.

Ultimately he chose to join Busan – but why?

Appearing on the *V2 Football Podcast* in 2014, Cooke said that he relished the challenge of such an unusual move. He had travelled to Korea to check out the club, and while there, decided to 'just pack up and go.' It was one year after the 2002 World Cup, which South Korea co-hosted.

'I took the opportunity after the World Cup. It was a big thing out in Korea, football was massive … and the stadiums, absolutely incredible.'

Cooke also explained to the Stoke City-themed *Wizards of Drivel* podcast why he decided to take the plunge on an uncommon offer from Asia.

'I was attracted to Busan ... there were other things I wanted to do in England, but I think I fancied a go at it,' Cooke said. 'It was ... a chance of a lifetime, I just thought I would give it a go, basically. And that's how it came about. And at the time, it was just too good to turn down. These opportunities didn't come around very often. I wasn't getting any younger, even though I still had plenty of prospects in England or anywhere else, but I just fancied a go at it, and that's how it came about.'

While Cooke's decision to voluntarily terminate his Stoke contract made sense from the perspective of wanting to play rather than sit on the bench, to the neutral observer his timing perhaps bordered on recklessness. English football was in the midst of financial panic due to the early collapse of ITV Digital. The nascent television channel had purchased broadcast rights to the Football League for an exorbitant sum, and many clubs responded by immediately spending the expected revenue windfall on players – before most of the cash had actually materialised. Then the TV channel collapsed, leaving clubs in a dire budgetary situation. Sixteen particularly profligate clubs entered administration less than a year after the channel's demise. Many were ruthless in cutting costs by refusing to extend player contracts and opting not to fill squad vacancies.

Needless to say, Cooke was fortunate that Ian Porterfield offered him an unexpected and highly lucrative contract in South Korea.

At Busan, the English striker was perhaps earning the highest salary of his career. It was a remarkable contrast from his early days as a footballer.

After youth apprenticeships at Shrewsbury Town and Telford United, Cooke moved to League of Wales side Newtown, where the wages were so modest he accepted a side job as an agricultural labourer building cowsheds and pouring concrete.

'It was hard work and boring as hell,' Cooke told the *Lancashire Evening Telegraph*. As the newspaper paraphrased the experience, 'The pay was a pittance, the hours were torturing, and the work was exhausting.'

Ascending from cowshed builder to professional footballer was quite the jump, although another foreigner who once graced the K League had an even more impressive tale of rags to riches. Brazilian striker Edinaldo Batista Libânio, commonly known as

Grafite, grew up in a poor household in rural São Paulo state, selling bin liners door to door as his first source of income. His first overseas football stint was with South Korea's Anyang Cheetahs in 2003, where after nine games without a goal, the striker was released mid-season.

But four years later Grafite signed a multi-year contract with German club Wolfsburg, where he scored a hat-trick during his UEFA Champions League debut. He even made a brief appearance for Brazil at the 2010 World Cup.

Evidently all Cookie had to do if he wished to suit up for the Three Lions on the world's grandest stage was to stop scoring in the K League.

After toiling away in Wales, followed by eight years as a pro in England, Cookie took the unconventional career step of accepting a playing stint in South Korea. He was 29 years old and married – and his wife Kate was pregnant.

'Through my career, the biggest decision I had to make was when I left Stoke City and then went to play in the K League in Korea,' Cooke later said in a 2008 interview. 'That was a massive decision as my wife was pregnant at the time. It was a great experience but you do have to think about family things.'

Unlike Hjelde's partner, who remained in the UK until her baby was delivered as she was already in the third trimester of her pregnancy when Hjelde signed with Busan, Cookie's wife was only in her first trimester. Still able to fly, she immediately accompanied him for their new life in Busan, despite expecting a baby.

What effect would family life have on Cooke's longevity in South Korea?

I also wondered how Cooke would get on with Porterfield. Earlier that year, just months prior to Cookie signing for Porterfield's Busan I'cons, Stan Ternent released his autobiography, which included a scathing chapter about working under Ian Porterfield. Cooke thought highly of Ternent, later referring to him as the best manager he ever played for. Had Cookie read Ternent's autobiography during the first half of 2003, prior to signing for Busan, it's possible he would have had strong concerns about playing under Porterfield and signing for Busan.

But while Porterfield already had public differences with Colombian striker Harry as well as several of his domestic Korean players, thus far there were no signs of strife between the Scottish manager and his trio of imports from English football.

The referee purses his lips around his whistle and blows, signalling full time. Busan squeak out a 1-0 home win over lowly Daegu, marking Busan's first consecutive wins of the 2003 K League season. Porterfield looks ecstatic. The players celebrate. Even the Pride of Pusan members appear awfully happy. It's an ephemeral moment to forget about the significant struggles and embrace optimism for the future.

Unexpectedly, a celebratory cake appeared in the stands. Two of the Pride of Pusan members were about to embark on their mandatory national military service, preventing them from attending Busan matches for the better part of two years.

My eyes scanned the faces within the group. Most members were young, with only two appearing to be older than early 20s. I couldn't help but wonder: was this, in all likelihood, the last Busan match for these two?

Judging by the lack of older faces, I had my doubts whether they would return. Careers in the cut-throat Korean corporate world would beckon, as would potential suitors and the prospect of raising a family.

This season had seen no shortage of drama – particularly off-pitch – at hapless Busan I'cons, involving management, players and fans alike. But this weekend I became aware of yet another angle in this grand sphere of strife: friction between the club and Busan Asiad Stadium management.

Colombian translator Leo Mendoza framed the issue succinctly, alleging that:

'What the stadium officials said:
- you can use Asiad Stadium for free;
- we'll promote the team;
- we'll sponsor your shirt;
- if you don't like Asiad, you can go back to Gudeok Stadium.

'What the stadium officials did:
- forced the club to pay extravagant fees for Asiad rental;
- completely ignored and avoided city-sponsored publicity;

- after the shirts were printed with the City of Busan sponsorship logo, refused to provide any money, instead offering a "discount" on the stadium rental;
- when the club suggested it would move back to Gudeok Stadium due to poor attendance, city council threatened lawsuits and retribution.

'End result:
- the club gave valuable shirt advertising to the city's "Dynamic Busan" campaign, and in return received absolutely nothing.'

An article in the *Kookje Shinmun* explained that while K League clubs such as Daejeon and Daegu received significant cooperation from their respective city governments, Busan I'cons had no such luck. For example, while one particular club only had to pay a paltry fee of £2,800 to use a World Cup stadium for an entire season, Busan I'cons had to fork over more than £275,000 to use Asiad Stadium, as well as pay more than £54,000 for pitch maintenance.

Despite such exorbitant rental costs, Asiad Stadium officials also restricted the amount of time Busan I'cons could use the field. When the club wanted to employ the pitch for a 90-minute practice prior to playing a friendly in Hong Kong against Kuwait's national team, stadium officials reportedly refused, citing the need to 'protect the pitch'. But when the Korean national Olympic team requested permission to utilise the same venue for three days of practice, the officials supposedly accepted without hesitation, according to the newspaper.

In summary: not only were Busan I'cons restricted by a meagre playing budget and suffering from minimal attendance, but so too were they having to battle with city government over their playing venue and promised sponsorship.

Meanwhile, the 2003 Summer Universiade – an international sporting event similar to the Olympics but only involving student athletes – had begun in Daegu. North Korea's participation would test some awkward taboos between it and the South, the host of the tournament. While the sporting events were unfolding well, politics flared between the two Korean states.

Several buses of North Korean archers and cheerleaders witnessed a shocking and unacceptable sight: four roadside banners created by the villagers of Yecheon County that welcomed North Korea's Universiade delegation to the South. According to the *Chosun Ilbo* and *JoongAng Daily*, the banners contained images of North Korean leader Kim Jong-il shaking hands with South Korean president Kim Dae-jung in 2000. One stated, 'We welcome you, North Korean athlete corps, with brotherly love.' Another displayed the unified Korea flag.

It turned out the rural residents of Yecheon were not well versed in the correct protocol for displaying images of North Korea's venerable leader. The banners were hung too low to the ground. They were left uncovered, risking a battering from the elements. They were placed too close to a scarecrow. And the images of the Northern leader had a seal stamped on them.

The North Koreans were outraged, and forced the South Korean bus drivers to stop – with one group apparently stepping on a driver's brake foot. They leaped off the buses and raced back to the four banners, removing and folding them impeccably, all the while crying and howling uncontrollably.

'The North Korean supporters were wailing loudly as they got on the bus, like women who had just lost their husbands,' a South Korean police officer told the *Chosun Ilbo*. 'People who were at the scene were saying that it was beyond their comprehension, and some even said it gave them the chills.'

ROUND 28

Busan **1-0** **Daegu**
Ulsan 2-1 Anyang
Gwangju 2-1 Bucheon
Daejeon 3-3 Jeonnam
[Seongnam vs. Pohang postponed due to inclement weather]
[Suwon vs. Jeonbuk postponed due to inclement weather]

K LEAGUE TABLE
Seongnam 58
Ulsan 54
Daejeon 42
Anyang 41
Suwon 41
Jeonnam 40
Pohang 40
Jeonbuk 38
Busan **28**
Gwangju 28
Daegu 19
Bucheon 11

Daewoo employees and their supporters clash with riot police during months of violent protests in early 2001. The Asian financial crisis led to the collapse of Daewoo, which had previously bankrolled Busan's football club. (Chung Sung-Jun/Getty Images)

2002 World Cup co-hosts South Korea celebrate after defeating Spain and advancing to the semi-finals, a fairy-tale run that included wins over Poland, Portugal and Italy. The Asian country had not previously won a single game at a World Cup. (Shaun Botterill/Getty Images)

Busan I'cons moved to Asiad Stadium ahead of the 2003 K League season. Like most new South Korean venues built for the 2002 World Cup, it was too large for club football. (Emmanuel Dunand/Getty Images)

Ian Porterfield (left) holds the FA Cup after scoring the only goal in Sunderland's 1973 victory over Leeds United at Wembley. The Second Division club's feat is considered one of the great upsets in the competition's history. (Bob Thomas/Getty Images)

Porterfield turned to football management after retiring, which culminated in his appointment at Chelsea of the Premier League. He then took charge of various teams overseas, including in Africa and the Middle East, before accepting a position in South Korea. (MirrorPix/Alamy)

Jamie Cureton celebrates in April 2002 after scoring the goal that promoted Reading to the second tier of English football. Cureton began his career in the Premier League with Norwich City, followed by successful spells at Bristol Rovers and Reading. (Chris Lobina/Getty)

Defender Jon Olav Hjelde helped Norwegian minnows Rosenborg win away to AC Milan and draw against Juventus in the 1996/97 UEFA Champions League. He was then plucked into English football by Nottingham Forest. (Tom Honan/PA Images)

Stoke City striker Andy Cooke (right arm raised) celebrates promotion after play-off victory in May 2002. Cooke began his career balancing semi-pro Welsh football with building cowsheds, before a dream move to Burnley. (Neal Simpson/PA Images)

One of Ian Porterfield's signing targets at Busan was Emmanuel Amunike, a former Barcelona winger and African Footballer of the Year who scored the winning goals at both the 1994 Africa Cup of Nations and 1996 Summer Olympics finals. (Bob Thomas/ Getty Images)

Ian Porterfield leads the Busan I'cons squad in a training session before the start of the 2003 K League season. The former Asian club champions finished the previous season second-bottom, an all-time low for the club. (Busan Ilbo)

Midfielder Noh Jung-yoon, who featured in both the 1994 and 1998 World Cups for South Korea, returned from Japan to captain Busan. (Busan Ilbo)

Andy Cooke thwarts the challenge of two Daejeon Citizen opponents. Would the former Burnley and Stoke City striker find success as a target player in South Korea? (Busan Ilbo)

At the start of the season, Busan featured four international players from Serbia and Colombia: (from left) Zoran Urumov, Tommy Mosquera, Dušan Šimić and Harry Castillo. However, manager Ian Porterfield had plans to import replacements from British football. (Busan Ilbo)

Cureton, a former England youth international, once turned down Alex Ferguson's offer to play for Manchester United's Class of 92. Would the Bristolian set the K League alight as a poaching striker? (Busan Ilbo)

(From left) Ian Porterfield, Jon Olav Hjelde and Andy Cooke share a smile, shortly after the pair of players from British football had arrived in South Korea.

Several Busan I'cons supporters hold scarves aloft as they chant club songs during a K League match.

A senior member of the Pride of Pusan, the most ardent supporters of Busan I'cons, holds a lit flare. Such pyrotechnics were technically illegal but would often be seen at football stadiums.

The Busan I'cons team bus is covered with graffiti, as administered by Pride of Pusan members. Ardent football fans are often asked to 'tag' the bus of their K League club, a behaviour unique to the Land of the Morning Calm. (FreeImages.com/Wonho Lee)

K League behemoths Busan Daewoo Royals changed their identity to become the Busan I'cons ahead of the 2000 season, due to being taken over by Hyundai Development Company.

Gwangju Sangmu supporter banners glow under daylight at the Gwangju World Cup Stadium, renamed the Guus Hiddink Stadium after South Korea knocked Spain out of the 2002 World Cup quarter-finals at the venue.

Author Devon Rowcliffe poses with an assortment of K League replica shirts and scarves, as well as the South Korean national flag.

Beondegi, *or silkworm pupae, is a common South Korean street food, marinated in sweet soy sauce and served in paper cups with a toothpick skewer. (Unsplash/Aigerim Kalysheva @sensotape)*

Large bronze bells, housed in ornately painted stone pavilions, can be found throughout South Korea. (Unsplash/Drew Graham@dizzyd718)

The Gwangandaegyo, or Diamond Bridge, opened just prior to the 2003 K League season, and has become synonymous with Busan's ocean views and sandy beaches. (Unsplash/Christopher Lee @chris267)

CHAPTER 23

BIG BUGS AND BODYGUARDS (OR, UNINTERESTED CLUB OWNERS)

BUSAN I'CONS VS. SEONGNAM ILHWA
CHUNMA (PEGASUS)
WEDNESDAY, 27 AUGUST 2003
K LEAGUE ROUND 12 (RESCHEDULED)
BUSAN ASIAD WORLD CUP STADIUM

JEONBUK HYUNDAI MOTORS VS.
BUSAN I'CONS
SUNDAY, 31 AUGUST 2003
K LEAGUE ROUND 29
JEONJU WORLD CUP STADIUM (A.K.A.
FORT JEONJU)

어떤 매미 한 마리가 거미줄에 걸려 처량한 소리를 지르길래 내가
듣다 못하여 매미를 날아가도록 풀어 주었다·
*'A cicada became ensnared within a spider's web and
cried out in distress; so unbearable was the noise that
I helped the cicada escape and fly away.'*
– Yi Gyu-bo, poet, 1168–1241 CE (Goryeo Dynasty)

SOUTH KOREAN summers pulse with vitality. Busan's typically temperate weather succumbs to semi-tropical swelter. With the increase in humidity, the climate becomes viscid, assuming an uncomfortably gummy quality.

The air is palpable, brewing dense monsoon rains and calamitous typhoons.

But perhaps the most vivid stimulus of Korean summers is an incessant background din.

Beside the concrete footpath, compacted dirt was pockmarked with a series of tiny holes. These were successful escape routes, from which small creatures arose from the earth to make their brief yet triumphant finale.

I looked up and noticed one on the trunk of a tree, mid-metamorphosis. Its exoskeleton was tearing apart, the back splitting open from the middle. Gradually the fully mature adult emerged, erecting itself to fill its new outer casing and wings with fluids before hardening. Rather than a scene from the movie *Alien*, this was an annual activity on the Korean peninsula: the moulting of cicadas, an insect the size of a small bird.

Although cicada nymphs that crawl out of the soil are silent, mature males found in Korea are equipped with sound-producing organs capable of reaching 75 decibels – louder than a television or vacuum cleaner. So harsh is their noise the cicadas temporarily disable their own hearing organs while generating a mating call.

Imagine a tree teeming with dozens of these noisy creatures, and the resulting cacophony can be loud enough to keep people awake at night. A summer stroll in Korea often carries the ambient drone of hundreds of buzzing cicadas.

Busan I'cons striker Jamie Cureton – now sporting a flamboyant, bleach-blond hairstyle – sat quietly in the bowels of Asiad Stadium preparing for today's match. Cureton had typically been one of the more convivial characters at the English clubs he had played for, joking around with other players and often providing music in the dressing room.

The language barrier as an Englishman in South Korea, however, was preventing Cureton from integrating with the squad, leaving him feeling isolated from the domestic players. Rather than being his usual extroverted and unrestrained self, Curo was mostly segregated and silent.

The Korean cicada's summer migration from the soil to the tree canopy transforms it into a voluble and social creature, and gifts it the ability of flight. Cureton's July move to South Korea had the opposite effect: gagging his voice, minimising his interaction, clipping his wings. It was an emasculating experience for a person so familiar with the limelight.

Still only one month into his K League stint, Curo would have to soldier on.

Busan were due to host Seongnam tonight. The league leaders were on impeccable form, winning their last five games. After capturing the K League title in 2001 and 2002, the northern club sought a third consecutive championship, which would equal the previous league record – also held by Seongnam.

Seongnam striker Kim Do-hoon had something to prove as well, the final player passed over by manager Guus Hiddink for South Korea's 23-member squad at the 2002 World Cup. Kim was now challenging for the 2003 K League golden boot, having already won it three years earlier.

Even worse, Busan would be without the suspended Cookie (one match for yellow card accumulation) as well as defender Jon Hjelde, who had temporarily returned to England for the birth of his first child. But in Busan's favour, they had just won consecutive matches for the first time this season.

Would the league behemoths make easy work of Ian Porterfield's ragtag team, or would Busan's recent success and tendency to over-perform against strong opponents allow the underdogs to prevail?

I hopped on the shuttle bus to Asiad Stadium offered by the club. Turning back after taking a seat, I noticed I was the only passenger.

Although Busan recently lowered the price of match tickets, the club was still resorting to additional discounts to boost attendance. Despite hosting the league's strongest club today, Busan decided to let punters in for only ₩1,000 (just over 50 pence) if they wore a red shirt. But would the rain foil this admission promotion?

Busan's starting line-up was displayed on the gigantic stadium screen. Cureton would start up front. Joining him would be striker Kim Chang-oh, who once had a brief stint at Antwerp in Belgium's Jupiler League but hadn't started a match for Busan in the last five months. There was also the usual shuffling of players, as well as one new face on the bench.

Early in the match, Serbian midfielder Šimić earns two yellow cards and is sent off. Busan find themselves down a man against in-form league leaders Seongnam.

Just moments before half-time, a handful of Seongnam away supporters – the Yellow Revolution Unity – finally arrive. By the day's end they'll have spent more than ten hours travelling across the country in the rain, to witness barely 45 minutes of football. They unfurl and hang a vast array of banners, several times as many as there are actual Seongnam fans. One features a portrait of Argentine Marxist revolutionary Che Guevara, an image that rarely musters any reaction in South Korea despite the country's strict National Security Act meant to prevent the spread of communism. It proclaims in English:

This Is Message
From Y.R.U!
Shout And Be Crazy
12th Players

Although the small collection of Seongnam fans are relatively quiet, they admittedly make more noise than the sex dolls that another K League club would mistakenly deploy in the stands in early 2020 during the COVID-19 pandemic lockdown, leading to overwhelming international media coverage and a fine from the league.

The half finishes 0-0, a good result for Busan. But without Cookie's presence, Busan are edentulous. Prospects appear bleak for anything other than a thumping in the second half.

Just eight minutes after the break, Seongnam score. Newly naturalised Denis Laktionov, now under the Korean name Lee Seongnam, launches the ball into the upper-right of goal, narrowly above the extended reach of lanky Busan goalkeeper Kim Yong-dae.

Busan obstinately hang on, restricting Seongnam to the 1-0 lead for most of the second half. But toward the end, Busan collapse. Two Seongnam defenders score within three minutes: another goal in the top corner, followed by an unlucky deflection that pinballs in. And just to remind Busan who the big boys are, golden boot contender Kim Do-hoon scores a fourth goal for Seongnam in stoppage time while on his backside.

Busan did try, but without an in-form striker to ping it home, Seongnam rarely looked perturbed. Worryingly, there were no signs of the quality Busan side that defeated Daegu just four days earlier. Jamie Cureton still appeared to be in a goalscoring funk.

At full time, several Pride of Pusan members moaned about Porterfield's managerial decisions. The Scot utilised only one of his three substitutions despite playing with ten men for most of the match. Even injury-challenged veteran Noh Jung-yoon, who rarely plays a full game, was uncharitably left on for the entire match.

The 4-0 thumping impaired Busan's goal difference, dragging them back down to third-bottom in the league table, below military side Gwangju. The attendance was even more dire: 1,047, a new season low for the entire K League.

* * *

코방귀만 뀐다
– To treat with disdain; to turn one's nose up
(literally, 'to fart from one's nose')

Andy Cooke was still in the honeymoon phase as an overseas footballer, and he relished visiting the impressive new World Cup stadiums during K League away matches. He spoke with the *V2 Football Podcast.*

'The World Cup ... was a big thing out in Korea, football was massive ... and the stadiums, absolutely incredible.

'[I was] so lucky to play in literally world-class stadiums every week ... Every time we drove to a [stadium], the bus would go down under the ground, because the car parks would be under the stadiums, literally a different world to rebuilt stadiums [in England]. Everything was just incredible.

'In the stadium, when you get into the changing rooms, you open the door, and there would be a huge warm-up area. You didn't have to go out on to the pitch sometimes, you could go in the warm-up area on AstroTurf, and warm up inside the stadium, underneath it. That's how far advanced they were.'

However, despite their fantastic amenities, Cookie also mentioned how absurdly large the stadiums were.

'It's very weird because the stadiums are so big. I remember playing in Seoul, and ... it was half-empty. It never looked [like there were] that many there. We never used to have that many at [Busan] games. We probably had about five or six thousand at home games, and it just looked absolutely empty our ground, because our ground was so massive, it was huge.

'The biggest [Busan attendance] was 20,000, and again it just looked like there was no one there because the stadiums were so vast.'

But with Cooke scoring goals for fun – and selected for the unofficial league 'best 11' for the month of August, along with Jon Hjelde, captain Noh Jung-yoon and Lee Jang-kwan – the Englishman probably wasn't too worried about the woeful attendances.

Cooke had scored four times in just six games for struggling Busan, twice as much as Jamie Cureton. After Busan were thrashed by Seongnam during Cookie's one-match absence, the club was delighted to have him back for the Sunday night away trip to opponents Jeonbuk.

I hopped on the supporters' bus for the long journey to Jeonju. Rather ominously, a hired bodyguard dressed in a black suit accompanied the Pride of Pusan. Jeonbuk supporters, known as the Mad Green Boys, had caused a few altercations in recent weeks and the Pride didn't want anything to do with them.

The bus stopped briefly at Asiad Stadium to pick up the Pride's banners and drums. Several males who weren't tasked with fetching items instead ventured outside to find the most menacing-looking long-jaw stag beetles and brought them aboard the bus to tease the girls. Feminine squeals punctured the humid afternoon air.

Towers began to rise from the earth as we approached Jeonju. The city endured an arduous history, renowned for resisting rule from other parts of the country. Jeonju was a primary site of Korea's Catholic slaughter in the 1800s, and spurred the Donghak Peasant Uprising – seen by some as an early democratic movement – in the 1890s.

The city was now a favourite of Korean food connoisseurs, as Jeonju invented *bibimbap* – rice bowls topped with an assortment of vegetables, beef and an egg – and offered the best *makgeolli* – milky rice wine.

Like Busan I'cons and Ulsan Tigers, Jeonbuk Motors were owned by a Hyundai subsidiary. But unlike Busan, Jeonbuk were fortunate to fall under one of Hyundai's wealthier arms: Hyundai Motor Company. While Busan struggled to lure talented footballers with their limited budget, Jeonbuk were flush with cash and superstars.

Surprisingly, the club didn't amount to much during their initial nine seasons in the K League. As of this weekend, Jeonbuk were in eighth place, above only the quartet of ineptness: Gwangju, Busan, Daegu and Bucheon.

Regardless of their un-intimidating record, Busan knew that Jeonbuk could be formidable opponents. Jeonbuk briefly held third place earlier in the season. Of the top-five attackers competing for the 2003 K League golden boot, two of them played for Jeonbuk: Brazilian strikers Magno Alves and Edmilson Dias de Lucena. Luckily for Busan, Edmilson wouldn't be used tonight, but Magno would, as well as two other attack-oriented Brazilians. Magno had scored a hat-trick over Busan in a 5-1 win back in round two, Porterfield's first K League loss. Busan's back-line would have to be at its best on this sticky summer evening. Unfortunately for Busan, Norwegian defender Jon Hjelde was still in England for the birth of his first child.

Jeonbuk once posted player profiles on the club's website in the hope of connecting with prospective fans. An English version was also included:

Park Young-mo
Ideal type of girl: Women of substances
Sung Jong-hyun
Motive to love football: I thought it would be fun
Lim Jong-hoon and Han Jong-sung
Ideal type of girl: Pure and poor
Kim Young-sam
Ideal type of girl: nice and cute lady
Experience and prizes: nothing
Kim Hyun-su
Ideal type of girl: obedient lady
Yoo Won-sub
Ideal type of girl: Too many

Our bus pulled in to the car park at the Jeonju World Cup Stadium. Despite not being burdened with a running track and having only two-thirds the capacity of Busan's ground, the venue was still absolutely massive, dominating the rural setting. From below, the roof looked like a *gayageum* – the Korean zither, a stringed musical instrument – while from above it took on the appearance of a *hapjukseon* – a traditional fan made from bamboo and mulberry paper.

But that's where the refined nod to traditional culture ended. The stadium's plastic seats came in garish pink and powder blue, giving the inner venue an aura more reminiscent of Hello Kitty than an intimidating football ground. To prevent football punters from getting K-pop withdrawal symptoms while walking between their car and the stadium, the car park was helpfully lined with speakers that pumped out upbeat tunes.

Dark clouds and a brisk chill washed over Jeonju an hour before the match, but the rain held off. Goalkeeper Kim Yong-dae, seemingly the darling of Busan manager Porterfield, was on the bench for the first time in months, likely due to the 4-0 massacre from Seongnam. And just like last match, another new face sat on the bench.

The Jeonbuk end was lively and packed with supporters outfitted in green. In the event their chants weren't intelligible to the families in the main stands, the club helpfully put lyrics on large electronic stadium screens to sing along to. Terrace karaoke!

Busan do well to hold off Jeonbuk's attacks, but eventually succumb to a goal in the 32nd minute. It's scored by Rodrigo Fernandes Valete, a midfielder on loan from Brazil. Jeonbuk's South American-inspired style of play is the polar opposite of Busan's kick-and-rush: composed, graceful and artistic. It's splendid to behold.

Jeonbuk defender Park Jae-hong scores in the 59th minute, while Brazilian striker Carlos Eduardo Castro da Silva – still at the tender age of 21 – finds the net minutes later. Rather abruptly, the home side are up 3-0.

Cookie becomes livid. It's hard enough carrying most of Busan's attack, but now he can't even depend on the rest of the squad to do their jobs. A ferocious glare on his face convinces his colleagues to keep a safe distance.

Pride of Pusan members are equally indignant. Several shout abuse at Jamie Cureton, who is having a frightful game. Due to the proximity between Jeonbuk's stands and the pitch, Curo hears the maltreatment, possibly for the first time, and stares at the Busan supporters for several seconds as he registers their antipathy.

Others focus their scorn at Porterfield. His old-fashioned tactics – as well as using players out of position and making questionable substitutions – ensure that winning over supporters will be next to impossible without winning games.

Unfortunately for Cureton, his reputation is tainted by association. Curo is Porterfield's signing, so if he isn't going to perform as well as Urumov and Harry had previously, the supporters' contempt for Porterfield will be channelled to Curo as well.

Cookie's saving grace is that he is scoring goals. In contrast to their treatment of Cureton, the Pride of Pusan will avidly chant Cookie's name if he misses a shot, hoping to lift his spirits and spur him on to that next important goal.

Curo, meanwhile, is struggling to settle, and the Pride have little patience. Rather than chanting his name to lift his spirits, the Pride instead mutter his name laced with obscenities – sometimes under their breath, but increasingly at a more audible volume.

It is all rather unfortunate for Cureton. It isn't his fault that fan-favourites Urumov and Harry had been shown the door just prior to his arrival. Nor did Curo benefit from Porterfield naively inflating expectations – the Scot had imprudently boasted that Cureton would score constantly. Further, Porterfield's decision to unveil Cureton during the 'showdown' meeting with supporters was also reckless, causing Cureton to be marinated in the stench of antagonism immediately upon joining the club. With such an introduction, it's no wonder the supporters had little patience for unsatisfactory performances from Cureton.

In just his eighth Busan match, a player already having difficulties settling into a foreign excursion recognises he has become the subject of scorn from his own team's supporters. This was a man adored at his previous clubs – Reading fans officially had a star in outer space named after him! But now, adding to the linguistic and cultural barriers, family and personal struggles, as well as poor playing form, Cureton will also have to contend with becoming the supporters' boo-boy.

'*Shovelling devil!*' one Pride member shouts at Cureton. The Korean expression combines the idiom 'shovelling' – someone incapable of achieving their goals yet futilely continuing to dig (in this case, unable to score) – and 'devil', referring to his ostracisation.

Being slated by fans of his current club is a completely alien prospect for Cureton. If any factor were likely to cause extroverted Cureton to retreat even deeper into a personal shell, this was it.

Did Cureton, determined to take a break from England, make the wrong decision by choosing to play in South Korea rather than

the United States? He would later admit he had enjoyed his trial at
D.C. United in Major League Soccer more than his introductory
time with Busan I'cons.

'I spent five days there [at D.C. United], loved it,' Cureton told
the *Non League Nosh* podcast. 'The boys [players] took me out. [I]
felt more comfortable there.'

Had Cureton opted to play stateside, his strike partner would
have been Hristo Stoitchkov, who featured in 175 matches for
Barcelona and won both the Golden Boot and Bronze Ball (third-
best overall player) awards at the 1994 FIFA World Cup.

'But Korea was sort of appealing,' said Cureton. 'It was different.'

Curo trudges on. Shortly after the third goal, fearsome Jeonbuk
striker Magno receives the ball in Busan's penalty box. He pivots
and blasts a thundering shot, scoring Jeonbuk's fourth. The Pride
of Pusan fall silent.

And then it's a fifth. Jeonbuk substitute striker Namkung Do
scores from almost the exact same spot as Magno. Busan goalkeeper
Jung Yoo-suk, playing for the first time in months, must wonder if
he'll see another game this season.

There's little work for Jeonbuk goalkeeper Lee Yong-bal, who
disappointingly opted not to wear any of his eccentric headwear
today. If ever there were an occasion to don one of his famous
top hats during a match, surely a one-sided blowout like this
would be it.

The referee finally ends the game. Busan have been routed 5-0,
the second time this season they've conceded five goals in Jeonju.

Pride of Pusan members dismantled their banner display
and quietly trudged back to the bus. A few moaned about the
inconsistency of the club: winning consecutive matches for the first
time this season, immediately followed by losing twice with a 9-0
aggregate scoreline.

The initial hour or two on the bus home was silent, but chatter
eventually percolated. One fellow remarked that club owners
Hyundai Development Company had little if any interest in Busan
I'cons doing well. That claim was intriguing. I knew the budget
made available to the team was relatively modest, but did the owners
genuinely not care about the performance of the club?

Former club translator Leo Mendoza offered some startling
allegations on the subject.

'I'Park corporate [Hyundai Development Company] took [Busan I'cons FC] as a burden, realising it was of no benefit whatsoever,' Mendoza wrote in an email.

'Busan I'cons yearly expenses [were] ... considered "lost money" by corporate. They knew very well that there would be no return on that cash. They basically were writing it off as a loss.

'Indifferent management with no incentive or desire to turn a profit ... no competition prizes that make any impact. ... [W]hether Busan I'cons finished first or last in the league, there would be no benefit for the corporation. ... [T]he grim reality is that [Hyundai Development Company] had no interest in a championship squad. They had no interest in anything from Busan I'cons.'

Although Hyundai Development Company was technically acting as a benevolent corporate citizen by bankrolling the club, it allegedly could not have cared less about how the team fared, according to Mendoza.

Today's lopsided scoreline was demoralising. After a promising start to his career in Korea, Andy Cooke was unable to score in two consecutive match debacles. He was noticeably annoyed at himself toward the end of both games.

Although Cookie successfully scored on his K League debut, he initially worried whether he had the ability to flourish in Asia. His first time on a pitch in Korea was at a K League reserve game. The weather was oppressively hot and he had not yet acclimatised to the subtropical summer conditions. Cooke told the *V2 Football Podcast*, 'I did not touch the ball for 25 minutes, and it was about 85°F [30°C] at seven o'clock at night in this game, and I thought, "What have I done here?" I couldn't get anywhere near [the other players], I couldn't touch the ball, it was hot ... and I thought, "What am I doing?"'

The intense heat even made training a brutal chore.

'We would train in the heat for two and a half hours in the mornings, three hours, then we'd have ... some lunch, and ... then a sleep. In the afternoon you'd get back, and we'd do another two and a half hours, three hours in the afternoon. And it used to absolutely kill me.'

Would Cooke be able to endure life in South Korea? Most concerning of all was the effect of the country's oppressive summer weather on his newly pregnant wife, Kate.

'Obviously I'm out all day. My wife was at home pulling her hair out. "What do I do?" She couldn't get out [during the summer when they arrived] because it was [extremely] hot in the day, so it was really, really tough.'

But a comment Cooke made to the *Wizards of Drivel* podcast about his time in South Korea was perhaps most revealing, 'Financially, it worked. Family-wise … it wasn't great timing.'

ROUND 12 (rescheduled due to inclement weather)

Busan	**0-4**	**Seongnam**

ROUND 29

Jeonbuk	**5-0**	**Busan**
Jeonnam	2-1	Anyang
Pohang	2-3	Ulsan
Bucheon	3-1	Daejeon
Gwangju	0-1	Suwon
Seongnam	2-0	Daegu

K LEAGUE TABLE

Seongnam	64
Ulsan	57
Suwon	44
Jeonnam	43
Daejeon	42
Jeonbuk	41
Anyang	41
Pohang	40
Gwangju	28
Busan	**28**
Daegu	19
Bucheon	14

CHAPTER 24

DIVORCES AND DRUBBINGS

GWANGJU SANGMU BULSAJO (MILITARY PHOENIX) vs. BUSAN I'CONS
WEDNESDAY, 3 SEPTEMBER 2003
K LEAGUE ROUND 34 (PLAYED EARLY DUE TO ASIAN CUP QUALIFIER)
GWANGJU WORLD CUP STADIUM (A.K.A. GUUS HIDDINK STADIUM)

개 밥에 도토리
– Something or someone that is out of place
(literally, 'an acorn in the dog's food')

TODAY WOULD mark Jamie Cureton's tenth match for Busan I'cons. The Bristolian was still struggling to find his form in South Korea. After making a promising start by scoring on his K League debut, Curo had only found the net in one other match thus far, creating just two goals in nine games. With Busan enduring consecutive drubbings, the club was desperate for the English striker to recapture the form that made him a favourite at Bristol Rovers and Reading.

Rumblings from inside the club suggested Cureton might not have been putting his full effort into training and that he carried a negative attitude.

Club translator Leo Mendoza sympathised, offering, 'Cureton had a whole lot of off-pitch problems that affected his work.'

As noted earlier, Cureton had split up with the mother of his two kids. The youngsters remained back in England. He missed them greatly.

Living in a country with a foreign language and culture can lead to homesickness, particularly for extroverted people. Was being away from his young children compounding Cureton's difficulty in settling professionally in South Korea?

Cureton later told *The Independent* that he pined for the buzz and atmosphere of English football – which he used to motivate himself on the pitch – during his time in Korea.

'What I missed was the English passion – I was used to playing in the Championship with everything full-on,' he said. 'It felt the pressure had got taken away.'

Although Porterfield set a high bar for Cureton early on, the striker's inability to comprehend Korean-language media coverage of the K League likely created an environment too serene for Cureton. Being unfamiliar with the league and its member clubs may have made it difficult to appreciate the relevance of each opponent or to get excited about upcoming fixtures.

'[Busan] didn't get massive crowds,' Cureton told the *Man Marking* podcast. 'I missed all that.'

Did Cureton also find pressure lacking from within Busan I'cons? Cureton previously mentioned that the team atmosphere was too relaxed during his trial at D.C. United, the American club he considered joining prior to choosing Busan.

Ian Porterfield was generally laid-back, a personality trait that suited the management of some teams and players but could be utterly ineffective with others. Was Porterfield being too soft on his favourite players, just as he had been at Chelsea? Was Cureton a poor fit for Porterfield's management style? Did Cureton require the so-called 'hairdryer treatment' – a verbal kick up the backside as motivation – every now and then from his boss? Was he not getting this at Busan? Was Porterfield astute enough to figure out the unique personality of each individual player and give them what they require? Or did Porterfield use more of an old-fashioned, one-size-fits-all style of dealing with his Busan playing squad?

Porterfield loved to talk. But did he enjoy listening? Did he actually get to know his squad?

Other minor factors may have worsened Cureton's situation. He initially expressed excitement to play in South Korea's World Cup stadiums; but other than Busan Asiad, Cureton didn't see another newly built venue until his ninth K League match – when he noticed the Busan supporters abusing him. The novelty factor had undoubtedly worn thin.

Cureton had also relocated to South Korea amid subtropical heat – a shock to any English body – and was obliged to play twice a week as well as train in such conditions due to the K League's congested 2003 fixture schedule.

Despite his challenges and frustrations, Curo had the opportunity to put things right tonight as Busan travelled to Gwangju for another match against the new military side. Oddly enough the newcomers were becoming a bogey opponent, as Busan had lost to Gwangju in both previous encounters. A win today would allow Busan to leapfrog above Gwangju again in the league table. Cureton hoped for a performance that would rectify his mindset and redeem the season.

Sadly it is not to be. Gwangju score in the first half with a goal from young striker Cho Jae-jin, who had just debuted for the South Korean national team two months earlier. Twenty-year-old Cho Won-hee, who would also go on to become a regular for the national side, scores in the closing half. The goals hand Gwangju a 2-0 win, their third victory over Busan this season, allowing the military team to surge three points above Busan in the K League table.

Despite Andy Cooke's return from suspension, Busan weren't able to score – their third straight goalless loss. Even Jon Hjelde's addition to the line-up after a brief trip to witness the birth of his first child wasn't enough to bolster Busan. It was one thing to struggle against wealthy K League clubs Seongnam and Jeonbuk, but poor displays against novices Gwangju didn't bode well for Ian Porterfield's tenure.

That evening, I browsed the news. FIFA announced an end to 'World Cup white elephants', no longer requiring host countries to construct monstrous stadiums. South Korea and Japan would purportedly be the last nations saddled with behemoth venues far too large for domestic club football.

Of South Korea's ten World Cup stadiums, only Seoul's Sangam Stadium – the Korean Wembley – was turning a profit; the *JoongAng Daily* pejoratively suggested the remainder 'resemble tombs'. But even the Seoul venue was still without a tenant club, causing Seoul City Council to hunt for suitors.

Two business conglomerates were rumoured to have an interest in starting a new club in Seoul: KT (Korea Telecom) and Hanwha (originally Korea Explosives).

The city ideally wanted two clubs to play at the stadium, but was only offering financial incentives for the creation of one new team. Essentially they were calling for an existing K League team to relocate to the capital.

'... [I]f an existing club changes its home to Seoul and another team is set up in Seoul, the city can have two teams,' Seoul city official Choi Seok-joo told the *Korea Times*.

Back in England, Wimbledon FC had not yet kicked a ball in Milton Keynes at this point, but Wimbledon's pending relocation had already been announced and more than a year had passed since the founding of AFC Wimbledon in protest. The painful topic of club relocation was fresh in many people's minds, including supporters of K League clubs.

South Korea's professional sports were unfortunately established upon the American franchise model. Just like in the USA, most Korean clubs didn't own their own stadium; instead, such venues were constructed and operated by government. Clubs were merely stadium tenants with leases. If a facility became too expensive, or entered a state of disrepair, clubs could simply leave to a different city. They would occasionally threaten to relocate unless local government upgraded existing facilities or built a new stadium. Many Korean sports clubs had such little history that most residents responded to their departure with a defeatist shrug.

To be fair, some K League teams were forced into involuntarily relocation. Three clubs played at Seoul's Dongdaemun Stadium until 1995, when the K League kicked them out due to poor attendance, hoping the teams could instead muster larger crowds outside the capital.

One of those teams moved to Cheonan when city officials promised their stadium would be renovated into a football-specific venue and equipped with floodlights. But when the agreed renovations didn't materialise, the club was on the move again just four years later, this time to Seongnam.

The second coming of lower-division side Hallelujah FC was also met with forced resettlement. Shortly after the club's triumphal entry into the city of Iksan for the K2 League's 2003 season, the team of born-again Christians were sent packing by a local council taken over by 'radical' Won Buddhists. Unable to compete in the second half of the season without a playing venue, the team moved to Gimpo for 2004.

But for every club whose hand was forced on relocation, there were several others that did so voluntarily. One such outfit in the semi-pro K2 League was Uijeongbu Hummel, which would become Icheon Hummel in 2006, then Nowon Hummel in 2008, and finally Chungju Hummel in 2010. Eventually the Hummel team folded. One wonders why.

Another K2 League side, Gimpo Kookmin Bank, not only relocated in 2003 but did so mid-season, shifting cities during the league's summer intermission.

With club relocation so prevalent in South Korean football, Seoul City Council's call for aspirant clubs alarmed hardcore fans. Of the three teams that were forced out of Seoul following the 1995 K League season (and became Seongnam, Anyang and Bucheon), Seongnam and Anyang remained in modest, ageing facilities. A brand new, football-specific World Cup stadium in Seoul was tempting for these two high-calibre clubs.

Several of Busan's professional sports clubs were acquired or relinquished through relocations. Basketball team Korea Tender Max 10 spent time in Gwangju and Yeosu before moving to Busan in 2003, while Busan's volleyball team – Samsung Fire & Marine Insurance (catchy name!) – would later depart for Daejeon.

Was there any chance Busan I'cons would entertain moving to Seoul? The club's relationship with Busan City Council – which owned both of the city's football stadiums – was rocky at best. Crowds at Asiad were low, rent was high, capacity was excessive, pitch time was limited, and promised sponsorship from the city was purportedly not forthcoming.

On the other hand, Busan were already playing in a brand-new stadium with modern amenities. Additionally, Seoul's World Cup stadium would come with the burden of an even bigger capacity than Asiad – more than 20 per cent larger.

Busan coach Choi Man-hee had been reassigned to the administrative role of investigating a football-specific venue for Busan I'cons. But surely that venue wouldn't be located on the other side of the country – would it?

ROUND 34 (played early due to Asian Cup qualifier)

Gwangju	**2-0**	**Busan**
Suwon	1-2	Daejeon
Seongnam	2-1	Ulsan
Bucheon	1-4	Anyang
Pohang	2-3	Jeonnam
Jeonbuk	2-1	Daegu

K LEAGUE TABLE

Seongnam	67
Ulsan	57
Jeonnam	46
Daejeon	45
Anyang	44
Jeonbuk	44
Suwon	44
Pohang	40
Gwangju	31
Busan	**28**
Daegu	19
Bucheon	14

CHAPTER 25

GREENER PASTURES AND MANITOBA DREAMIN'

BUSAN I'CONS VS. SUWON SAMSUNG
BLUEWINGS
SUNDAY, 7 SEPTEMBER 2003
K LEAGUE ROUND 30
BUSAN ASIAD WORLD CUP STADIUM

쥐구멍에도 볕 들날이 있다
*– Every cloud has a silver lining (literally, 'even in
a rat hole there are days when the sun shines')*

BUSAN'S SAJIK-DONG neighbourhood was awash in royal blue shirts, but these weren't retro tops of the former Busan Daewoo Royals. Today, Busan I'cons would host Suwon Bluewings, and the area around the stadium was teeming with away supporters.

After dropping three matches on the trot, this was an important fixture for Ian Porterfield. Suwon were reigning Korean FA Cup holders and recent back-to-back Asian Club Championship winners. However, they were uncharacteristically also in the bottom half of the K League table and had lost their previous match. Could Busan avoid assembling their longest losing streak of the season and instead gain points against the club crowned continental champions just 17 months earlier?

The David versus slightly rickety Goliath encounter was set. Adding further significance to the match were fresh memories from the 1998 dugout-emptying brawl between the two clubs.

Kick-off. With both clubs inspired, the match is tense. The ball rarely gets the opportunity to leave the midfield. Players battle tenaciously. Tackles are fierce and swift, uncharacteristic for the K League. From the opening minutes it's obvious this match won't finish as a 0-0 draw.

Suwon push forward. Romanian midfielder Gabriel Popescu, formerly of Spanish giants Valencia, surges toward Busan's goal and is taken down by a defender in panic. The referee points to the penalty spot. The Pride of Pusan members sigh and mutter with exasperation. Up steps Nádson Rodrigues de Souza, who just months earlier made several appearances for Brazil's senior national team. He places the ball down on the penalty spot, takes a quick shot and hands the visitors the lead.

1-0 Suwon.

Busan rush forward, launching a quick response. The ball is pushed up the right flank and crossed to Busan elder Noh Jung-yoon, who is waiting to shoot. A Suwon defender gets to the ball first, but his clumsy attempt at a clearance instead puts the ball into his own net.

1-1. The referee soon blows for half-time.

Despite the equaliser, Jamie Cureton's head drops. His neck remains in a droop as he returns with his team-mates to the dressing room.

The planned striking partnership between Cureton and Andy Cooke established more than five weeks ago shows little sign of maturation. It's perhaps ironic how things turned out at Busan for the English duo. When Curo signed for Busan, Reading fans swamped an online internet forum with praise for their former striker. In sharp contrast, most Stoke supporters didn't seem to care much that Cookie had left – in fact, many seemed relieved. But the move to Korea was instrumental in revitalising Cookie's desire to score. Sunderland fanzine *A Love Supreme* wrote in an unpublished article about Cookie's time in South Korea that his 'goalscoring success came as a surprise to Cooke himself'.

Busan win a corner just seconds after the restart, which lands at the feet of Cookie near the right post. Employing his wiliness for scoring, Cookie eschews shooting toward the guarded near post and instead rapidly smacks the ball toward the uncovered left side of goal. It rockets into the back of Suwon's net.

2-1 Busan.

Busan's players race back to the centre circle, exchanging high-fives in celebration. Even Jamie Cureton has a huge grin on his face, such is the relief of Busan leading for once.

But 40 minutes later, with just five minutes remaining, Suwon equalise. Have Busan thrown away a rare opportunity to defeat a normally formidable opponent?

Ageing Busan captain Noh Jung-yoon is awarded a free kick deep in Suwon territory. He crosses a low, floating ball that sails across the entirety of the six-yard box. Cookie comes running in and takes possession in the same spot as his earlier goal. Just like last time, he forgoes shooting to the near post in favour of the far side, again left unmarked. The ball bulges the net. Busan have their third goal. Cookie runs toward the small but jubilant crowd, pumping his fist in celebration.

A child's song is unexpectedly blasted over the loudspeakers:

C is for Cookie, that's good enough for me,
C is for Cookie, that's good enough for me,
C is for Cookie, that's good enough for me,
Oh, Cookie, Cookie, Cookie starts with C.

Suwon goalkeeper Lee Woon-jae, who guarded South Korea's net during the 2002 World Cup, spins around in anger, looking for a defender to shout at. Finding none, he resorts to shaking his fists at the clouds.

3-2 Busan.

With just seconds left and a Busan win all but sealed, the Pride of Pusan members are ecstatic. Suwon, after all, is the club they despise most.

To my surprise, the Busan supporters light a flare. Then another. And another. Soon seven such incendiary devices are burning, cloaking the Pride of Pusan in a hellish, deep-orange glow. A thick column of white smoke rises toward the gaping hole in Busan Asiad Stadium's roof.

The referee whistles for full time. Busan have halted their losing run by defeating a superior opponent. The upset would see Busan goalkeeper Kim Yong-dae selected for the league's unofficial 'best 11' of the week, despite having sat on the bench for the earlier midweek match.

After scoring the brace that lifted Busan to victory, Cookie was delighted and circled the pitch to applaud the sparse crowd.

Cookie had held his K League opponents in high regard since joining Busan, praising their ability.

'Technically, they're very, very good players,' he told the *V2 Football Podcast.* '[They're] more comfortable on the ball.'

However, he had supposedly sussed out a way to capitalise on lapses in concentration by some of his opponents.

'I found that I could always find a little bit of space, they'd switch off for a split-second, and it'd be easier to get half a yard to score.'

Although Cookie was initially humbled by the intense summer heat that left him questioning his ability to transition to the rigours of the K League, his play was beginning to flourish.

'When I was [in Korea], I was the fittest I've ever been in my life, easily,' Cooke told the podcast. 'The condition I was in when I was there ... I wish I could have got myself in the condition I was [in Korea] back in [England].

'I've never probably peaked as much as I did out there. So there's something to say for it, whether it's the science of it, or the way we were training, I would say I was very fit out there.'

Unfortunately, Jamie Cureton's stint at Busan was headed in the opposite direction. He was substituted out of the match with more than ten minutes remaining. The game-winning goal was scored while Curo sat in the dugout.

As previously mentioned, Cureton was unhappy in South Korea due to being apart from his young children. He was also missing his extended family. The Bristolian hadn't considered the full consequences of moving to the other side of the planet.

'I didn't realise by doing it [signing for Busan] and moving [to Korea], how much of a massive life change it would be ... being stuck on your own, not seeing family, just being able to speak to them on the phone, not seeing my kids,' Cureton said to the *Full Core Football 24* online video channel. 'That change was huge and I didn't anticipate [it], I wasn't prepared for it.'

'I was a bit depressed ...' Cureton told *The Independent.*

'I was missing my kids. They were only two and four [years old],' he told the *Non League Nosh* podcast, 'so not seeing them, finding it hard to speak to them because of the time difference ... there was no [video chat software back then], trying to speak to them on the phone, and my little one could hardly speak. So I found that difficult. Speaking to my mum and sister, I used to cry nearly every day speaking to them.'

'[I was] sat in South Korea in an apartment, not enjoying life, not enjoying football, crying most days,' he told the *GasCast* podcast.

'And ... after a month I thought, "What have you done?"'

Cureton's recent girlfriend, who had joined him for an adventurous life in South Korea, had returned to England. Cureton was now living entirely on his own.

'In the end, she went home, and my life at the time ... was a mess, to be honest,' Cureton told BBC Radio Berkshire's *Reading FC* podcast.

'I was in a bad [psychological] place,' Cureton said to the *GasCast* podcast, 'stuck a million miles away on [my] own from everyone, and just not enjoying life at all.'

'The football side [of Korea] was good,' Cureton told the *Full Core Football 24* online video channel, 'every facility, everything, the standard was fine. But my off-the-field was just still all over the shop.'

Shortly after Cureton arrived in South Korea, he noticed the locals staring at him whenever he ventured out in public. With all the attention, living in Korea as a visible foreigner in the early 2000s could sometimes feel like being a human exhibit, especially outside of the more cosmopolitan capital, Seoul.

During this period, many South Koreans entertained leaving the country for a purportedly better life overseas. An entire industry sprang up to aid their escape. Migration agencies quickly proliferated. The Hyundai Home Shopping Network, a television channel, broke sales records when it offered emigration packages to the Canadian prairie province of Manitoba, an underpopulated area as exciting as Nuneaton.

Struggling in South Korea, would Cureton be tempted to join the exodus by leaving the country prior to the end of his two-year overseas contract?

But even if Curo were to see out the remainder of his time in South Korea, he still might have no choice but to leave Busan. After months of protracted and futile negotiations with Busan's stadium management and city council, Busan I'cons Football Club formally announced their application to relocate to the Seoul World Cup Stadium, some 300km away in the opposite corner of the country.

ROUND 30
Busan	**3-2**	**Suwon**
Ulsan	1-0	Daejeon
Jeonnam	1-1	Gwangju
Jeonbuk	2-1	Bucheon
Pohang	0-0	Daegu

[Anyang vs. Seongnam postponed due to inclement weather]

K LEAGUE TABLE
Seongnam	67
Ulsan	60
Jeonbuk	47
Jeonnam	47
Daejeon	45
Anyang	44
Suwon	44
Pohang	41
Gwangju	32
Busan	**31**
Daegu	20
Bucheon	14

CHAPTER 26

FOOD POISONING AND A 335KPH BREEZE

DAEJEON CITIZEN VS. BUSAN I'CONS
SUNDAY, 14 SEPTEMBER 2003
K LEAGUE ROUND 31
DAEJEON WORLD CUP STADIUM (A.K.A.
PURPLE ARENA)

SEONGNAM ILHWA CHUNMA (PEGASUS)
VS. BUSAN I'CONS
SUNDAY, 21 SEPTEMBER 2003
K LEAGUE ROUND 32
SEONGNAM STADIUM (A.K.A. MORAN
STADIUM)

BUSAN I'CONS VS. GWANGJU SANGMU
BULSAJO (MILITARY PHOENIX)
WEDNESDAY, 24 SEPTEMBER 2003
K LEAGUE ROUND 33
BUSAN ASIAD WORLD CUP STADIUM

비 온 뒤에 땅이 굳어진다
— *Adversity strengthens the sufferer (literally 'the
ground hardens after a rain')*

SUPER TYPHOON Maemi – named after ear-splitting cicadas
– was destined for South Korea. Its trajectory would carve directly

through Busan during the Chuseok (Korean Thanksgiving) holidays. The storm was classified as a 'category five', the strongest possible on the Saffir-Simpson scale. To put that into perspective, the weaker category four was accompanied by the warning, 'Catastrophic damage will occur.' Maemi would be the strongest typhoon to hit Korea since the country began keeping records in 1904.

Three days prior to landfall, while the super typhoon still hovered above the Pacific Ocean, Maemi hit its peak with wind gusts estimated at 335kph (205mph). As it struck Jeju Island, the storm set records for fastest wind speed and lowest air pressure ever measured on Korean soil.

Maemi soon decimated and flooded its way through to Busan, a city of 3.7 million inhabitants. Winds slowed considerably to a steady 154kph (with gusts estimated up to 190kph, or more than 50m per second) by then, still vigorous enough to be the second-fastest ever recorded in the city.

I was in my apartment when the storm hit. The building shook fiercely, winds battering it like a piñata. By 7pm the electricity went out. Throughout Busan, windows were sucked out of buildings, sometimes frame and all, adding potentially lethal panes of glass to the downpour.

The winds increased in intensity around 10pm and lasted through half the night. Damage to the city was substantial, exacerbated by the typhoon hitting land during high tide. Container cranes made from steel were twisted like origami paper, while shipping containers were hurled across the port. A large oil rig under construction in neighbouring Ulsan was dragged out to sea. A cruise ship was flung ashore at a popular beach. At least 82 vessels sank; many of those that remained afloat were found either on their side or partially submerged. Trees, poles and power lines hung haphazardly across the urban landscape like celebratory streamers after an overindulgent party. Roads crumbled, bridges buckled, and a train was derailed by a landslide. Cars were tossed around like toys; those foolish enough to park their vehicle near the harbour likely found it floating in the water. Flooding was extensive.

Super Typhoon Maemi killed 16 people in Busan and claimed an additional 101 lives elsewhere in South Korea due to drowning, electrocution, mudslides and other causes. Numerous large buildings collapsed. Two dozen people were trapped in a basement karaoke bar when a structure buckled in Masan, killing most of the occupants. In total, 25,000 people were left homeless. A government statement claimed that damage was valued at more than US$1.4bn.

The storm also sheared several panels of roof membrane from Busan Asiad Stadium, leaving conspicuous gaps. Although it seemed crude to trivialise the extensive loss of life and property destruction, I couldn't help but see the typhoon as a metaphor for Busan I'cons' jarring announcement that they had applied to leave the city.

With their current stadium in need of storm-damage repairs, Busan rather fortuitously were scheduled to play away to Daejeon that weekend. Daejeon were enjoying their breakout season, currently in fifth place and on almost 50 per cent more league points than Busan. But Busan had unexpectedly beaten Daejeon 2-0 back in June; combined with last week's win over former Asian champions Suwon, the Busan squad were optimistic.

The arrival of autumn meant a return to 3pm weekend kick-offs, although the weather remained incredibly hot.

The first half is uneventful, finishing scoreless. Early in the second, Brazilian Alex Chandre de Oliveira (known as 'Tico') brings the ball into the right side of the 18-yard box, then slices it through to striker Gong Oh-kyun loitering on the left of the goal area. Gong smashes it with his left foot past Busan goalkeeper Kim Yong-dae. The only goal of the match, Daejeon pick up the 1-0 win. Jamie Cureton is substituted off just 58 minutes into the game.

Normal programming had apparently resumed for Busan I'cons.

Several days later, Vivi Fuhr Hjelde finally arrived in Korea with her newborn son, Leo. They had come to live with the new father, Jon.

Vivi had never stepped foot in Korea before moving there with her young baby. Would she enjoy living in the country? Would raising her first child in an unfamiliar environment prove too challenging? Would she be able to cope without the assuring presence of family and friends? She had already spent several years away from Norway living in Nottingham, but would Busan prove too drastic a change, especially with a newborn in tow?

Meanwhile, up at the Seoul World Cup Stadium that Busan I'cons intended to move to, the South Korean national team hosted an Asian Cup qualifying match. The Korean public had gone mad for football during the 2002 World Cup, particularly their country's unanticipated run to the semi-finals. But less than 15 months later, the national team couldn't even fill one third of Seoul's giant new World Cup venue. This was the city and the stadium that Busan I'cons were threatening to move to? A venue more than 20 per cent larger than the gargantuan Busan Asiad Stadium?

Next for Busan was an away trip to league leaders Seongnam, undefeated in their last nine matches – earning 25 of a possible 27 points – and romping toward their third straight K League title. On paper, this would be Busan's most difficult fixture of the season.

The one bit of optimism for Busan was that they had earned an unexpected draw from their previous visit to Seongnam in May. Could the unfancied visitors sneak away with points again?

In short: yes. Seongnam score first when former Busan Daewoo Royals forward Saša Drakulić feeds the ball to Brazilian midfielder Irineu Ricardo, lurking in the goal area. But eight minutes later, Busan auxiliary striker Hwang Cheol-min sets up an easy goal for Andy Cooke. The match finishes 1-1. Busan amazingly earn a point from both of their visits this season to league behemoths Seongnam.

Only six Busan supporters made the trip north for this midweek match, the bus cancelled due to lack of interest. Jamie Cureton didn't start, instead appearing as a sub during the final ten minutes. In his place, Hwang Cheol-min played up front.

It's worth putting Porterfield's decision to play Hwang instead of Cureton in context. Hwang was the Scottish manager's go-to choice for unused sub this 2003 season. Busan picked up Hwang in the 2001 K League draft as their penultimate selection; he was taken 52nd overall of the 53 chosen players. All other K League clubs waived the opportunity to select a player by that 11th round. Fast forward to this 2003 season, and it wasn't until August that Hwang received his first start of the year.

Today, that player was chosen for Busan's starting 11 ahead of a former England youth international who Alex Ferguson had attempted to lure to Manchester United. That was how badly Curo's season was unravelling with Busan.

The performances of Busan's two English strikers, Cureton and Cooke, couldn't have been further polarised. I struggled to make sense of it. I was aware of Cureton's personal issues, but somehow that didn't seem enough to explain the stark contrast.

Could their early careers have been partly responsible? Cookie started from the bottom: playing semi-pro football while toiling away in blue-collar drudgery. Cureton, however, was groomed in a Premier League academy.

Did the adversity of Cookie's early years in football better prepare him mentally for the challenges of living in Korea? In contrast, did Curo's lofty professional beginnings leave him ill-equipped to deal with the combination of personal and professional struggle? To be fair, Cureton's time in the Premier League was before the money and pampering had reached absurd levels. But would a more humble career start have better prepared Curo for playing in Asia during a time of personal turbulence? Had Cureton's admitted early-career over-indulgence in late nights and alcohol – rather than hard graft – left him without the obstinate resolve to muster on?

I picked up a sports newspaper and opened the football section. Hooliganism was worsening across the league, with 2003 the most violent season yet. The Pride of Pusan hadn't become entangled in any conflicts this year, thanks to their anti-alcohol policy. But some of the Seoul Capital Area-based supporters' groups were engaging in occasional skirmishes, as were followers of Jeolla's two older clubs, Jeonbuk and Jeonnam.

At the recent Suwon–Anyang derby, Suwon fans rained bottles down upon a linesman. But it all kicked off at the subsequent Suwon–Ulsan game: the Ulsan manager allegedly put his hands around the neck of the referee, provoking a melee that involved both benches. Two Suwon fans joined the skirmish by invading the pitch and supposedly whacking Ulsan veteran Kim Hyuns-uk.

Elsewhere that same day, a Bucheon player made rude gestures towards the Jeonnam supporters after scoring a late equaliser. In retaliation, five of them invaded the pitch and threatened the Bucheon squad. Soon after, fisticuffs broke out between the Jeonnam and Bucheon fans. Jeonnam's mob then surrounded the Bucheon supporters' bus for one and a half hours, preventing it from departing. They finally turned their attention to the Bucheon dressing room, surrounding the exit door and demanding that the offending player come out to apologise – which he eventually did.

Referee abuse was spiralling out of control, supporters were becoming increasingly belligerent and tensions were rising across the league.

The *Korea Times* argued that the lack of punishment for supporters was culpable for the deterioration in behaviour. It noted there were no penalties for pitch invasions as long as players or match officials weren't assaulted, and that miscreants were typically only ejected from the stadium rather than charged for offences.

The newspaper spoke with Suwon Bluewings official Lee Ho-seung, who bemoaned the lack of police at K League matches.

'Unlike European countries, South Korea doesn't deploy police at [club] matches, saying they are commercial games and that those benefitting financially must take charge of security,' said Lee. 'But … our stewards, numbering less than 100 and without any power to arrest or suppress troublemakers, can't single-handedly ensure safety. Fans are starting to become more aggressive, knowing our stewards can't overpower them even if they cause problems in the stadium.

'Fans caught up in the emotion of a game can be extremely dangerous. The K League needs a police presence.'

If K League club supporters were enjoying the increasing ferocity of the matchday experience, they could blame the traditional Korean contest of *seokjeon*, or 'stone battles'. These began as military training exercises but eventually evolved into a popular activity for civilians. Combatants would be armed with stones, metal bars and wooden clubs, and wore only light armour made from animal hides or plants.

These 'stone battles' often featured neighbouring villages or feuding clans. Participants would begin with macho hooting and hollering, with alcohol consumed prior to fights commencing. They would proceed to beat the living daylight out of each other – often resulting in horrific injuries or even deaths. Fights could last several days.

If the football supporters of Greater Seoul or Jeolla were increasingly interested in argy-bargy, perhaps it was as much an effort to re-establish traditional Korean culture as it was to emulate European hooligans.

Yeah, right.

That evening I enjoyed a Western meal at a restaurant – a plate of nachos slathered in cheese, served with a pint of Korean stout. It caused my first experience of food poisoning, with projectile emissions from both ends. My guess was that the cheese had gone off during the hot Korean summer.

Busan's next K League opponents, Gwangju Sangmu, would live through a similar experience several seasons later. In 2008, the Gwangju squad enjoyed a team dinner highlighted by a traditional Korean dish made from raw beef and rice. Sure enough, the entire squad came down with food poisoning, resulting in the first-ever postponement of a K League match due to mass illness.

But it was still 2003, and with the players in good health, Busan was about to play its fourth and final match against Gwangju this season. Busan had somehow managed to lose to the newcomers in all three of their earlier meetings. Porterfield was desperate not to hand this nascent club a league quadruple over his southeastern side.

Interestingly, Gwangju Sangmu – a team comprised of players from other K League clubs on loan to fulfil their mandatory national military service – were not the first military team in South Korea. That honour went to Yangzee Football Club, created in 1967 when dictator Park Chung-hee demanded the South keep up with the exploits of North Korea's national team, which had advanced to the quarter-finals of the 1966 World Cup in England. The South's best players were rounded up, housed in the Korean Central Intelligence Agency (KCIA) barracks, supplied with the best available food and trained on pristine grass pitches.

The team's name (alternatively spelled 'Yangji'), meant 'sunlit land', a reference to the KCIA motto, 'We work in the dark to protect the sunlit land.' Players were subjected to harsh conditions meant to increase their resolve, such as a one-hour run every morning at 6.00 prior to football training. They were paid only a small stipend, but were rewarded with large financial bonuses for winning performances. Perhaps more importantly, playing for the team fulfilled their national military service obligation.

So when Gwangju Sangmu was established as a K League team in 2003 after years as a works-league side, it offered a similar benefit to players: the opportunity to satisfy their military service requirements as a K League footballer instead of as a soldier.

Busan hosted Gwangju at Asiad Stadium this evening. In addition to Busan's poor record against Gwangju, the visitors were enjoying a rare streak of good form, going undefeated and winning three of their last four matches – including an earlier game against Busan.

In a desperate bid to finally beat Gwangju, Porterfield was not only rotating his starting 11 but also shuffling some of their positions. Jung Yoo-suk would make a rare appearance in goal. But the truly baffling change was striker Gwak Kyung-keun – obtained during the close season by a rare transfer fee from Busan – being listed as a defender.

The Pride of Pusan members were in disbelief at Porterfield's decision. Two became livid, shouting obscenities toward the far-away dugout until they were calmed by their peers.

But then came an even greater surprise. As the substitutes' names were listed on the stadium screen, one familiar name prominently appeared: Harry. Colombian striker Harry Castillo had returned and was apparently kitted up on Busan's bench. It had been more than ten weeks since Harry last featured for Busan after Porterfield declared him banished from the squad.

A month earlier, translator Mendoza posted online that Harry was still under contract with the club. It now appeared that Porterfield and Harry had been able to mend their frosty relationship.

But what would Harry's return mean for the European trio that recently joined the club? Under K League rules, only three foreign players could play at the same time for one team. Cureton hadn't scored in seven matches. Was his position now under threat? If so, Curo would have the opportunity today to prove himself, as he would start up front for Busan.

The Asiad Stadium pitch is in rough shape, cradling several yellow patches. Attendance is sparse yet again. The match is hard-fought but isn't one for purists, containing a profusion of long balls and missed passes.

Just 15 minutes into the match, Busan veteran Noh Jung-yoon is inadvertently kicked in the ribs by an overly enthusiastic Gwangju player. Noh is forced to leave the pitch in severe pain.

Early in the second half, Busan midfielder Jeon Woo-keun acquires possession. As he bounds toward goal, none of the numerous white Gwangju shirts behind the ball mark Jeon. Inexplicably, the Gwangju player closest to Jeon instead runs over to Jamie Cureton to mark him tightly. With a plethora of space, Jeon takes a rare crack at goal. It's a hard strike, curling violently to the right as it sails low, just above the pitch. With the goalkeeper beaten, the ball smacks the right post and barrels into the net.

1-0 Busan. It's Jeon's first goal of the season.

With five minutes remaining, Cureton is substituted. It's now been eight matches since he's scored. He plods himself down on to the far end of the dugout bench, on the side opposite from Harry.

The match finished as a 1-0 win for Busan. Porterfield looked relieved. Victory from this 'six-pointer' prevented Gwangju from claiming a league quadruple over Busan, and enabled Busan to climb up to just three points behind Gwangju in the heady K League battle for fourth-bottom.

At the game's conclusion, Cookie was bestowed the club's 'most valuable player' award for the month of August, which followed his earlier unofficial league 'best 11' selection.

The Pride of Pusan members, however, remained concerned. Today's victory required an uncharacteristic goal from a midfielder who rarely scores.

'I bet Harry will start instead of Cureton next match,' one Pride member said.

Veteran Noh's injury wasn't serious – a case of inflamed ribs – but he would miss two important games against Seongnam and Suwon.

Perhaps the greatest worry was today's attendance: 726. It was the lowest crowd of the season, both for Busan and indeed the entire league. In fact, it was the first gate below 1,000 anywhere in the K League for years.

To Busan's owners, the stadium grass up in Seoul must have certainly looked greener.

ROUND 31

Daejeon	**1-0**	**Busan**
Bucheon	1-2	Pohang
Gwangju	2-0	Jeonbuk
Jeonnam	1-2	Seongnam
Suwon	2-0	Anyang
Daegu	1-1	Ulsan

ROUND 32

Seongnam	**1-1**	**Busan**
Pohang	0-1	Jeonbuk
Jeonnam	3-3	Bucheon
Gwangju	1-0	Anyang
Suwon	2-2	Ulsan
Daegu	2-1	Daejeon

ROUND 33

Busan	**1-0**	**Gwangju**
Daejeon	0-0	Suwon
Ulsan	1-1	Seongnam
Anyang	2-0	Bucheon
Jeonnam	1-0	Pohang
Daegu	0-0	Jeonbuk

K LEAGUE TABLE

Seongnam	72
Ulsan	63
Jeonbuk	51
Jeonnam	51
Suwon	49
Daejeon	49
Anyang	47
Pohang	44
Gwangju	38
Busan	**35**
Daegu	25
Bucheon	15

CHAPTER 27

BASEBALL RIOTS, VANISHING NEPALESE AND FURIOUS CHICKENS

BUSAN I'CONS VS. SEONGNAM ILHWA
CHUNMA (PEGASUS)
WEDNESDAY, 1 OCTOBER 2003
K LEAGUE ROUND 35
BUSAN ASIAD WORLD CUP STADIUM
고래 싸움에 새우 등 터진다
*– The weak are hurt by the actions of the powerful
(literally, 'when whales fight, the backs of shrimp
are easily snapped')*

LEE SEUNG-YEOP of the Daegu Samsung Lions approached home plate. One home run was all it would take for him to break the Asian single-season record. Despite Lee playing for the away team, the home Busan Lotte Giants fans were eager to witness baseball history.

So when the Giants' pitcher intentionally walked Lee – denying him the opportunity to hit the ball – the home crowd went ballistic. Spectators turned anything they could get their hands on into projectiles, showering the field with rubbish and debris. Some of the objects thrown from higher up in the seats didn't quite reach the playing surface and instead struck fellow fans in the back of the head, including one woman hospitalised after being injured by a flung piece of wood. Numerous fires lit in the stands were used to

259

set objects ablaze before hurling them on to the field, causing the pitch to ignite in several spots. The disturbance took 90 minutes to clear, including riot police entering the stands and dragging numerous fans away. By the time the match finally resumed, the stands were virtually empty.

If the K League was hoping to differentiate itself from the plethora of other Korean spectator sports, nascent hooliganism apparently wasn't a unique selling point. The *Korea Times* opined, 'Vandalism and abuse are now an integral part of the local sports fan's experience.'

Meanwhile in football, the South Korean national team thrashed Nepal by an embarrassing 16–0 scoreline during an Asian Cup qualifier, after which three Nepalese players went missing – presumably either to seek asylum or to live amidst the shadows in the Hermit Kingdom.

It was within this atmosphere of sporting turbulence that Busan I'cons were due to once again host K League leaders Seongnam. Busan had inexplicably earned points from both of their away matches at Seongnam this season, including their previous meeting just ten days earlier. Although Seongnam had accrued an impressive 11-match undefeated streak, most of their results were either narrow wins or draws. True, Seongnam were running away with the league, but their margins of victory were less intimidating, and Busan seemed to understand how to thwart them.

But worrying for Busan was that veteran defender Lee Lim-saeng didn't get his kit on, and was said to be suffering from chronic injury.

Seongnam's playing style is truly a joy to watch. The ball is kept on the pitch, whisked around by intelligent, rapid passes. Their players caress the ball, confidently turning away from pressure as if to arrogantly deny its existence. Almost every attempt at goal stems from an elaborate build-up that involves at least half of the team.

Busan are the polar opposite. Imagine an ungainly donkey using its hind legs to kick out at an old leather football, sending it flying only to land with a dismal thud. Busan's play is direct, often bypassing the midfield as balls are hopelessly rocketed up toward goal. It has no aesthetically redeeming qualities. It makes no pretence of style or sophistication. There is no joy or revelry to it. Busan's efforts are simply a crude attempt to put the ball over the goal line by any feasible means. It reeks of desperation, if not resignation.

Busan are the underdogs, but not in a valiant way like a small club facing superior opposition in a knock out competition. Instead, they're a once-mighty side in decline, mouldering with decay. Some hapless teams attract masochistic fans; but with Busan, even that sort of person would likely avert their gaze in embarrassment. Imagine Manchester City's 1995/96 relegation season, but without the respite of dropping down and renewal in a lower division. Instead, Busan were condemned to perpetually flounder near the bottom of the top division.

Attendance is more than double last week, but at less than 1,500 it's still pitifully low and stands out as the smallest K League gate of the round.

Thirty minutes into the match and visitors Seongnam are up 3-0. Former Busan Daewoo Royals striker Saša Drakulić is involved in all three goals, scoring the first and then – in less than two minutes – setting up the subsequent pair.

Kind Seongnam FC,
How charitable they are!
They could score seven goals,
But they only scored three goals.
How charitable they are!

This was a tongue-in-cheek chant oft heard in K League stadiums when dominant Seongnam came to visit. To be accurate, their scorelines rarely reached such heights in recent months, but Busan seemed happy to roll over for the league leaders today.

Earlier this week I was reminded by Colombian-American translator Leo Mendoza that Porterfield's imported trio were by no means his first-choice overseas signings.

'[Porterfield] wants to employ the English system,' Mendoza wrote in an email. 'Come the end of the English seasons, he has to scour the drains of the English Championship [second tier] to see who was left out of contract. This results in signing Andy Cooke and Jamie Cureton. ... Andy is a great bloke, motivated, and ready to use his size and power. But Jamie is a psychological wreck. He has ... personal problems with his lady ... and the desire to get as far as possible from England. Neither player was on Ian's first-choice list.

'Needless to say, Ian's makeshift imports were less than ideal. But that was all he could get on the cheap signing bonuses and no transfer money.'

Nor was the Scot's assistant manager at Busan, Aberdeen legend Drew Jarvie, his first choice for the position. Porterfield had wanted Tom Jones, a player he plucked from English non-league obscurity and inserted into Aberdeen's squad in the late 1980s. It was perhaps an odd choice, as Jones had just resigned as manager of Swindon Supermarine after leading the club to its worst-ever start to a season, and the pair hadn't spoken in almost 15 years.

But the club's tight-fisted ways even dictated who Porterfield could appoint as his number two. Jones did briefly join Porterfield in late 2002 to help lead Busan during the Korean FA Cup campaign, but the English coach's contract negotiations collapsed when he and the club couldn't agree on the cost of several perks, such as housing and education for Jones' children.

The referee whistles for half-time. Thirty-five kilometres to the north, Ulsan are hosting Suwon. Apparently also harbouring animosity toward the northern club, an Ulsan home supporter releases several live chickens on to the pitch bedecked with tags featuring the names of Suwon's prominent players. He then also hurls some eggs for good measure. Perhaps this is a tentative first step toward de-escalation from hooliganism that the K League hoped for?

Another prominent half-time substitution: Jamie Cureton comes out, making way for Harry – the first action for the Colombian since his return to the club. Curo has now gone nine matches without a goal. Replacing the player Porterfield claimed 'will score more goals than anyone in this country' with a striker he banished from the club just 75 days earlier must have served as some leathery crow for the Scottish manager to chew.

Harry scores an opportune goal as consolation, but that's all Busan can muster in a 3-1 thrashing by the K League giants. Elsewhere, Gwangju defeat Anyang, an opponent from the top half of the K League table. This leaves Busan six points behind the military newcomers, albeit with a match in hand.

How would Jamie Cureton react to being pulled off at half-time, as well as his replacement scoring? Pressure was mounting for the Bristolian.

Earlier that year, Cureton had been a cherished member of the Reading squad back home in England. But just a few months later, he found himself in unfamiliar circumstances: struggling at the sport he loved and had previously always dominated, while attempting to live in an alien country.

'What I should have done is re-sign for Reading,' Cureton later said to the *TNC Podcast*. 'I was loving every minute of it.'

Cureton had spent the last seven years desperately trying to climb back to the Premier League. Did leaving Reading sabotage those plans?

'I look back and [think], "I'd had just stayed at Reading, signed a three-year contract,"' Cureton later told the *Back of the Net* online video channel. 'They got into the Premier League within that period. Things would have been different.'

But did Cureton specifically regret coming to South Korea? In a 2014 interview with *The Independent*, Curo would refer to his time in the Land of the Morning Calm as 'another big mistake' in his career.

'It [moving to Korea] was the wrong decision,' Cureton later said to the *GasCast* podcast. 'Should never have done it, but I did.'

'I was still scoring goals in the Championship, and I had an opportunity to stay at Reading or go to other [Football League] clubs, so it was foolish for me [to go to Korea], really,' Cureton would say to Exeter City FC's online video channel.

'I was too young to leave what I had [in English football],' Cureton later told the *Full Core Football 24* online video channel. 'My career was flying. And I just hit a brick wall in the end, when I went out there [Korea].'

'Football-wise, [Busan] was okay,' Cureton later said to *Back of the Net*. 'The place was beautiful. I have nothing against South Korea. I lived on a beach in a lovely apartment. Training facilities, stadium, everything was unbelievable. But I was just not in the right place [psychologically]. I was too young and it just didn't work.'

'I was … mentally drained from living on my own and I was struggling being away from my kids, so it was probably the wrong move, really, at the … wrong time,' Cureton later told Exeter City FC's online video channel.

'After two months, I knew I'd made the wrong move,' he would tell the *Singing from the Nest* blog.

'I was probably at the lowest point in my life, really,' Cureton later said to the *Man Marking* podcast. 'It was just a case of trying to get through it, and just counting the days down.'

Twenty-one months still remained on Cureton's two-year contract with Busan I'cons.

Online rumours began to swirl of Cureton leaving for West Ham United as Alan Pardew, the manager Cureton played for at Reading prior to moving to Busan, had just taken the reins at the East London club.

Meanwhile, Cookie told the British media that Korea was a 'great experience' and that he's 'so glad' he came. He mentioned that he was learning a bit of the Korean language, including the *Hangeul* alphabet. Speaking later with the *V2 Football Podcast*, Cookie said the country was home to a 'fantastic culture'.

South Korea's national flag, the *Taegeukgi*, features a prominent *yin-yang* circle, representing opposite forces in the natural world. Cooke and Cureton certainly seemed to be having inverse experiences playing for Busan I'cons. Cookie had scored in more than half his matches and won awards, and made efforts to enjoy his stay despite some family-related challenges. Curo, however, was struggling to find the net, found his playing time seriously reduced and didn't seem to be enjoying life overseas.

Did the rumours of a quick departure back to England for Cureton contain a hint of truth?

I looked at the sports news. Seoul City Council had announced that none of Korea's wealthy business conglomerates were willing to bankroll a new football club in Seoul.

This was devastating news. The Korean Football Association's preference was for a new club to be established. But since there were no takers by prospective ownership groups, Seoul city officials switched tactics: solely to convince an existing K League club to relocate to the capital.

Only one club had submitted an application to move to Seoul thus far: Busan I'cons.

ROUND 35

Busan	**1-3**	**Seongnam**
Jeonbuk	1-2	Pohang
Jeonnam	0-0	Bucheon
Anyang	1-2	Gwangju
Ulsan	0-2	Suwon
Daejeon	3-2	Daegu

K LEAGUE TABLE

Seongnam	75
Ulsan	63
Jeonnam	52
Suwon	52
Daejeon	52
Jeonbuk	51
Anyang	47
Pohang	47
Gwangju	41
Busan	**35**
Daegu	25
Bucheon	16

CHAPTER 28

SMASHING CHAIRS AND PERILOUS BUSES

DAEGU FC VS. BUSAN I'CONS
SUNDAY, 26 OCTOBER 2003
K LEAGUE ROUND 39
DAEGU CIVIC STADIUM
독 안에 든 쥐
– There is little hope for escape (literally,
'a mouse in an earthen jar')

IAN PORTERFIELD'S Busan I'cons limped through their congested schedule into October, the penultimate month of the K League season, with matches against three difficult opponents: Suwon, Daejeon and Ulsan.

Although they would receive a battering against Samsung-bankrolled Suwon, Busan pluckily earned narrow victories against both Daejeon and Ulsan – marking just the second instance this season of Busan winning consecutive matches. Busan were now only one point below Gwangju, still with a match in hand. Cookie, Harry and goalkeeper Kim Yong-dae were named in the league's unofficial 'best 11' for the week.

But Jamie Cureton's on-field woes continued. He was inexplicably employed as a midfielder against Suwon, perhaps the first instance in his adult life. Curo's playing time was also beginning to dwindle, as he was pulled with 25 minutes remaining against Daejeon and only played the final five minutes as a late substitute against Ulsan.

The club was also dealt some bad news: Lee Lim-saeng's chronic injuries had become so bad that the veteran defender decided to retire. Busan had paid a rare transfer fee to obtain him from Bucheon's fire sale of talent during the close season, yet were only able to utilise his services for less than a single year.

As Seongnam were running away with the league title, perhaps the most captivating contest by this point was for the K League golden boot. Five players were realistically in contention: Seongnam's Kim Do-hoon and four Brazilians. Kim scored a hat-trick during round 36, equalling the all-time K League goals record of 21. But with eight rounds still to play, a new record was inevitable.

In the subsequent round, Jeonbuk striker Magno Alves – who had scored the most goals for storied club Fluminense in the 2001 Brazilian Série A – earned a brace to also reach the existing goal record and go level with Kim. The five-way contest was quickly narrowing into a two-way race between Kim and Magno.

Magno's close pursuit was causing Kim some consternation, who ruffled feathers by stating he didn't want a non-Korean to set the new K League goal record.

'I don't want to lose the title to foreign players,' Kim told the *Dong-A Ilbo*. 'I will break the record without fail.'

Kim's decision to twist the tight goal race into a patriotic battle of 'Koreans against foreigners' wasn't helping South Korea earn a cosmopolitan image. Nor was Kim unique for transposing such a nationalistic context on to an otherwise benign contest.

Over the centuries, Korea had developed a persecution complex, the natural consequence of being geographically surrounded – and occasionally subjugated and even colonised – by larger powers. When China wasn't coercing Korea's royal family to formally honour the Chinese emperor, aggressive Japanese forces were intruding instead.

It wasn't a coincidence that Korea became the Hermit Kingdom: it needed to keep the outside world at bay to protect itself from imperialist conquests.

The determination to defeat stronger outside forces implanted a David-against-Goliath narrative into Korea's national psyche. And despite South Korea's rapidly developing economy, many locals still harboured an 'aggrieved underdog' mentality against the international community.

There was little appetite or tolerance for criticism of South Korea in 2003. Perceived slights, even if unintentional, occasionally sparked international incidents. When South Korean speed skater Kim Dong-sung passed the finish line first at the 2002 Winter Olympics but was disqualified for 'blocking', the gold went instead to USA skater Apolo Ohno. As an American of Japanese descent – the two least-favourite nationalities of South Korean jingoists – Ohno was made the scapegoat. He was inundated with death threats and told he would be attacked if he attended a future skating event in South Korea. The on-ice incident became such a powerful analogy of the oppression of Korea by larger powers that at the FIFA World Cup just months later, a goal for Korea against the USA was celebrated by mimicking speed-skating motions.

The term *pihae uishik* (피해 의식)' – or 'victim mentality' – was used to explain surprisingly emotive reactions to what would seem benign incidents to most outsiders.

Even locals weren't immune to their country's patriotic backlash. During the 2006 World Cup, Korean football commentator Shin Moon-sun suggested that a Swiss goal against South Korea was not offside and should stand. The response from his fellow citizens was that he was a national traitor. Three days later, he was summoned back to Korea in the middle of the tournament and relieved of his commentating duties.

Conversely, whenever a foreigner praised anything Korean during this era, it served as a source of tremendous pride and self-assurance. Korean food – or more specifically, foreigners' fondness for Korean food – was a frequent topic of curiosity. When Brazilian manager Arthur Bernardes was appointed boss at a K League side in 2008, the news media felt it necessary to mention that he enjoyed eating *kimchi jjigae*.

The 2002 World Cup had served as an opportunity for South Korea to illustrate that it could compete with the best of the world, and with each subsequent surprise win, the streets of Korea filled with an increasing number of fans who were more captivated by the nationalistic celebrations than the football.

After midfielder Park Ji-sung joined Manchester United, the signing was used to assert that Koreans were good enough to play for the best football clubs in the world, and Park was transformed into a national icon.

The subsequent generation of Koreans, much more self-assured and cosmopolitan, would derisively refer to such nationalistic self-congratulation as '*guk bbong* (국뽕)', or 'nationalism meth'. But this generation still wanted nothing but for Korea to finish on top.

This was the patriotic context for Seongnam striker Kim Do-hoon's assertion that he didn't want a foreigner to set the new K League goalscoring record. In wasn't just that he *personally* wanted to create the new record – he wanted to set the record *because he was Korean*. He wanted to protect the domestic league's pride and virtue by preventing a non-Korean from sullying it.

This wasn't so much about a football record as it was about nationalistic pride.

While Busan played away to Ulsan, Seongnam hosted Jeonbuk, a match that pitted the teams of the two primary golden-boot aspirants – Kim Do-hoon and Magno Alves – against each other. Magno scored but Kim did not, giving Jeonbuk's Brazilian the new record of 22 K League goals. However, several rounds of the K League were still to be played; the record-breaking certainly wasn't finished yet.

Another foreign striker enjoying life in South Korea was Busan's Andy Cooke. After acclimatising to the heat he was finding success on the pitch and even learning the local language. But despite such efforts, Cookie and his wife Kate were starting to feel some pangs of homesickness. Cooke, who later spoke with the *V2 Football Podcast* about this period, said, 'Koreans are such lovely people, and the culture and the food is fantastic, so that helps, but there was some lonely, lonely time there.'

Cookie told the podcast that the location of their beach-resort house in Busan was not ideal, requiring a several-hour commute each day.

'I'd have to drive for an hour – well, it was only about five or six miles to the house, across the city – but it would take me about an hour-and-a-half because the traffic was crazy,' said Cooke. 'It was really, really tough.'

He also mentioned that having all of their family and friends back home created a feeling of isolation.

'We didn't really get to know that many expats … Ian [Porterfield] spoke English, and the assistant manager at the time [Drew Jarvie] spoke English, and that was about it,' he told the podcast. 'I was constantly on the computer. I think that's down to loneliness at times, or being out there, you want to keep in touch.'

Cooke had similar comments when speaking with the *Stoke Sentinel* toward the end of the 2003 season.

'I'll be glad to get home for a bit because you do miss family and friends out here when you're a 12-hour flight away and there's a nine-hour time difference,' he said.

'And obviously there is little TV to watch in our language, so we must have watched 500 videos since getting over here.'

With Cooke's first child on the way, and loneliness starting to take a toll on both him and his wife, would the English striker be able to complete the entirety of his two-year contract with Busan I'cons?

After a two-week international break, Busan were due to play away to newcomers Daegu FC on a Sunday afternoon. Busan had one loss, one draw and one win thus far against Daegu, an improvement in each subsequent fixture. The I'cons were also on a two-match winning streak. However, Daegu had only lost twice in their last eight matches – a run that included a win over Jeonbuk (now in third place), as well as draws home and away against second-placed Ulsan. While this fixture might have looked an unappealing second-bottom versus third-bottom match at first glance, both sides were on strong form and the game offered the allure of a hard-fought six-pointer.

After driving for 30 minutes, traffic slowed as larger vehicles were required to roll across a weight scale. As the Busan supporters' bus rode over, an official waved for our driver to pull over to the side of the road alongside several large trucks.

Uh oh.

'Everyone up front!' barked our driver. The Pride of Pusan members obliged, marching up the aisle toward the front half of the vehicle. Apparently our bus was too rear-heavy, and so the clever driver – who had no doubt been through this scenario before – had sussed out a way to beat the system and keep his vehicle on the road. So, technically speaking, our supporters' bus was probably unsafe, unfit for the motorway as it carried dozens of passengers. I recalled the news from last week that a bus fell off a road up near Daegu. I reached for my seatbelt – and realised there wasn't one.

Gulp.

We finally arrived at the Daegu Civic Stadium, an old ground constructed prior to the Korean War but renovated just one month before this match.

Peculiarly, neither Cureton nor Harry start. The match is tense. Daegu score first in the 13th minute, thanks to a young winger in his debut K League season. Cookie has several opportunities but just can't quite tuck one past Daegu's goalkeeper.

At half-time, Cureton comes on as a substitute. Unfortunately the English striker doesn't amount to much. The Busan supporters have a new banner that proclaims 'poetry on the pitch', but sadly, it's anything but.

Then, disaster. Norwegian defender Jon Hjelde takes a nasty knock and is taken off the pitch by stretcher. It's obvious he will have to be substituted. Porterfield has to think fast: replace him with another defender – such as 1998 World Cup participant Jang Dae-il – or thrown on a more attack-oriented player instead? He opts for the latter, bringing on Colombian goal-poacher Harry.

The substitution doesn't work. With Busan's back-line weakened, Daegu quickly score.

The match finishes as a 2-0 win for Daegu, now just nine points behind Busan at the arse end of the K League table, with only lowly Bucheon below. The result gives newcomers Daegu FC a home league double over Busan, former champions of Asia.

Elsewhere, Gwangju only manage a draw away to bottom side Bucheon, but it's one more point than Busan manage this round, allowing Gwangju to widen their lead above Busan to two points.

More noteworthy: Seongnam lifted the 2003 K League title, their third straight championship. It's a romp of a season, with Seongnam almost 20 points ahead of second-placed Ulsan.

Neither of the two main golden boot challengers – Kim Do-hoon of Seongnam nor Magno Alves of Jeonbuk – managed to score this round.

But there was another development in the Seoul World Cup Stadium relocation saga. Anyang Cheetahs announced they had also applied to move to the country's capital. Anyang's stadium was built on the cheap in the mid-1980s, toward the end of the country's dictatorship era when construction was often rushed and wanting in quality. Despite being less than two decades old, the stadium was already dilapidated, its concrete terraces crumbling.

The Korea Football Association and K League responded to Anyang's application by releasing statements reiterating their desire for a new team to be created rather than an existing team being relocated. But with no business conglomerates expressing an interest by the previous deadline, that scenario looked improbable.

'We are in the position to think about long-term measures for the development of Korean football,' an unnamed K League official told the *Korea Times*. 'If the Cheetahs come to Seoul, it could possibly create a temporary boom in Seoul. But what will happen in Anyang? We should take a long-term view to solve this matter.'

Just one month earlier, Wimbledon played their first match in Milton Keynes after being relocated against fans' wishes. The parallel in South Korea was striking. Anyang fans were livid at their club's application announcement.

The K League's board of directors would soon make the final decision as to whether Busan I'cons or Anyang Cheetahs would be granted permission to move to Seoul.

ROUND 36

Suwon	3-0	Busan
Daejeon	1-1	Ulsan
Seongnam	5-1	Anyang
Jeonnam	1-0	Gwangju
Bucheon	2-3	Jeonbuk
Daegu	0-1	Pohang

ROUND 37

Busan	1-0	Daejeon
Pohang	4-1	Bucheon
Jeonbuk	2-0	Gwangju
Jeonnam	0-0	Seongnam
Anyang	1-2	Suwon
Ulsan	0-0	Daegu

ROUND 38

Ulsan	1-2	Busan
Daejeon	3-0	Anyang
Suwon	1-2	Jeonnam
Seongnam	1-2	Jeonbuk
Gwangju	1-1	Pohang
Daegu	1-0	Bucheon

ROUND 28 (rescheduled due to inclement weather)
Seongnam   1-0   Pohang

ROUND 39
Daegu   **2-0**   **Busan**
Anyang   1-1   Ulsan
Bucheon   0-0   Gwangju
Jeonbuk   2-2   Suwon
Jeonnam   2-1   Daejeon
Pohang   0-1   Seongnam

K LEAGUE TABLE
Seongnam   85
Ulsan   66
Jeonnam   62
Jeonbuk   61
Suwon   59
Daejeon   56
Pohang   54
Anyang   48
Gwangju   43
Busan   **41**
Daegu   32
Bucheon   17

CHAPTER 29

FOOTBALL HOOLIGANS AND PICNICKING FAMILIES

BUSAN I'CONS VS. JEONBUK HYUNDAI MOTORS
SUNDAY, 9 NOVEMBER 2003
K LEAGUE ROUND 42
BUSAN ASIAD WORLD CUP STADIUM

시작이 반이다
– Starting is half the job

K LEAGUE HOOLIGANISM was increasing to unprecedented levels this season, yet authorities had done little to remedy the trend. They presumably hoped it would fizzle out on its own.

But when Jeonbuk supporters – several armed with steel pipes – ran on to the pitch, attempted to invade the away team's dressing room and smashed windows, the league had had enough. These rampaging wannabes were scaring off the bread and butter of the K League: passive adults and picnicking families.

Jeonbuk hardcore weren't the only naughty fans, as unsavoury incidents had become a regular occurrence across the country. In a scene reminiscent of professional wrestling, Daejeon supporters threw a table and several rubbish bins down from the stands, and hurled bottles and a live flare toward the opposition goalkeeper.

At a Daegu–Suwon match during the summer, Daegu supporters threw lit flares on the playing surface. Stewards helpfully replied by launching them back into the crowd.

With matters starting to get messy, the K League took action – or at least talked a tough line. Officials promised to identify and prosecute the responsible parties, fine the relevant clubs, and force clubs whose supporters engage in violence on two occasions to play behind closed doors. Was the announcement the beginning of a crackdown, or yet more empty threats to be ignored by those who enjoyed a bit of argy-bargy?

But back to the actual football. Busan would finish October and begin the final month of the season with a pair of away matches at rapidly improving Jeonnam as well as a home match against faltering Anyang. Busan would lose both games against Jeonnam, 4-1 and 3-0, allowing the Jeolla side to complete a 'league quadruple' with a 12-1 aggregate scoreline. Fortunately Busan were able to salvage a point from a goalless draw against Anyang.

Cureton commenced this set of matches yet again as a substitute – his third consecutive game on the bench – but didn't even make the squad during the two subsequent encounters. Conjecture that Curo would break his contract prematurely and leave Busan intensified.

Cookie was scoring regularly, but his efforts weren't enough to single-handedly earn victories for Busan. Meanwhile, Hjelde was involved in a nasty collision during the last match of October, which would rule him out for several games.

Was coming to South Korea worth the risk for foreign players?

'It's a big gamble, and it's a huge commitment, moving to the other side of the world,' Cooke later told the *V2 Football Podcast*. 'It's not an easy thing to do, by no means.'

On the bright side for Busan, at the conclusion of the three matches, they had reduced Gwangju's lead to just a single point.

Meanwhile, in the K League golden-boot race, Seongnam's Kim Do-hoon had scored once while Jeonbuk's Magno found the back of the net twice, giving the Brazilian a two-goal lead over the native Korean striker with just three matches remaining.

Elsewhere in the K League, rumours were swirling that business conglomerate SK intended to cease its ownership and funding of Bucheon. Was this yet another club ripe for relocation to Seoul?

* * *

Busan I'cons supporters must have wondered whether Ian Porterfield's British revolution was a ruse. The club was now winless in their last four matches, while the much-heralded Jamie Cureton – whom Porterfield attested would score more goals than anyone else in the league – had still only scored twice.

After Busan's recent match, midfielder Jeon Woo-keun joined defender Shim Jae-won in declaring he had registered to fulfil his national military service and thus would spend the next two seasons playing on loan to Gwangju. Pride of Pusan members speculated whether Jeon's decision was an indirect criticism of Porterfield's management and an attempt to avoid playing under him.

With just three rounds remaining in this overloaded season, Busan would host Jeonbuk Hyundai Motors next. The visitors were high in the league table but had won only once in their last four games. Perhaps this was a chance for Porterfield to earn points against a strong opponent.

Cureton was pencilled in to start the match, dampening rumours of him leaving for West Ham. Cookie also returned after serving his one-match suspension for cautions, while Hjelde's injury kept him out for the third straight game.

The first half-hour is largely uneventful, although Busan look dangerous with the combined efforts of Harry, Cookie and Curo. In the 37th minute, Harry crosses the ball across the face of the penalty area. Curo gets his head on to it and thuds it into goal. The Bristolian has finally broken his dry spell of almost three months. Curo's celebration is ecstatic, with Harry rushing in to congratulate him.

1-0 Busan.

Just seven minutes later, Busan are back on the attack. Curo gets his head on a cross into the box, directing the ball at the left of goal. He almost gets his second goal of the match, but the ball bounces softly off the post. Luckily, Cookie rushes forward unchallenged and easily hammers the ball into the top right of the net.

2-0 Busan. This was Busan's best start to a match in almost three months.

Ten minutes after the break, Busan are at it again. Defender Shim Jae-won strays up front with possession and rushes toward goal, surprising Jeonbuk's back-line. Yet again, the ball is crossed across the face of the penalty area. This cross is lower, so Cureton sticks out a boot to direct the ball toward the net. It rockets up into the left side of goal.

3-0 Busan.

This was becoming quite the result, as today was the first time Busan had been up by such a scoreline all season. In fact, you had to look back to July 2002 – more than 15 months earlier, prior to Porterfield's time in charge – for the last occasion Busan acquired such an emphatic lead.

For Jamie Cureton, it was surely relief. In less than an hour he has doubled his goal tally for the season. Will this silence his critics and put rumours of his return home to rest?

But four minutes after Busan obtain their 3-0 lead, Jeonbuk pounce. Brazilian striker Edmilson scores for the visitors. Just two minutes later, Magno Alves – the player involved in the golden boot race and who scored a hat-trick against Busan back in March during Porterfield's first K League defeat – adds to Jeonbuk's tally.

3-2 Busan. In a spell of just two minutes, Busan's biggest lead in more than a year almost completely evaporates.

Just as pessimism begins to set in among Busan fans, Jeonbuk score an own goal under pressure. It extends Busan's lead into a less anxious, two-goal buffer: 4-2.

The Pride of Pusan fans chant the responsible Jeonbuk player's name in mock congratulation. Tempting fate, they even start to chant 'we want five!' This, of course, angers the K League gods, whose wrath should not be tested. Toward the end of the match, Jeonbuk pick up another two goals in a three-minute spell, again by Brazilians Magno and Edmilson.

4-4.

Now pessimism *truly* sets in. The early three-goal lead has been eradicated. Jeonbuk continue to pressure, looking for the winner. This is starting to resemble the Premier League match from 2001 in which Manchester United came back from being 3-0 down against Tottenham to actually win. Are Busan about to chuck this game away?

The conclusion of the match is intense. Instead of Busan sitting back and hoping for the draw, both clubs strive for the victory. Each team leaves themselves exposed after charging forward, causing repeated counter-attacks. It's enthralling for neutral observers, but nerve-wracking for the Busan faithful. They pray for the whistle – anything to earn Busan a point and prevent an embarrassing loss.

The referee finally concludes the game after a tortuous length of time. Although it finished as a draw, it was one of the most exciting ends to a football match I had ever witnessed. A pity that fewer than 1,000 people bothered to turn up to watch – already the third time Busan could only attract a three-figure crowd that season.

Despite being tremendous entertainment, the result was woeful for Busan considering the early, three-goal lead. It was now the fifth match on the trot without a win for Busan.

On the bright side, Jamie Cureton had finally conquered his goal drought. Would this help him overcome his depression and adjust to life in Asia?

Worryingly, however, Curo looked to be sporting an injury again after the match as he walked gingerly back to the dressing room.

Another positive from this weekend was that Busan earned a point on a night that Gwangju lost, putting Busan level with Gwangju in the much-coveted fourth-bottom K League position. These heights were the stuff of nosebleeds.

Second-bottom Daegu miraculously attained a 3-3 draw against champions Seongnam, but with only two matches remaining they could no longer mathematically catch up with Busan. If the true objective of Busan's season was simply faring better than the two new teams, Busan were halfway there.

Busan's two remaining fixtures were away to Pohang and at home against basement club Bucheon, while Gwangju would host resurgent Daejeon and play away to dominant Ulsan. Busan looked to have the easier games lined up, but would likely have to overcome their winless ways to ensure a finish above Gwangju.

In the golden boot race, although Magno scored twice against Busan, Seongnam's Kim Do-hoon managed a hat-trick against Daegu, narrowing Magno's lead to a single goal. A tense finish awaited.

Several days later, the K League board of directors held a meeting at their headquarters in Seoul. On the agenda was whether to allow an existing team to relocate to the Seoul World Cup Stadium, which would require amending the league's existing policy. The fans got wind of the meeting agenda, resulting in some 300 Anyang and Busan supporters protesting outside the meeting venue despite it being held on a weekday during business hours. They were determined to publicly display their opposition to the league potentially sanctioning a club move. The fans' protest wasn't appreciated, with a large police presence greeting them. Irate supporters attempted to force their way into the league office, leading to several scuffles between officers and protesters.

Despite the commotion outside, the K League's board of directors ultimately voted unanimously to allow one existing club to relocate to Seoul. But would it be Busan or Anyang that move to the capital, abandoning their fan base and community?

ROUND 19 (rescheduled due to inclement weather)
Jeonnam **4-1** **Busan**

ROUND 28 (rescheduled due to inclement weather)
Suwon 2-0 Jeonbuk

ROUND 30 (rescheduled due to inclement weather)
Anyang 2-2 Seongnam

ROUND 40
Busan **0-0** **Anyang**
Ulsan 0-0 Jeonnam
Seongnam 1-1 Bucheon
Daejeon 1-0 Jeonbuk
Suwon 0-0 Pohang
Gwangju 0-2 Daegu

ROUND 41
Jeonnam **3-0** **Busan**
Gwangju 3-4 Seongnam
Bucheon 3-1 Suwon
Pohang 3-0 Daejeon
Jeonbuk 3-1 Ulsan
Daegu 0-2 Anyang

ROUND 42
Busan **4-4** **Jeonbuk**
Anyang 1-0 Jeonnam
Ulsan 1-2 Pohang
Daejeon 1-0 Bucheon
Suwon 1-0 Gwangju
Daegu 3-3 Seongnam

K LEAGUE TABLE

Seongnam	91
Jeonnam	69
Ulsan	67
Suwon	66
Jeonbuk	66
Daejeon	62
Pohang	61
Anyang	56
Gwangju	43
Busan	**43**
Daegu	36
Bucheon	21

CHAPTER 30

MATCH FIXING AND FAREWELL LETTERS

POHANG STEELERS VS. BUSAN I'CONS
WEDNESDAY, 12 NOVEMBER 2003
K LEAGUE ROUND 43
POHANG STEEL YARD (A.K.A. BLAST
FURNACE)

BUSAN I'CONS VS. BUCHEON SK
SUNDAY, 16 NOVEMBER 2003
K LEAGUE ROUND 44 (FINAL
LEAGUE MATCH)
BUSAN ASIAD WORLD CUP STADIUM

망건 쓰자 파장된다
*– Too little, too late (literally, 'just as you
finishing fastening your headband, the state
examination ends')*

Jamie Cureton's noticeable limp at the conclusion at Busan's previous match turned out to be more serious than initially thought.

'I picked up an injury in the last game I played ... and I've been struggling,' Cureton told the website of Reading FC, his English club prior to moving to South Korea.

'It's been a bit weird not knowing what the actual problem [is] because of the language barrier.'

After suffering from being separated from his young children in England, the inability to engage in his usual extroversion while in a foreign country, depression, and a goal drought, Curo finally improved his fortunes by scoring a brace against K League powerhouse Jeonbuk. But with an unknown injury to his ankle, pessimism likely came flooding back after brief respite. Only two league matches remained; would Cureton receive another opportunity to add to his four-goal tally before the winter close season?

Throughout the past few months, Andy Cooke had coped much better than Cureton with life in South Korea. Cookie was scoring regularly and the subtropical heat had finally eased, enabling his pregnant wife Kate to venture outside their beachfront apartment more often during daytime. There was now a tranquil feeling to Cookie's interviews. He told the *Stoke Sentinel*, 'I've managed to do quite well so far. Out here I'm more relaxed as a player and focusing on goalscoring – maybe I should have been more selfish in that respect at Stoke.

'... [T]here are certainly no regrets in giving it a go here [in South Korea]. Life is a lot more relaxed and football isn't in your face all the time here because we can't read the newspapers or follow the TV the same.

'I'd certainly recommend [South Korea] to any other player with the chance to come out and play here.'

Busan's final away match of the season would be a Wednesday trip to the Steel Yard to face mid-table Pohang Steelers. The fixture looked arduous. Busan were shouldering a five-match winless streak. Conversely, Pohang were undefeated in their last three games, and had only lost against league-winners Seongnam in their last nine games. But in Busan's favour, they had fared reasonably well against Pohang thus far this season, earning one win, one draw and a loss.

Cookie and Harry both start up front. Cureton is out nursing the injury he picked up after finally scoring again last match. Hjelde returns to the squad after missing three games due to a knock on his knee. Ageing midfielder Noh Jung-yoon doesn't make it. Once again, Porterfield is forced to cobble together a makeshift starting 11.

Jeon Woo-keun, the attacking midfielder who disliked Porterfield's kick-and-rush tactics and recently announced he was leaving Busan I'cons for the next two seasons to fulfil his military obligation on loan at Gwangju Sangmu, scores a rare goal in the

89th minute after a pass from Harry. It was as if a weight were lifted off Jeon's shoulders. This player, who was once expected to represent South Korea at the 2000 Olympics but had lapsed into a K League utility role under mediocre managers, today looked relaxed and confident. Was playing for woeful Busan really such psychological drudgery that the prospect of playing elsewhere next season was enough to lift one's spirits?

Busan's season had been stripped of success many months ago, but a moral victory was still possible for the former Asian champions – to finish at least in ninth place, above K League newcomers Gwangju. Unfortunately, Busan's 1-0 away win at Pohang in this penultimate round wasn't enough to lift them above tenth as Gwangju also secured a victory, snapping a six-match winless streak. If Busan were to finish above Gwangju, they would have to leapfrog the new team on the final day of the season.

For Porterfield, lifting Busan above the newly formed military team wouldn't just be a consolatory victory – it might be his last opportunity to salvage his K League employment.

As much as Busan I'cons seemed a cursed club, the fixture gods were smiling upon them at the twilight of this lamentable season. Busan's final K League match would be at home against bottom-dwellers Bucheon, in theory the easiest possible game they would face all year. Gwangju – rivals for the illustrious fourth-from-bottom position – faced a daunting challenge: playing away to second-placed Ulsan. Would Busan be able to exploit the final day's pairings and leap into ninth, or would they manage to bugger up even this advantageous scenario?

Once again, Cureton wouldn't feature due to injury. Hjelde was also absent, despite having just played a full game after returning from a knock to his knee.

Half an hour into the match against basement Bucheon, Busan earn a free kick. As the ball is about to be struck, three Bucheon defenders rush away from goal, hoping to catch a Busan player with the offside trap. It looks like a cheeky ploy rehearsed on the training ground. With Bucheon's season all but over, they have little to lose.

While it's possible that a couple of Busan players are offside, Cookie is clearly onside. The referee's assistant doesn't raise his flag. Cookie races toward goal and collects the incoming ball at the corner of the six-yard box. By now the three Bucheon defenders realise their ruse has failed and look back in helpless horror, hoping for a miracle from their goalkeeper. But there are to be no such heroics: Cookie smashes the ball into the goal.

1-0 Busan. It's a comical end to a season of inadvertent slapstick.

With the game complete, the Busan players and coaching staff crowded around a mobile phone to watch for the final score in the Gwangju match. It was 0-0 at half-time, making for a tense second half in Busan. But relief washed over their faces as they saw the updated result: Ulsan 5-0 Gwangju. Yes, *five* goals scored in the second half. Gwangju's late collapse made it official: Busan finished the season in a heady ninth place, pulling ahead of the new military team for the first time in months.

Ian Porterfield smiled faintly, yet knew he had much work to do to turn this team around – if he even survived the close season. Despite finishing above Gwangju and Daegu, Busan's pitiful goal difference of -30 was worse than both of the new teams.

For Andy Cooke, his excursion to South Korea galvanised his career as a goalscorer. The Salopian striker tallied 13 goals in 22 games, finishing as the tenth-highest scorer in the league, despite joining halfway into the season. Only Brazilians and native Koreans scored more than him, as Cookie contributed more goals than several other foreign attacking players who had contested the entire season.

For Jamie Cureton, moving to Busan had a very different outcome: just four goals in 21 games. Having left Reading on a relative high, he had been sought after by numerous clubs. But now, his ability to perform was in doubt. Life away from his young children was difficult and he found it challenging to adjust to a foreign country where he couldn't be his gregarious self. Would he want to spend another year and a half in Korea as he was contractually obligated? Did Porterfield still want his services?

Busan I'cons would require a tremendous amount of effort – and luck – to rebuild. The former champions of Asia barely ascended to the height of fourth-bottom, only above a new military team, a team that set a league record for consecutive winless results and another woeful expansion side. Their record stood at 13 wins, ten draws and 21 losses.

Going into the final round of the season, jockeying for the golden boot were Magno Alves of Jeonbuk (with 27 goals), Kim Do-hoon of Seongnam (26), Ricardo 'Dodo' Lucas of Ulsan (23), and Itamar Batista da Silva of Jeonnam (23) – three Brazilians and one Korean. Kim scored during the first half of his match, bringing him level with Magno. In the second half, Dodo scored an impressive (and possibly suspect) four goals, including three goals in four minutes, also bringing him up to 27. But Kim scored again in the second half, notching him at 28. With no goals from Magno or Itamar, Kim achieved his desired feat: ensuring that a Korean set the new all-time K League scoring record. The Korean sports media revelled in the accomplishment.

Almost immediately after the final whistle, a whisper campaign began. There was no doubting that Kim Do-hoon was a superb striker, but had he received some 'assistance' in his achievement, as some were alleging? He had managed to close the 2003 season by scoring six goals during three winless matches. A 3-3 draw against lowly Daegu, in which Kim scored a hat-trick yet Seongnam didn't manage to win, raised the most eyebrows. However, no credible evidence of any wrong-doing was ever presented.

If Busan's 13 wins seemed feeble, Bucheon only mustered three victories in this marathon 44-match season. From a points-per-game perspective, it was the worst performance in the 21-year history of the K League.

After more than a year of Bucheon supporters demanding that club owners SK sell the under-funded club, it looked like they might get their wish. SK declared they wanted out. Soon an Argentina-based multinational corporation heavily involved with casinos expressed an interest in purchasing Bucheon, which would potentially make it the first K League side bankrolled with foreign money. Chinese super club Dalian Shide also publicly mulled over whether to acquire the struggling Korean team.

Although the managerial merry-go-round was thankfully absent from Korean club football, Suwon Bluewings sacked Kim Ho after eight seasons in charge since the founding of the club, and replaced him with Cha Bum-keun, arguably South Korea's best-ever footballer. Cha had recently completed a multi-year ban from involvement in Korean football due to making accusations that match-fixing and corruption were prevalent in the Korean game, allegations he made shortly after being sacked as the South Korean national team manager when the country was dumped out of the 1998 World Cup.

With mumblings about whether some of Seongnam's achievements had been 'genuine', many Koreans were reminded of the accusations of impropriety that led to Cha's ban half a decade earlier. Were crooked events really part of Korean football, and were they still occurring?

As the years rolled on, nefarious activities continued. A match-fixing scandal would be exposed in 2011 that involved coaches and organised crime rings serving as brokers. More than 50 players were implicated; 41 were given lifetime bans from football while 39 people in total were imprisoned. The national government warned that the league would be shut down if it didn't sort itself out.

Gyeongnam FC president Ahn Jongbok was accused of bribing two K League referees during the 2013 and 2014 seasons. He resigned in disgrace and the club was docked ten points.

A Jeonbuk scout was indicted for paying a bung to two referees, also during the 2013 season. The club claimed he was a rogue employee acting on his own volition and that they were completely unaware of his misdeeds.

To be fair to Korean football, most Asian countries struggled to eradicate match-fixing, and the scourge was also present in other Korean sports – even professional video-gaming.

Back in the K League, Busan's application to relocate to the Seoul World Cup Stadium in the opposite corner of the country looked like a done deal, despite the league not yet making a formal announcement. Club staff posted a public apology to the fans that served as a goodbye letter:

'We, the Busan I'cons, have been encouraged throughout these times with you. Through joy and sorrow, excitement and pain, we could not have been there without you. We will never forget the beautiful times we have shared with you.

'The Busan I'cons bought out the bankrupt Busan Daewoo Royals in the year 2000 to boost the level of K League interest, and for the success of the 2002 World Cup. We have also invested US$60m over the past four years (even through Korea's financial crisis) for the club to regain its stature as a traditional and powerful football club.

'We have tried our best for the better of the league and the team. ... We have also implemented a youth system and have tried to spread football infrastructure around the city.

'However, the lack of a football-specific stadium and other challenging circumstances made us predict deficits in the future that could threaten the very existence of the club.

'Therefore, despite the passionate support and love of Busan's citizens, we, the Busan I'cons have chosen the unfortunate option of moving out of Busan for the future success and the survival of the club. We have decided that a move to Seoul will increase Korea's overall football infrastructure, and the fact that it is the capital city with a population of ten million gave us the aspirations of transforming ourselves into a pure, citizen-owned football club. Although we are deeply saddened by our decision to move, we believe that you will understand and accept our difficult decision.

'Finally, we express our grief to the citizens of Busan, who gave us their unwavering belief and support. We will strive forward to become a better football club in the future so we can step closer to the football fans from this point on. Thank you.'

Incensed, the Pride of Pusan members rushed to Busan City Hall and staged a protest, determined to make their displeasure publicly known.

Busan City Council panicked. If the only football club in South Korea's second-largest city – a club with formidable pedigree – were to flee for greener pastures, Busan's municipal politicians might foot the blame and take a bollocking in the next election.

Meetings were set up between Busan I'cons and the city. Council officials offered the club a plethora of enticements in the hope of convincing them to stay put: a reduction in stadium rent, kit sponsorship, additional financial support and repairs to the old Gudeok Stadium. Mostly things that had allegedly already been offered to the club earlier but not delivered upon.

Would the club take the bait?

One anonymous Busan city official told the media, 'If needed, we can change the laws to help football expand in Busan, and we will support Busan I'cons in the long run.'

But an uninterested senior club official responded, 'We are confident. We want this Seoul move and I have never thought about failing this decision.'

While Busan played its last match of the season at home on a Sunday afternoon, Seoul city officials, the Korean Football

Association and the K League met to discuss the relocation bids from Busan and Anyang. A final decision was imminent.

As flies to wanton boys are we to th' gods,
They kill us for their sport.

– William Shakespeare's *King Lear*: act 4, scene 1

ROUND 43

Pohang	**0-1**	**Busan**
Seongnam	2-4	Suwon
Gwangju	1-0	Daejeon
Bucheon	0-1	Ulsan
Jeonbuk	3-1	Anyang
Daegu	1-1	Jeonnam

ROUND 44

Busan	**1-0**	**Bucheon**
Jeonnam	1-1	Jeonbuk
Anyang	1-2	Pohang
Ulsan	5-0	Gwangju
Daejeon	3-2	Seongnam
Suwon	2-1	Daegu

FINAL 2003 K LEAGUE TABLE

Seongnam Ilhwa Chunma (Pegasus)	91
Ulsan Hyundai Horang-i (Tigers)	73
Suwon Samsung Bluewings	72
Jeonnam Dragons	71
Jeonbuk Hyundai Motors	69
Daejeon Citizen	65
Pohang Steelers	64
Anyang LG Cheetahs	56
Busan I'cons	**49**
Gwangju Sangmu Bulsajo (Military Phoenix)	46
Daegu FC	37
Bucheon SK	21

CHAPTER 31

SEASON OF SORROW

KONKUK UNIVERSITY VS. BUSAN I'CONS
FRIDAY, 21 NOVEMBER 2003
KOREAN FA CUP, ROUND OF 32
NAMHAE SPORTS PARK

용두사미 (龍頭蛇尾)
– Come in with a bang but go out with a fizzle
(literally, 'dragon head, snake tail')

AUTUMN 2003 was a time of intense change in South Korea. Its first bullet train was about to launch, the ban on Japanese cultural goods was being rescinded and the government had just signed a free trade agreement with Chile.

And after just four months in the Hermit Kingdom, Jamie Cureton was returning to England.

The football calendar hadn't quite concluded yet, as Busan I'cons were still to compete in the post-season Korean FA Cup, which could run as long as five matches. But with 20 months still remaining on his contract, Cureton decided to leave.

He wouldn't be coming back.

'Curo just does not like the lifestyle [in South Korea] and he's struggled with the language,' said his agent, Nick Ellis.

'It was different, a completely different way of life,' Cureton later told Exeter City FC's online video channel. 'We'd finish a game, and they'd go straight for a meal. It was like a mad rush; there was no team talk after a game, they just sat in a restaurant. So it was different.'

'I've had a stint abroad now, seen what it's about and learnt a lot about myself,' Cureton told the Reading FC website.

Years later, after self-reflection, Cureton was less critical about the country had been stationed in.

'It's a shame it didn't work out,' Cureton told *The Guardian*. 'It was probably just the timing of when I went. I was too young. I'd just had three good years at Reading and it's probably the one decision where I should have stayed at a club.

'I was there on my own and missing my two kids,' he said. 'I didn't think I could handle going back [to Korea] and needed to get out of my contract. It was just too much. If I had settled down and maybe been in my 30s, it would have been perfect but it was bad timing.'

'I was never going to be a success playing [in Korea] because my outside life was all over the place,' Cureton told the *Full Core Football 24* online video channel.

'If I was like I am now – I'm married and got a little one – if I went with a family, and with [today's] technology [video chat software], I probably would have stayed three or four years, not a problem,' Cureton said to the *Non League Nosh* podcast.

'It was the one time where football wasn't enough [to overcome off-pitch challenges],' Cureton told the *Man Marking* podcast, 'and I felt I needed to get home.'

'I had another [18 months remaining] out there, and I said [to my agent], "I can't go back, I don't enjoy it, I'm not happy,"' Cureton told *Full Core Football 24*. 'I'm really focused now, so it's a case of finding the best possible move for me in England,' Cureton told the Reading FC website, shortly after leaving Korea.

Sunderland fanzine *A Love Supreme* was much more blunt in its assessment in an unpublished article.

'The more cynical among the I'cons fans thought he was treating the I'cons and the K League as a paid holiday for him and his girlfriend away from the [ex-spouse] and kids.

'Perhaps Cureton realises he wasn't mature enough, or dedicated enough to play in a foreign league. It won't be any consolation though to I'cons fans to know that he's really focused now.'

To some in England, Cureton would always be a treasure, a hero. He personified triumph, victory. Success, promotion. Perhaps even swagger.

But to most in Busan, Cureton was a shadow of a player. He represented failure. He mirrored the current plight of this once-mighty club. Rather unfairly, he came to embody what had gone wrong at Busan over the past four years, even though he had barely been in Korea for four months.

Cureton was condemned to be an outsider at Busan – not because he wasn't Korean, but because he was portrayed as the face of the new regime. He was Hyundai Development Company, not former owners Daewoo. He was the ill-fitting Asiad World Cup Stadium, rather than the comforting and familiar Gudeok. He was the futile Busan I'cons, not the dominant Busan Royals.

It felt so re-assuring for the supporters to make a scapegoat out of him. But the relief was ephemeral, failing to satiate the disgust among supporters that ran much deeper. The self-loathing.

The Pride of Pusan members saw unflattering flashes of themselves in Cureton. He personified their despair. And they despised him for it.

Most discomforting was that he and they were one and the same. His adversity on the pitch mirrored their distress in the stands. He was running from his past, while they were futilely clinging to theirs.

They had converged paths for but a sliver of their lives, circling each other briefly in an uncomfortable dance until both were flung out toward an uncertain and unfamiliar future.

While Busan were willing to let Cureton depart before the end of his contract, they weren't about to simply let him walk away. He would have to pay back part of his signing bonus, at the very least. Despite Cureton already returning to the UK, his contract termination – particularly financial matters – had yet to be finalised.

Perhaps more pressing for Ian Porterfield was how this would affect Andy Cooke, a player who had been brought in merely to assist Cureton but unexpectedly became the star striker. Cookie mentioned he had developed a good friendship with Cureton during his first few months in an unfamiliar country.

'It was really good that [Cureton] was over at the time,' Cooke told the *V2 Football Podcast*.

Would Porterfield need to bring in another British – or at least English-speaking – player to prevent Cooke becoming homesick? With it now being November and part-way through the English football season, how would Porterfield be able to pick up a decent signing without any transfer money available? Could a player out of work during the English season possibly be better than Cureton, a former Premier League striker? Did Porterfield have any realistic hope of improving the squad before next summer and keeping Cooke socially content in Korea?

But before he could plot any close-season acquisitions, Porterfield had the Korean FA Cup to contest. This was only the eighth instalment of the young competition, played late in the year after the conclusion of the K League season. Most Korean clubs didn't take the FA Cup very seriously, although it did come with an enticing prize: qualification for the Asian Champions League.

True to Korean football, the competition was organised at the last minute. Fixture dates for the third round proper – the juncture when K League clubs entered – were announced just two weeks in advance of matches. Busan's opening encounter would be played on a Friday afternoon during business hours in a neutral city, ensuring attendance would be negligible.

At least the final had been scheduled with fans in mind: a weekend at the Seoul World Cup Stadium. Back in 2000, the final was played on a Wednesday afternoon in Jeju, a remote island in the south-west of the country.

The final five rounds of the Korean FA Cup were to be played within ten calendar days, giving some indication why the competition didn't hold much clout. No wonder some smaller teams had won the cup during the same season they finished bottom of the league.

If Busan were to advance to the final, they would play at the venue they were currently bidding to relocate to in the capital. What an awkward day out that would be for the Pride of Pusan.

For Busan's opening knockout game, they had been drawn 'away' to Konkuk University, a school in Seoul. The match would be played at the neutral Namhae Sports Park, a venue just a short stroll from the rugged southern coastline. Although winter was still technically a month away, the Pacific Ocean winds were howling. The small contingent of Busan supporters naively thought they had come sufficiently dressed for the gruesome weather – with some wearing four layers of clothing – but it still wasn't enough to shield them from the brutal, piercing bluster. They clustered together in a fruitless attempt to remain warm as the stormy winds pelted them without relent.

The *Dong-A Ilbo* published an article one day earlier that yearned for a cup upset, waxing romantically about the 'miracle' of amateurs Calais Racing Union advancing to the Coupe de France final in 2000.

Busan I'cons had to be concerned about stumbling early against an amateur opponent. Konkuk had just lifted the national university football autumn championship, their eighth half-season title since the mid-1980s. Prior to that they won the national football championship (a competition since merged into the Korean FA Cup) on two occasions. Konkuk had also produced a number of notable professionals, including 2002 World Cup stars Lee Young-pyo (later of Tottenham) and Hwang Sun-hong.

Although the Korean FA Cup was still a fledgling competition, Busan were no strangers to being dumped out by amateurs. Six years earlier, Busan Daewoo Royals were defeated by Housing and Commercial Bank after extra time and penalties – marking the first occasion that a K League side was upset by lower-division opposition.

Prior to the match I spotted Porterfield and assistant Jarvie wandering in. Jarvie gave me a big grin and waved, while Porterfield – remembering our earlier encounter – shot me a stern look every bit as piercing as the ocean gale.

Just four minutes in, there's a goal. Midfielder Kim Hyung-bum slots the ball in comfortably, appearing every bit the professional.

Unfortunately for Busan, Kim is but a mere student. Konkuk University have taken an early lead against their K League opponents.

Porterfield, Sunderland's FA Cup giant-killing hero from three decades earlier, doesn't panic. Although Cureton is no longer part of the Busan squad, Cookie and Harry are playing up front for Busan, while Jon has returned to the team's back-line. League all-star goalkeeper Kim Yong-dae is reassuringly between Busan's posts. Porterfield's favourite defender and midfielder – Lee Jang-gwan and Kim Tae-min – both start.

Busan pounce in retaliation and almost score in the 21st minute, hitting the post. But Konkuk University continue to press against their professional foes, nearly scoring just three minutes later from a ball that slowly floats toward goal, carried by coastal winds.

Soon it's half-time. Players and fans alike flee for cover from the ruthless elements.

Porterfield's season is falling apart. While he had successfully steered his skint squad above Bucheon and the two K League newcomers, would losing to amateur opposition be the last straw for fans and club brass? Would such a humiliating loss be impossible to ignore? I didn't envy the Busan players, who were no doubt receiving a bollocking in the dressing room from the normally calm Scotsman.

Seven minutes after the break, Cookie scores an equaliser with a thundering shot. He's pleased but doesn't waste time with celebration, trudging back to the centre circle with his head bowed in concentration.

Moments later, in the 58th minute, another goal. Striker Chu Hyung-chul makes it 2-1 – for the university team. It's a stunning header by the player who had laced up for hosts South Korea at the recent Summer Universiade.

Porterfield begins to pace by the touchline. Okay, that opening goal wasn't a fluke. Konkuk are serious opponents. What to do?

Busan storm back, minutes later hitting the post for the second time. Then advantage shifts toward the students, who almost score their third.

In the 70th minute, Colombian striker Harry scores to pull Busan level once again. Ten minutes later, Konkuk goalkeeper Kim Jung-gook hurls himself against the driving winds to make a superb save, keeping the scoreline even. On the resulting corner, Kim again does well to prevent a goal from the professionals.

By this time, with just minutes left to play, Busan start to relentlessly hammer the students, taking five corner kicks within three minutes. It seems inevitable that the K League side will snatch a late, cruel victory. Busan hit the post for a third time, and Cookie buries the rebound, giving the professionals the lead. The Busan supporters, nearly frozen solid at this point from the unrelenting gale, leap into the air in celebration.

But no goal. It's called back for offside. The students continue to hang on, putting their entire effort into thwarting Busan's attack. All they can do is resist the onslaught, by this point entirely one-way traffic.

The whistle blows. Konkuk University have hung on. The match will advance to sudden-death golden goal play, still used by FIFA during this period. Whichever team scores first will win and progress.

Extra time mirrors the last period of regulation time: Busan continue to maul the university opposition. The professionals' superior fitness is evident. Busan create chance, after chance, after chance, but squander them all. After 120 minutes, still deadlocked at 2-2, the match proceeds to penalty kicks to determine the winner.

Porterfield can't believe it. The day's earlier match at this same venue finished as a rout for K League newcomers Daegu FC: a 5-0 thrashing over Myungji University. Yet here were Busan, who finished above Daegu in the league, unable to surpass their student opponents.

Konkuk shoot first. To Porterfield's great relief, Busan continue their dominance into the penalty kicks. Konkuk fail to convert their first two attempts, while Cookie and attacking midfielder Hwang Cheol-min score for Busan. It seems this will be a quick, smooth end to the match for normally hapless Busan.

But the professionals begin to wobble. Konkuk score their next two, while Busan's mediocre defender Lee Jung-hyo and fill-in midfielder Doh Hwa-sung both fail to convert their attempts. After four rounds, it's level at 2-2.

Then comes the pivotal fifth round. Up steps Cho Yong-hyun, who five months later would be declared 'most valuable player' at the national university football spring championship. He scores for Konkuk, effortlessly. It's now up to Busan. Score and they level it; fail and they're out.

Centre-back and former captain Yoon Hee-joon will take it. Yoon had turned 31 years old earlier that month, and was in his ninth season at Busan. Porterfield looks comforted that someone of Yoon's experience will take this critical shot.

Goal. No celebration. Yoon marches back to his team-mates, who are relieved rather than jubilant. We proceed to the sixth round, deadlocked.

Konkuk striker Kim Yong-bum plants the ball on the penalty spot, steadying it from the on-rushing wind. After some delay, he finally takes the shot. He misses. He cannot believe it, and sinks to his knees in disappointment. The Busan players smile and start moving about, looking rejuvenated.

Colombian striker Harry wades forward to take his shot. Porterfield flashes a small grin. Busan only have to score this attempt and they've won. Although Porterfield and Harry had a major falling-out earlier in the season, Harry returned to the squad and is one of the more reliable Busan players, already scoring in open play earlier today.

Harry looks up at the young goalkeeper and takes his shot. It goes wide, trailing off harmlessly into the fencing. The intimate stadium becomes a cacophony of gasps. Players and fans alike cannot believe it. The star foreign striker has missed. Busan haven't won. After six rounds of penalty kicks, the teams remain level at 3-3.

Next up is Konkuk striker Ha Seung-ryong. He scores. Then giant Norwegian defender Jon Hjelde converts his. Still level after seven attempts each.

Midfielder Han Byung-yong takes Konkuk's eighth shot. It's good.

Busan's attacking midfielder Lee Yong-ha, just shy of his 30th birthday, advances to the penalty spot. He hasn't featured much for Busan this season, playing only half of their matches and absent for two long stretches during the latter period of the year.

Lee looks apprehensive. After some consideration, he takes his shot. It would be his last time to kick a ball as a professional player.

Lee misses.

Konkuk University players are ecstatic, leaping into the air. Their entire bench rushes on to the pitch to join the celebration.

Busan I'cons have been dumped out of the Korean FA Cup by amateurs. Some of the Busan players drop to their knees, some put their hands on their head, others stare vacantly in shock.

The Busan supporters are silent, but their faces display an array of emotions. Sadness. Rage. Disbelief. Shame.

A typical matchday for them, really.

Andy Cooke is irate, and storms back to the dressing room. By the touchline, Ian Porterfield hides his hands inside his trouser pockets, looks down at the ground and sighs. His expression betrays an increasingly forlorn soul.

The Pride of Pusan tear their flags down from the barriers and proceed back to the bus for the agonising ride home.

Looking out the window as our vehicle passed through the winding hills of Namhae, many of the town's elderly women hung

seaweed to dry in the autumn breeze. The supporters remained
silent well into the journey.

Busan's humbling loss marked the first occasion in five years
that a K League club was knocked out by university students. But
more embarrassment was to come. The next day, both Anyang
and Suwon were also dispatched by scholarly amateurs, setting a
new Korean FA Cup record for giant-killing. Blame the 44-match
K League season.

It was a biting autumn across North East Asia for many
professional clubs. Over in Japan, Yokohama F. Marinos – crowned
J.League champions just weeks earlier – came excruciatingly close
to being knocked out of the Emperor's Cup (Japan's version of the
FA Cup) by a secondary school team, which would have been the
greatest upset in the competition's 83-year history.

But it was an African football result that likely caught
Porterfield's attention.

Kumasi Asante Kotoko, the Ghanaian club that Porterfield
had managed for several months the previous year until a vicious
falling-out with the chairman, won their league title just two
days after Busan were dumped out of the Korean FA Cup by
amateurs.

The winning goal for Kotoko was scored by Michael Osei, the
impressive striker Porterfield signed for Busan but was forced to
relinquish after it was revealed Osei was still under contract with
the Ghanaian club.

If a different chairman had been in power at Kotoko, would
Porterfield still be there today? Would the Scot now be receiving
credit for winning Ghana's league title, instead of being knocked
out of South Korea's national cup by students?

Or, had Osei properly transferred to Busan – instead of being
presented to the Korean club as an unattached player despite still
being under contract in Ghana – would Busan's K League season
have unfolded differently? Would Osei have formed a successful
partnership up front with Urumov and Harry, or perhaps later with
Cureton or Cookie?

* * *

The weeks passed and winter came to South Korea. During *Seollal*,
the Lunar New Year celebrations, many residents returned to their

home towns to pay respects to family elders and deceased ancestors. The exodus from Seoul left the capital eerily quiet.

For Busan I'cons fans, they were still left wondering whether their club would head in the opposite direction: a permanent move *to* Seoul. The capital's gravitas enticed many South Koreans to relocate for opportunity; now it threatened to even inhale celebrated sports clubs.

The month of March arrived, and Busan I'cons organised a media conference for an announcement.

This was it.

After months of negotiations with Busan City Council, the I'cons declared they would remain in Busan. The city's government had offered the club sufficient enticements to convince them to stay.

There would be no relocation to Seoul – at least not for Busan. Anyang LG Cheetahs, the sole remaining club that had applied to move to the capital, would go instead. Approved by the league and Korean Football Association, the deed was done.

Anyang supporters were distraught. Their club was to become the Milton Keynes Dons of South Korea. Their derby with Suwon Bluewings – which had grown to become the fiercest in the K League – was now effectively dead. Eight years of football culture built in the city of Anyang was eradicated with the stroke of a pen by some suited fellow who probably couldn't name three of the team's players.

With Busan I'cons remaining put, Busan fans began to speculate whether the club had genuinely wanted a move to Seoul, or if it may have simply been a ruse to leverage greater concessions.

Ian Porterfield was later interviewed and asked if the relocation application had been legitimate. While Porterfield was never told the inside story by senior club officials, he had assumptions.

'In all honesty, it was a good marketing exercise,' he said to *Soccerphile*'s John Duerden. 'I was very happy that the I'cons stayed in Busan.

'I think that this [proposed relocation] was a message to the people [city officials] here ... Since that situation came about, maybe a few people have sat up and took notice and offered more help and support which is very much needed.

'At the end of the day, [relocation to Seoul] was never going to happen. That was my thought.'

2003 KOREAN FA CUP, ROUND OF 32

Busan	**2-2 (4-5 p)**	**Konkuk University**
Suwon	2-3	Kyunghee University
Anyang	1-2	Korea University
Mipo Dockyard	3-3 (3-1 p)	Kwangwoon University
Police	0-0 (3-0 p)	Hong-ik University
Ulsan	3-2	Soongsil University
Jeonnam	1-0	Incheon Korean Rail
Bucheon	2-0	Seosan Citizen
Seongnam	5-3	Ajou University
Daegu	5-2	Myongju University
Suwon City	3-0	Bongshin Club
Daejeon	3-0	Hannam University
Goyang KB	5-0	Pai Chai University
Pohang	5-0	JEI Education
Gwangju	9-1	Yong-in University
Jeonbuk	walkover	Seoul City

EPILOGUE

십 년이면 강산도 변한다
*– In ten years, even the rivers and
mountains change*

Dalian Atkinson – First British footballer to play in the K League retired in 2001 after just five matches in South Korea. Killed in 2016 after West Mercia Police shot him with a Taser.

Lee Dong-gook – Gwangju Sangmu forward who gave Busan nightmares signed for Middlesbrough of the Premier League in early 2007 on an 18-month contract. Sadly, never scored during league play and returned to Korea. Won the K League golden boot during his first full season back. Eleven years later, with the world watching during COVID-19 lockdowns, earned the first goal of the 2020 K League season at the age of 41. Scored in the K League across four separate decades.

Daewoo chairman Kim Woo-jung – Fled South Korea to avoid arrest and lived abroad for almost six years, including as the guest of Sudanese president Omar al-Bashir, a dictator later accused by the International Criminal Court of genocide, crimes against humanity and war crimes. Returned to South Korea in 2005 and was sentenced to ten years in prison for embezzlement and accounting fraud, and had US$22bn of his fortune seized. Less than two years later was granted amnesty by South Korea's president. Died in 2019.

Busan I'cons FC – Squad would be slashed to 37 players for 2004, and down to 30 players in 2005, eliminating the reserve team. Club renamed Busan IPark ahead of the 2006 season, an attempt at free publicity for Hyundai Development Company's apartment construction wing, IPark. Built temporary stands on Asiad Stadium's running track starting in 2008 in an effort to bridge the monstrous venue's gaping chasm between the seats and the pitch. In 2015, became the first conglomerate-owned K League club to be relegated. Moved back to the old Gudeok Stadium in late 2016, meaning that Asiad World Cup Stadium spent a grand total of 14 years hosting football, despite costing £163.7m to build (the equivalent of £280.1m in 2020 after inflation). Earned the dubious distinction of being the first lower-division club to lose the promotion-relegation play-off, doing so twice, before finally returning to Korea's top flight for the 2020 season.

Emmanuel Amunike (midfielder) – Barcelona alumnus and Olympic gold medallist made little progress with injury rehabilitation and decided to part ways with Busan in August 2003. Three months later, after a potential deal with a United Arab Emirates club collapsed, he signed for unfancied Jordanian team Al-Wehdat and partook in 2003/04 Arab Champions League. Coventry City attempted to sign Amunike for 2004/05 season, but he failed to secure a UK work permit and retired.

Kim Jee-hyuk (goalkeeper) – Didn't see any playing time in 2003, and would only make three match appearances in more than half a decade at Busan. Banned from Korean football for life in 2011 when found guilty of involvement in a match-fixing scandal.

Shin Young-rok (defender) – Despite a promising start to his career in Belgium, the 'lesser Shin' (compared to his namesake at Suwon who became a star) left Busan in 2005 and continued playing in the lower divisions.

Jung Yoo-suk (goalkeeper) – Left to complete his military service on loan with Gwangju Sangmu at the earliest opportunity. Remained at Busan through the 2009 season, then served a couple more years as a pro elsewhere before retiring. Became goalkeeping coach of the South Korean women's national team.

Ahn Hyo-yeon (forward) – One of the two young players Ian Porterfield took an early shine to, Ahn overcame injury and blossomed into a fruitful striker during the 2004 season. Suwon offered him a lucrative signing bonus he couldn't resist – a situation typical of what Porterfield and Busan I'cons faced in trying to build a winning team on a low budget. Bounced around the K League, Japan and South East Asia before retiring in 2013. Became manager of Dongguk University.

Lee Yong-ha (midfielder/forward) – After missing the final penalty shot in Busan's embarrassing FA Cup loss to Konkuk University, Lee retired from football just days following his 30th birthday, having played six seasons at Busan.

Ryu Byung-hoon (defender) – His 20 matches in 2003 would be his most active season in a decade as a peripheral player at Busan. Ryu didn't see any playing time in 2004 and was subsequently cut by Porterfield. Then played another eight seasons for second division giant-killers Goyang Kookmin Bank (renowned for knocking top-flight sides out of the Korean FA Cup) before coaching a few second-division clubs.

Lee Jung-hyo (defender) – Porterfield's arrival at Busan in 2003 marked the middle of Lee's decade at the club. After retiring he spent four years coaching at a university, then at several K League clubs.

Doh Hwa-sung (midfielder) – He remained with Busan for another half a decade. Doh's claim to fame was scoring the longest-distance goal in K League history in 2005, a 65m shot, which remained a league record for almost a decade. Was banned from Korean football for life in 2011 when found guilty of involvement in a match-fixing scandal. Was then fined by a court in 2019 for football agency fraud.

Shim Jae-won (defender) – Wanted to move to another K League club when his contract expired after 2008, but league rules meant Busan were entitled to a transfer fee. Instead played two seasons in China, but Busan still wanted a fee. Spent half a season in Korea's semi-pro league in 2010 before deciding to retire. Became a part-time football commentator on local TV while dabbling in catering and tourism.

Jang Dae-il (defender) – Mr 'Handsome XI' retired after the 2003 season due to injury and in 2004 was arrested on suspicion of drink-driving, according to SBS News. Later that year made his acting debut as a Japanese gangster in a sitcom and dated a famous actress. Made another attempt at playing football with a third-tier club in 2008, then faded into obscurity.

Jeon Woo-keun (midfielder) – Remained at Busan through to 2008, then played abroad in China and Singapore. After retiring, Jeon entered football management at high school and university levels.

Gwak Kyung-keun (forward) – Never scored for Busan despite two seasons at the club, bizarrely being converted into a defender by Porterfield. After 2004, Gwak received an MRI scan and was told he could be killed if he received another hard knock to the head, forcing him to retire. After managing at a high school for eight years, Gwak moved back into the professional game with phoenix club Bucheon FC. He was fired that same year without compensation, accused of allegedly embezzling public funds meant for the club and inappropriate selection of players. In response, Gwak took the club to court and won. After briefly managing the uniquely named KKK Football Club, he served as a coach at Chinese side Tianjin Teda and filled in as caretaker manager, overseeing such players as former Chelsea midfielder John Mikel Obi.

Noh Jung-yoon (midfielder) – The 2003 captain played three additional K League seasons. Noh then retired to the USA with family in Los Angeles, where he was rumoured to be working on coaching qualifications but remained low-key.

Lee Lim-saeng (defender) – Retired before the end of the 2003 season due to chronic injury. Served as coach for half a dozen years at Suwon. Spent the subsequent half-decade as manager of Singapore club Home United, becoming longest-serving foreign manager in S-League history. Then worked alongside former team-mate Gwak in China as a coach and caretaker manager at Tianjin Teda. Subsequently became chairman of the Korean Football Association's technical development committee (overseeing national youth teams), but soon resigned. Anointed manager of Suwon Bluewings for the

2019 season and won the Korean FA Cup, but received abuse from Suwon fans for lack of tactical nous.

Kim Tae-min (midfielder) – Porterfield's most-used midfielder of 2003 would attend the 2004 Athens Summer Olympics and remained with Busan for another four seasons. Kim would spend a further five years in the K League before becoming a journeyman in China, Thailand and Hong Kong. As of 2020 he was senior coach at a Vietnamese club.

Yoon Hee-joon (defender) – Yoon remained with Busan through 2005, playing 11 seasons at the club and regaining the captain's armband during his final year. After one additional season with Jeonnam he retired and turned to coaching at several K League clubs.

Kim Yong-dae (goalkeeper) – Named 'most valuable player' of the 2004 Korean FA Cup. When K League giants Seongnam came calling for Kim's services after the 2005 season, he jumped at the chance, leaving Porterfield without his star player. Appeared at the 2006 World Cup, won three K League titles and three Korean FA Cup medals, named 'K League best goalkeeper' twice, and earned an Asian Champions League runners-up medal. Made an appearance in the 2017 all-star game and finally retired after the 2018 season.

Lee Jang-kwan (defender) – As the most-used player in 2003, Lee would break Busan's record for most games played (256) the following season. In 2005, he was rewarded for his long-term loyalty by being offered a ten-year contract despite being 31 years old. The next year he was made captain. But in 2007 he departed the club with ill feelings when he was pushed to retire before he was ready, even though he still had more than seven years remaining on his contract. He reluctantly parted ways with Busan, having played 348 games and earned one broken heart. In 2011 he was named manager of Yongin University, where he won the national university championship in 2015 and 2018.

Dušan Šimić (midfielder) – Left Korea after the 2003 season. Played several more years in Hungary, Romania and Serbia.

Trialled for Real Salt Lake of Major League Soccer in 2008, but failed to earn a contract offer and retired.

Tommy Mosquera Lozano (forward) – After having his short-term loan terminated by Porterfield partway through the 2003 season, Tommy returned to South America for lower-division spells in Colombia and Argentina. After one last contract in China in 2006, Tommy retired and eventually became a coach at a youth club in Colombia. He caused a brief scare in 2017 when he disappeared from his home in Bogotá, leading to frantic pleas in the newspapers and social media for assistance locating him. The next day he phoned his mother to inform everyone he was okay.

Zoran Urumov (midfielder/forward) – After leaving for greener pastures with Suwon in mid-2003, the Serbian drinking machine scored the only goal in a 2004 friendly between Suwon and Barcelona, causing the Catalonian visitors great embarrassment. Suwon then won the second stage of the 2004 K League, and Urumov scored Suwon's last penalty in their championship play-off final victory over Pohang. Returned to Europe and played several more seasons in Serbia, Greece and Montenegro before retiring in 2010. After serving as sporting director at Serbian second-tier club FK Sinđelić Beograd, he became a player agent.

Harry German Castillo Vallejo (forward) – After missing his penalty in Busan's FA Cup loss to Konkuk University, Harry signed for reigning K League champions Seongnam, where he saw little playing time. He returned to his native Colombia in 2005 with Millonarios, the club that allegedly stitched up Tommy years earlier. Then it was back to South Korea for the debut season of Gyeongnam FC, followed by another four years in Colombia before retiring in 2011. Opened his own football school in 2013 and later hired Tommy as a coach.

Choi Man-hee (coach) – The man with the beaming smile left Busan to become a coach with Suwon for half a decade (2005–2009). In 2011 he became the first manager of newly established Gwangju FC. Unfortunately one of the nicest men in football walked into an unfortunate situation: players weren't being fed, their accommodation wasn't heated/cooled, supplies such as boots obtained by the club were not given to players, the club had no training ground (they practised in a public park), and the chairman interfered in player selection (including an order to freeze out one particular foreign player). After leaving that regrettable position in 2012, Choi rejoined Busan in 2017 as the club's chief executive.

Drew Jarvie (coach) – The Scot left South Korea after the 2003 season. There were rumours Jarvie might become manager of Peterhead in Scotland's fourth tier, but nothing came of it, and he instead worked for his son's electrical business in Aberdeen. In 2008 Jarvie nearly died, but life-saving heart surgery brought him back to health. He then served as a matchday ambassador for Aberdeen FC.

Jon Olav Hjelde (defender) – The towering Norwegian intended to remain in South Korea, but acquired a nasty knee injury during pre-season that kept him out for the first half of 2004. Without having played a single match by the summer, he asked Busan for an early release from his contract, which the club agreed to. He then returned to England and soon trialled with Queens Park Rangers and Nottingham Forest – causing some bitterness back in Busan. Hjelde signed a one-year deal with Forest, but was released when they were relegated.

He then spent two seasons with nearby Mansfield Town in England's fourth tier before retiring. Returning to Norway, Hjelde acquired two university degrees, then worked as an independent distributor for a coffee company and as a coach for a local fourth-tier club's academy. Remained the only Norwegian to play in the K League until 2018.

Andy Cooke (forward) – After a highly successful debut in the K League, the Englishman returned for the 2004 season wearing Busan's number ten shirt (the squad number Cureton had wanted). Despite featuring in the K League's all-star game that season, Cooke was no longer as prolific a goalscorer, with a goals-to-games ratio at roughly half of the previous year. Now with a young child, longing to spend more time with family and friends, and still not enjoying the relentless summer heat, Cooke and his wife returned to England after the 2004 K League season.

'The culture in Korea was a great experience and I'm so glad I went there,' said Cooke.

Of the three Britain-based players Porterfield signed in 2003, it was Cooke – the only of the three without Premier League experience – who performed the best and remained in South Korea the longest.

Perhaps building cowsheds also builds character.

Upon returning to England, Cooke joined recently relegated Bradford City in England's third tier. Although he played alongside Dean Windass, who scored 28 goals and was co-winner of the League One golden boot, Cooke just couldn't seem to score.

In 2006 Cooke started a property business that converted barns into luxury houses, and also played for Shrewsbury Town in the fourth tier of English football. He scored twice in the League Two play-off semi-final, earning his team the opportunity to play at the new Wembley Stadium just months after it opened.

After a couple of seasons he was released by Shrewsbury. When it became clear that no other Football League clubs were interested in the 34-year-old, he retired.

Cooke subsequently emigrated to Canada and briefly worked in the insurance industry, but soon returned to England. He then became director of football and player at Market Drayton Town, his local non-league club, for a couple of years. Cooke later obtained the UEFA A Licence and in 2017 opened his own football school, while also serving as the director of an air-conditioning company.

Jamie Cureton (forward) – After returning to England in late 2003, paying most of his up-front signing bonus back to Busan I'cons and improving his injured ankle, Cureton entered into negotiations to sign with third-tier Queens Park Rangers. But then came the realisation that Busan were demanding a transfer fee around £100,000. QPR couldn't afford it, so the deal looked to be off. Curo appeared on Sky Sports shortly afterward, pleading for some British club to rescue him. Still without a team by late January 2004, Cureton admitted to the *Reading Evening Post* that he was worried about the future. The transfer window was about to close, the K League pre-season was approaching and Curo remained technically under contract with Busan.

'I've got to sit tight and see what happens but hopefully I can sign [for an English club] by [transfer] deadline day,' said Cureton. 'I won't be happy if I have to go back [to South Korea] – it will be a nightmare.'

'[My agent and I] spent basically December until the end of January trying to get out of my contract, which thankfully we did,' Cureton told the *Man Marking* podcast.

QPR were able to successfully raise the money for the transfer fee through fan fundraising, and signed Cureton mere hours before the transfer window closed. Four months later, QPR were promoted to the second tier and would compete in the inaugural season of the rebranded Football League Championship. Unfortunately, Cureton would struggle and be released at the end of the 2004/05 season. A local newspaper, the *Ealing Gazette*, selected Cureton as QPR's 'most disappointing player' of the year.

'I think I'd lost a couple of years from going [to Korea],' Cureton told the *Non League Nosh* podcast. 'I lost the year I went [to Korea], and I lost the year coming back because I was still [psychologically] all over the place … [my] off-the-field life still wasn't settled. Joining QPR, they didn't ever see the best of me at all. I signed [for] 18 months there and they were like, "what a waste" because I was still mentally not right.'

'I think [people] thought I was on the decline,' Cureton told the *Back of the Net* online video channel.

'By moving out there [Korea], I probably wasted two seasons of my career in England, to be honest,' Cureton said to the *Full Core Football 24* online video channel.

He would then bounce around the Football League for the next 11 seasons, with some success. This included stops at Colchester United, where Cureton rediscovered his scoring form, winning the 2006/07 Championship golden boot and lifting the club to its best-ever finish; his boyhood club Norwich City; Devon side Exeter City; Leyton Orient, near his home in Essex; Cheltenham, where he scored his 250th senior goal and played his 20th season as a professional; and Dagenham and Redbridge, where he was the oldest-serving outfield player in the top four divisions (Ryan Giggs and Kevin Phillips had just retired), and became the second-oldest player ever to score a Football League hat-trick at the age of 39 years and 222 days – agonisingly, just one day shy of the record held by Phillips.

Dagenham and Redbridge were relegated from the Football League in 2016. Cureton was keen to continue his career as a professional footballer, but he was now 40 years old and offers were scarce.

Cureton temporarily joined Farnborough, a local club down in the eighth tier of the pyramid, as he sought to keep his fitness up while seeking a return to the Football League.

'I'll still carry on trying to get back to the Football League,' Cureton told the *Non-League Paper*. 'I'll still hold on to that dream until it's gone – it's where I made my name and I'm not quite ready to give that up just yet.'

'A league club basically signed me,' Cureton told *GloucestershireLive*. 'We had phone calls and meetings [but] it was the chairman who blocked the move – because of my age.'

Unfortunately it wasn't to be – Cureton would spend the remainder of his playing career in non-league football.

'I'd love to be playing high but age gets to you a bit and I decided to drop down and keep going as long as possible,' Cureton told talkSPORT, as reported by *DevonLive*. 'I spoke to a lot of friends who have retired ... and they have all said, play as long as possible. As long as I can still keep going I will. I get the same buzz. I keep running around trying to do myself justice.'

In 2017, Cureton won what was surprisingly his first silverware in senior football: the Southern League Division One Central (eighth-tier) play-off trophy. That was followed by winning the World Cup for England – or at least the 2018 Veterans World Cup during a summer tournament in Thailand.

The next year at Bishop's Stortford, Cureton appeared in his 1,000th senior match, becoming only the 29th player in the world to do so. He also became the first player to score in each of the top nine divisions of English football, after finding the net for Enfield FC.

'In front of 60,000 or 60, the buzz of a goal still feels the same,' he told *The Telegraph*.

As he continued playing, the English striker also spent several years coaching Arsenal's academy teams on a part-time basis. He received the UEFA B coaching badge, made numerous media appearances in preparation for a possible career in football media, and was considering taking a sporting director course with the Professional Footballers' Association.

Cureton remained an active player as of the 2020/21 season, his 27th year of senior football. Although this book was published long after the 2003 K League season concluded, the delay wouldn't outlast Cureton's determination to continue his playing career.

'I've made mistakes and done things that I wish I wouldn't have done,' Cureton told BBC Radio Berkshire's Reading FC podcast, when asked about his expansive career. 'But you … think, "well, this is your life" … you make decisions, right or wrong, you've gotta stand by them. … I have to back the decisions I've made. Yeah, I would have changed some of them, but I'm here now, I'm still playing … which is, you know, unbelievable at my age [44 years old]. I've met a lot of very good people along the way. So … it doesn't keep me up [at night], but I do think about it, without a doubt.'

Ian Porterfield (manager) – After a difficult initial K League season in 2003 and the departure of Jamie Cureton (along with 19 other players), Porterfield lured veteran midfielder and former Southampton captain Chris Marsden to Busan. Known fondly as the 'bald Beckenbauer' or 'Chris Marsden, football genius' by Southampton fans, Marsden signed a two-year contract in Korea. He scored the first goal of the 2004 K League season, against the newly relocated FC Seoul.

'I think a lot of English players don't come abroad because they have a problem adjusting their mindset to how people's cultures and countries operate differently,' Marsden told Reuters in April 2004. 'It's all about us adapting to the Korean way and not Korea adapting to the British way – and I'm happy with that.'

The next month, Marsden would quit Busan and return to England, citing 'family reasons'. The Sheffielder would spend even less time in South Korea than Jamie Cureton.

'My wife was desperately unhappy, she couldn't settle at all,' Marsden told the *Korea Times*. 'I was coming home from training, and some days she would be in tears, so the best solution for my wife was to return home.'

Four months later, shortly before the launch of Australia's new professional soccer league, Porterfield managed to snatch promising Aussie youngster Ahmad Elrich to Busan. Elrich was reportedly paid US$3,000 every week by Busan, in addition to a large signing bonus and the use of a house and car.

Yet just two months later, Elrich would join the swelling ranks of players from Western countries walking out on Busan. Tottenham Hotspur attempted to sign Elrich, but Busan wanted a significant transfer fee for the youngster. Tottenham refused, causing Elrich to resent Busan and storm out of South Korea in a huff. Still contracted to Busan, he would be frozen out of football for five months until Fulham eventually agreed to pay a fee for him. Elrich would see little playing time in England and was eventually released. He returned to Australia to play in the A-League, and in 2011 was jailed for four years in a maximum-security prison for gun and drug offences.

That same season (2004), the Pride of Pusan held a 'silent support boycott', demanding that Porterfield resign.

Despite a merry-go-round of Western imports, no money for transfer fees and a restrictive budget for signing domestic players, Porterfield was able to improve Busan I'cons. They finished in the top half of the K League table during the 2004 season's second stage, and went on to win the post-season Korean FA Cup – a feat Busan still haven't been able to repeat 15 years later.

'I had an incredible feeling of happiness within myself, to know that they'd benefited from my guidance,' Porterfield told the *Northern Echo*.

There was a rumour Porterfield might leave to become manager at Dundee United, but it turned out to be an internet prank. Unaware of the tomfoolery, the *Scottish Sun* phoned Porterfield in Asia to ask whether his rumoured return to Scotland was true.

'What I won't be doing is going to Dundee United and saying I want the job,' Porterfield confidently responded. 'I don't have anything to prove to anyone.'

As the Dundee rumour made its rounds, Busan offered Porterfield a two-year contract extension. Busan started well and would win the first stage of the 2005 K League season. Porterfield's chest inflated as the Korean sports media speculated whether he would be snapped up to lead the South Korea men's national team.

From the earlier FA Cup win came entry into the 2005 Asian Champions League. Busan would thrash their group-stage opponents, becoming only the second club to win all six matches, the first team to score 25 goals (surpassing the record set by Seongnam in 2003), the first team to earn a +25 goal difference (a record still unsurpassed 17 years later), and the first Korean side to keep clean sheets in all six games. Busan subsequently brushed aside Qatari champions Al Sadd in the quarter-finals with a 5-1 aggregate scoreline.

Suddenly everyone in Asian football was asking: who is this Ian Porterfield?

With rumours intensifying that Porterfield would leave for better opportunities overseas, Korean fans pleaded with him to stay at Busan, posting complimentary messages online.

> *Don't be back your country.*
> *I hope you stay here. Busan fighting!*
> *Ian fighting!*
> *and this is the last chance.*
> *Asian champs cup is Busan's.*
> *for the winner*
> *for the star of the Asia*
> *for the crowded stadium.*
> *Let's go to the victory.*
> *Busan is the best.*
> *Porterfield is the best of the best.*

But just as quickly as Porterfield had built Busan into a formidable team, his project unravelled spectacularly. Already qualified for the 2005 K League championship play-offs by the season's halfway point, Busan sputtered immediately in the second stage of the season. In the Asian Champions League semi-final, Busan lost by a staggering 7-0 aggregate scoreline, including a humiliating 5-0 home defeat in the first leg. Matters didn't improve in the K League, where Busan whimpered across the second-stage finish line without a single win. They were then knocked out of the play-offs in the first round by K League newcomers Incheon United.

With 2006 not starting any better for Busan, Porterfield began to apply for jobs elsewhere in earnest, including at Sunderland and the India men's national team. Busan's winless streak continued unabated, and people began to whisper whether Busan might break the unenviable K League winless record set by Bucheon over the 2002 and 2003 seasons (a record that ended when hapless Bucheon defeated Porterfield's Busan in 2003). Busan would eventually equal the embarrassing record, but before Porterfield could set a new low, he resigned as manager. Despite the club chairman's efforts to retain the Scot, Ian Porterfield left South Korea.

Given the difficult conditions Porterfield faced managing Busan, some fans still revere him as a hero. Busan was Porterfield's most successful spell in his career as a football manager, and his second-longest job in management. He was one of only three foreign managers to lead a K League side to a major trophy triumph. Porterfield directed the second-longest reign as a foreign manager in the history of the league, and led Busan longer than any of his predecessors or successors to date, Korean or foreign.

Perhaps Porterfield's biggest achievement at the club was orchestrating the rebuild of a robust youth academy, soon imitated by the league's powerhouses.

Ultimately, Porterfield's record at Busan wasn't great: 30 wins, 40 draws and 53 losses – or a 24 per cent win ratio – from 123 league and cup matches. In stark contrast to his final months in charge, his temporary replacement would win his first four matches.

'To me, the more I've stayed outside the UK, the better coach I've become,' Porterfield told the *Northern Echo*. 'If a job was offered [to me in the UK] there's no doubt I could be up for it, but I think it would be at a lesser club now. It would be nice to be back in the UK, but it's not something I linger over.'

After an idyllic break in Florida with his wife and several months off from the stress of football, Ian Porterfield was announced as the new manager of the Armenian national team in August 2006. A former member of the Soviet Union, Armenia were ranked 104th in international football, behind Botswana and narrowly ahead of Singapore.

Under Porterfield, Armenia got off to a slow start in Euro 2008 qualifying, winless in their first five matches.

Before the fifth match, Porterfield went for a routine prostate check and doctors found an irregularity. Receiving a full scan, he was informed that there was a cancerous tumour in his colon. After surgery he began chemotherapy, but was determined to quickly return to work (against doctors' advice) and later that month attended Armenia's fifth qualifier, a 1-0 loss away to Poland. The day prior to the match, he told the *Sunderland Echo* he wouldn't be able to travel due to his cancer treatment, yet somehow he managed to sneak in the flight to Poland.

Rather unexpectedly that summer, the team's fortunes improved dramatically. Armenia would win away to Kazakhstan, and days later won at home against Poland.

'This is history for Armenia,' Porterfield told *The Independent*. 'They have never ever won two games in a row. They've beaten teams like Andorra but never a big team like Poland before.'

'It's wonderful for the people here. The flags are out in the street. The president came to see me. Och, it's lifted this country so much. It's just what this country needs.'

The next month, after visiting Russian health specialists, Porterfield was told that his cancer had returned. His prognosis was grim. The Scot underwent additional surgery, followed by chemotherapy and radiotherapy treatment at the Royal Brompton Hospital in London.

One month later, by now in ill health that continued to worsen, Porterfield boarded an aeroplane for Armenia. He was determined to be in the technical area as his team faced Luiz Felipe Scolari's Portugal. The visitors carried a daunting reputation: runners-up at Euro 2004 and fourth place at the 2006 World Cup. Porterfield refused to miss it, regardless of the consequences to his personal health.

'It was the day before the Portugal game, we'd just finished our training session for the day at the stadium,' said Tom Jones, Porterfield's primary assistant at Armenia, in Robert O'Connor's book, *Blood and Circuses: Football and the Fight for Europe's Rebel Republics*. 'All the media were there and everyone could see that Ian was struggling. He had a colostomy bag and god knows what else. He could barely stand. Then he got everybody together in the middle of the pitch and he said "link hands". He got everybody with hands up in the air and he said, "This. This is for us. Together."'

As the Armenian players warmed up prior to kick-off, fans chanted the name of Ian Porterfield, still in disbelief that their team had won consecutive matches. They wondered what magic they might witness tonight against one of the world's football's giants.

Porterfield stood wearing a black trench coat over a white dress shirt and red tie. His face looked gaunt, the curves of his cheekbones and chin protruding more than usual.

From the very beginning the Armenians pressure the visitors, repeatedly coming close to scoring. In the 10th minute, after an inswinging free kick, 22-year-old centre-back Robert Arzumanyan heads the ball low. It lands near the feet of Portugal goalkeeper Ricardo and bounces into the net.

1-0 Armenia. The stadium erupts in euphoria. The former Soviet country takes the lead against juggernauts ranked eighth in the world.

Some 25 minutes later, Manchester United striker Cristiano Ronaldo equalises for the visitors. But Armenia would hold on, earning a historic draw against one of the best teams on the planet.

As *The Scotsman* put it, Porterfield 'could lift sides to great feats'.

Three weeks later, Ian Porterfield died in a hospice in Surrey, aged 61. The president of Armenia released a statement of condolence.

'It was with a deep sorrow that I learned about Ian Porterfield's premature death,' the statement read. 'During a very short period of time, as he managed Armenia's national team, he succeeded in giving it a new breath, to become a unifying centre that conveyed resolution to the players and advanced the team spirit and the idea of victory.'

Fans of Porterfield from his various teams over the decades flooded to the BBC website to leave messages of condolence:

'Ian Porterfield dragged Sheffield United up by the bootlaces and is the foundation of our modern day team. He took us up from the old Fourth Division with a (then) record number of points after just one season, and then again to the old Second Division. He was one of this country's most under-rated coaches and astute managers, and all clubs who have been fortunate enough to benefit from his services are today that much richer.'

'I am fan of Kumasi Asante Kotoko, two-time African Champion. We had the privilege of having Ian as a Coach for one Season. We will miss this gentleman. RIP Ian.'

'It was with a deep sense of loss that the news of Ian's death broke in Zambia. Remembering that he came here in 1993 when we lost our entire national team in the fatal air crash off the coast of Gabon. Under his charge we came out second in the African Cup of Nations Championships of 1994 losing out to Nigeria by a 2-1 scoreline. Ian thanks for standing with us in our time of need.'

'My family lived close to the Porterfields in the 1970s. I was one of many ardent Sunderland fans who hung around his front gate. Ian would regularly come out and have a kick-around with us. He will never know how much pleasure he gave to a bunch of scrawny kids hanging around his house.'

'So long, Ian, and thanks for all the great memories. [Your FA Cup-winning goal in 1973] was the only time I've ever seen my miner father cry.'

SOURCES

Information was sourced from the following media outlets, books and individuals. A sincere thanks to each of them.

A-League.com.au
A Love Supreme
AllAfrica
Asian Football Confederation
Back of the Net online video channel
BBC News
BBC Radio Berkshire's Reading FC podcast
BBC Sport
Blood and Circuses: Football and the Fight for Europe's Rebel Republics, by Robert O'Connor (Biteback Publishing, 2020)
Chosun Ilbo
Daily Record
DevonLive
Dong-A Ilbo
Duck Magazine
Ealing Gazette
Exeter City FC's online video channel
Financial Times
Full Core Football 24 online video channel
GasCast podcast
Ghanaian Chronicle
GhanaWeb
GloucestershireLive
The Guardian
The Impossible Dream, by Ian Porterfield with John Gibson (A.K. Publications, 1973)

The Independent
#innspark podcast
Inter-Asia Cultural Studies (Kim Hyun-mee, translated by Hong
    Sung-hee. 'Feminization of the 2002 World Cup and women's
    fandom,' volume 5, issue 1, 2004; reprinted by permission of
    Informa UK Limited, trading as Taylor & Francis Group, www.
    tandfonline.com)
JoongAng Daily
KLeague.com
Kookje Shinmun
Korea Times
Lancashire Evening Post
Lancashire Evening Telegraph
Leo Mendoza
Man Marking podcast
Modern Ghana
NewsInGhana.com
Norwegian Broadcasting Corporation
Northern Echo
OhMyNews
Pan African News Agency (*Panapress*)
QPRnet
Reading Evening Post and *GetReading* (now *BerkshireLive*)
Reading Chronicle
ReadingFC.co.uk
Reuters
ROKfootball.com (R.I.P.), particularly Mark Trevena, Andre
    Zlotkowski and Jamie Murdoch
SBS News
Scottish Sun
Singing from the Nest blog
Sky Sports
Soccerphile and John Duerden
Sports Chosun
Stan the Man: A Hard Life in Football, by Stan Ternent (John Blake
    Publishing, 2004)
Sunderland Echo
The Star (Gauteng)
Stoke Sentinel

Sunday Mirror
talkSPORT
The Telegraph
The Times
TNC Podcast (Talk Norwich City)
Trinidad Guardian
Trønder-Avisa
Tygodnik Płocki and former K League midfielder Tadeusz Świątek
V2 Football Podcast
Wizards of Drivel podcast
WorldSoccerNews.com
Yonhap News Agency